TITHE WAR
1918-1939

The Countryside in Revolt

Carol Twinch

Media
ASSOCIATES

By the same author:

Plain and Simple Egg Production
So You Want to Keep Sheep
Poultry: A Guide to Management
Women on the Land: Their Story During Two World Wars
In Search of St Walstan: East Anglia's Enduring Legend

FIRST EDITION 2001

Published by Media Associates, Norwich, Norfolk
Front cover The Boardroom Design Studio
Printed and bound by The Lavenham Press, Lavenham, Suffolk
Distributed by GLF Books, PO Box 36, Saxmundham, Suffolk IP17 2PS

ISBN 0 9521499 2 3

CONTENTS

INTRODUCTION

'All the tithe of the land, whether of the seed of the land or of the fruit of the trees, is the Lord's; it is holy to the Lord. If a man wishes to redeem any of his tithes, he shall add a fifth to it. And all the tithe of herds and flocks, every tenth animal of all that pass under the herdsman's staff, shall be holy to the Lord. A man shall not inquire whether it is good or bad, neither shall he exchange it; and if he exchanges it, then both it and that for which it is exchanged shall be holy; it shall not be redeemed.'

(Leviticus 27:30)

IN SALISBURY CATHEDRAL there is a small and innocuous plaque dedicated to Gilbert Burnet, Bishop of Salisbury 1689-1715, Chairman of Committee of the Bill of Rights and Organiser of Queen Anne's Bounty. It was erected in 1960 by one of his descendants, a one-time Governor of New York, New Jersey and Massachusetts. Yet the Bounty of Queen Anne, which Bishop Burnet was instrumental in founding, was not at all innocuous and its power and influence could not be guessed at from the three small words 'Queen Anne's Bounty'.

The 'bounty', or QAB as it become known, began life in 1704 as 'Queen Anne's Bounty for the Augmentation of the Maintenance of the Poor Clergy' and comprised the royal revenue from First Fruits and Tenths. These revenues were, roughly, a tenth portion of a landowner's produce and had been confiscated by Henry VIII in the 1540s and distributed to other bodies and institutions, many of them outside the Church. The fact that it was a tithe on agricultural produce resulted, eventually, in an almost singular form of what had once been a universal and voluntary giving of the first tenth for support of a clergy by the whole community. Tithe, under the auspices of QAB, endured in one form or another for almost three hundred years.

In the years between the Reformation and the dawn of the 20th century, the question of tithe was raked over continuously and the legislation affecting it adjusted and re-adjusted. At the time of the Suppression of the Monasteries Henry VIII inadvertently created more tithe, as much of the land formerly owned by the monasteries, which passed to lay ownership, was tithe-free but reverted to the common law once the exempt monastic body was removed. For the first time tithe was payable to those outside the Church, institutions and individuals thereafter called lay impropriators.

With tithe so deeply enshrined in both civil and ecclesiastical law it is hardly surprising that no consideration was given to its abolition. Not only would the legislation immediately surrounding tithe need reforming, which in itself was complicated enough, but there were also income tax and rating implications to be considered.

It might idly be supposed that the great man of the people Oliver Cromwell would have reviewed or reformed it; but he was unfortunately a tax and tithe collector by profession and meddling in the bottomless complications of tithe held little appeal. When, as Lord Protector, he involved himself in the issue of episcopacy and other religious matters the Commonwealth Government had its work cut out formulating a clear ecclesiastical policy to accommodate the swell of religious fanaticism. Tithe was then also paid to many lay impropriators, not just to the Church, and did not form part of its revenue in the way that it did after 1704. In her fictional account of the draining of the East Anglian marshlands, *Land from the Waters*, Doreen Wallace wrote:

> 'Through the death of an uncle, Oliver had succeeded to some property and the post of tithe-farmer to [Ely] Cathedral. This entailed organisation of the collection of tithes throughout the Isle. It was not hard work, for once the organisation was complete there was no more for Oliver to do except look after the accounts and hand over the money – or apply for the Sheriff's men to be put in, did a tithepayer turn recalcitrant. It was strange employment for him who had so often spoken against Church practices, to be garnering the moneys of the church.'

At the Restoration Charles II used tithe revenue as provision for his mistresses and 'natural' children, and so it limped on until 1704 when

Bishop Burnet persuaded Queen Anne to take a personal interest in the plight of the country parson. [For a comprehensive study of QAB see *The Foundation and Early Years of Queen Anne's Bounty* (Savidge, 1955) and *Temporal Pillars* (Best, 1964).]

This book is not a history of compulsory tithe, nor is it about the modern principle of voluntary tithed income: tithe history is international, its origins obscured by time, and its passage through the centuries as long and complicated as that of humanity itself. It is accompanied by prolific and vast volumes of legislation that extend wider than the general 'tithe', which for the purposes of this book is taken to be that deriving from the land. Since, however, some knowledge of the background to tithe is necessary, an outline chronology is included in Appendix I.

There is no proof that tithe as such was ever intended to be a tax purely on agriculture. Tithe in its purest sense applied to everyone, of whatever profession, as evidenced in *Bohun's Law of Tithes*, written in 1744 by W Bohun of the Inner Temple. The City of London from very early times levied a house tax to pay the clergy and in medieval times an oath had to be sworn in respect of the value of a personal tithe, on which the parish rector remarks in Chaucer's *Canterbury Tales*. Chaucer's 'plowman' and Friar also tell of the power of the bishop and the archdeacon in the matter of unpaid tithes at a time when defaulters were dealt with in the King's Ecclesiastical Court and subject to ex-communication for non-payment. Bohun makes it clear that tithe was also once the responsibility of tradesmen, professional men, wage earners, etc., the only exemption being the ill-gotten gains of 'rogues and vagabonds'. But by the 1830s tithe fell only on those who could not pick up their assets and run, namely owners of land that carried an historic obligation.

Since 'time immemorial' there has been a special link between the twin paths of agriculture and religion. Both deal with recognised basic human needs, the one temporal the other spiritual, but while the rural clergy had much in common with their farming parishioners it was also the very thing that drove a wedge between them. The curate (and later author) A Tindal Hart witnessed a tithe distraint sale in Kent during the 1930s and wrote:

'Despite all the centuries-old frictions and disputes occasioned between the clergy and their people in the collection of tithes or the raising of rents, the close association of the parson with the soil has in the past provided a deep and close bond uniting him with his parishioners. At first as a peasant

himself he laboured alongside them in the open field ... as the receiver of the tithes and the landlord of the glebe farm ... he could always rejoice with them in a successful season ... and sorrow at a bad harvest in which all again would suffer.'

A romantic, one-sided view of tithing day and its accompanying feasts is immortalised in James Woodforde's *The Diary of a Country Parson* (1758-1802) and illustrates payment of tithe in kind through one parson's eyes. Woodforde saw nothing wrong in the ritual of farmers paying tithe but he acknowledged their reluctance to pay and did not take kindly to the 'insolence' of one Mr Forster who showed resentment at having to pay tithe. Forster undoubtedly spoke for others who dared not cross the parson but nevertheless harboured fierce, on-going resentment. Such frolics as went on in Weston Longville were not mirrored across England and Wales with even half as much jollity. Many parsons gave little back to the tithepayers in the nature of 'frolics' and, conversely, others had to use all their wit and ingenuity to get what tithe was due to them, especially when farming was in its almost permanent slough of despond.

Reverend Francis Kilvert, too, recounts his Tithe Audit, although by 1878 farmers paid not in kind, but in cash:

About 50 tithepayers came, most of them very small holders, some paying as little as 9d.'

In similar vein to Parson Woodforde, Kilvert recounts that after they had paid their tithe the farmers retired to the back hall and were regaled with bread, cheese and beer, some of them eating and drinking the value of the tithe they had paid. Farmers, of course, attended Tithe Audits to avail themselves gleefully of as much food and drink as they could consume at one sitting as their only means available of literally getting their own back.

In 1870 Kilvert makes amused reference to the poem *The Yearly Distress* written in 1779 by William Cowper for the Reverend William Unwin, whose distress at having to receive the tithe was, wrote the young curate, as great as it was for those who gave it. Cowper replied encouragingly to the young Unwin, who had complained of being miserable about accepting tithes (the receipt of which was 'burdensome'):

'... you sent away your farmers in good humour ... and now you have nothing to do but to chink your purse, and laugh at what is past. Your delicacy makes you groan under that which other men never feel, or feel but slightly.'

Unwin, however, continued to feel badly and in Cowper's poem, subtitled *'Verses addressed to a Country Clergyman complaining of the disagreeableness of the day annually appointed for receiving the Dues at the Parsonage'*, he writes:

> *'The priest he merry is and blithe*
> *Three quarters of the year,*
> *But oh! It cuts him like a scythe*
> *When tithing time draws near.'*

Cowper takes a cynical view of farmers, and for Unwin's sake calls them bumpkins, clumsy swains with bald pates, and coarse individuals, who were out to cheat the parson if he could. Many farmers did, of course, practise time-honoured ways of reducing the tenth portion, some of which found their way into Cowper's poem:

> *'One talks of mildew and of frost,*
> *And one of storms of hail,*
> *And one, of pigs that he has lost*
> *By Maggots at the tail.'*

It was the Tithe Act of 1836 that brought the Tithe Frolics as described by Parson Woodforde to an end, and the centuries-old tradition of collecting the tenth share of a farmer's produce in kind ceased.

The clergy had long complained of the inconvenience of collecting tithes, especially in parishes that were spread out, and increasingly farmers found ways of reducing the tenth share. Farmers, for their part, were invariably hampered by the non-appearance of the titheowner at, say, haymaking time or at harvest. The farmer was required (and risked a lawsuit if he failed) to give notice to the titheowner that his tenth share was ready for harvesting, but if no one came to take the crop the remaining nine-tenths could not be harvested. His late arrival could mean a delay in harvesting, then late ploughing, and thus leave the farmer ever more dependent on the vagaries of the weather.

In revenge, farmers would often alert the titheowner to the impending harvest, be it hay, turnips, corn, the weaning of a sow, or the milking of a cow. When he came to collect, however, the parson found that it had been 'too wet' to harvest, or the crop was poor, or the cow 'gone dry'. Sometimes the farmer would draw ten turnips, give one to the tithing man saying that was all he intended to harvest that day. Indeed, if a farmer was lucky enough to have a plot of land tithe-free, he would farm it to the best advantage and let the tithed land go to ruin or reduce the crop by indifferent husbandry.

In 1836 Lord John Russell, who steered the Tithe Bill through Parliament, warned the House of Commons that agricultural tithe was fast disappearing in the same way that personal tithes had lapsed through widespread refusal to pay them, or the laxity of titheowners in collection. The eventual Act began with personal tithes, but ended with all being dropped bar agricultural.

For those interested in the 1836 Tithe Act there can be no better instruction than Eric J Evans' *Tithes: Maps, Apportionments and the 1836 Act* and *Tithe Surveys of England and Wales* by Roger Kain and Hugh Prince. Eric Evans explains:

> *'... tithe values were converted into rent charge payments by assuming that each sum had been used to purchase equal quantities of wheat, barley and oats at prices published annually in the London Gazette (cl 56-57). The scale was first fixed in December 1836 when £100 of tithe would purchase 94.95 bushels of wheat, 168.42 of barley and 242.42 of oats. These calculations were used by valuers throughout the country to obtain the initial rent charge, and the figures appear at the end of the preamble to each tithe apportionment.*
>
> *'Procedure for recovering rent charge was also stated clearly in the Act. If payment had not been made within 21 days of falling due, the titheowner could enter the defaulter's lands and distrain for the amount outstanding (cl 81).'*

This was the essence of how tithe was to be collected for the next hundred years though this short explanation does meagre justice to the Act. Suffice it to say here that the 1836 Tithe Commutation Act did not abolish the archaic practice of tithe. Instead it converted a tenth share of agriculture produce to a cash payment and re-named it Tithe Rentcharge.

The implications were eventually catastrophic for farming. Although technically still linked to the produce of the land, come rain or shine, good harvest or bad, the titheowner would have his 'tenth share' in hard cash – even if there was, in truth, nothing to share. As the rentcharge was to be a fixed and on-going charge, there was no more sharing of a seasonally bad harvest, pestilence or disease. A slice of a man's profits was to go to a newly created 'shareholder' who had made no monetary or other practical investment, where dividend was not dependent in any way on the profitability or otherwise of agriculture.

Since the titheowner with the lion's share was the Established Church, tithepayers of other denominations were obliged to contribute to the

Anglican clergy. This did not go down well in Wales with its history of non-conformity in the Wesleyan tradition. Although the Welsh fight was to move away from the Church in 1919, when tithe there was secularised, an annuity was still paid so the effect on tithepayers was the same. The tithe war that began in England at the end of the First World War had already been fought in Wales during the late 1880s.

Given its anachronistic nature and the fact that its peculiar evolution meant that tithe came to be levied on land and not on the produce of the land, it might be thought that somewhere along the line of British history such injustice would have attracted political notice. Imagine a Bill placed before a modern Parliament for a new tax called tithe. It is to be applied arbitrarily, the only proviso being that tithepayers shall be chosen at random and own agricultural land. Annual demands for this tax shall bear little relation to net or gross income. This fixed sum is levied indiscriminately on parishioners inside and outside the Church of England with the bulk of the revenue used by the Church to pay its rural clergy. No investment is required on the part of the recipient who also has no responsibility towards the tithepayer or the land. But, as Doreen Wallace warned her readers at the start of her novel *Old Father Antic*, they must not suppose *'that Law is based on Reason and designed for the better regimentation of men's lives'.*

By 1900 almost every nation, including Scotland and Ireland, had reformed or abolished tithe, but thanks to the exceptional efficiency of the 1836 Commissioners in drawing up their maps, and regularising all tithe, it flourished in England and Wales. Not only did the 1836 Act convert 'kind' to 'rental' but it also had the effect of reviving it, since, as a mathematical calculation, it was more easily collected. Numerous instances of tithe liability had, for a variety of reasons, lapsed, but were resurrected when titheowners realised what was happening and were quick to register their claim, thereby creating a tangible form of real estate from nothing more than a happy circumstance.

In most cases it was the Great Tithes, those that derived directly from the soil, which formed what became known as 'agricultural tithe', many of the Small or Mixed Tithes having been redeemed before or shortly after 1836 (see Glossary). Corn land carried the most valuable tithe and accounts for why it was that, later, the anti-tithe agitation was strongest in the corn-growing east and south of England. The old hop fields of Kent, Surrey and Essex were subject to Extraordinary Tithe but no longer grew hops, although the high value tithe remained. Since farming in the north of England tended towards livestock, or other Small Tithes, the tithe was much smaller. There was no tithe in Scotland, it having been abolished at the Reformation.

The 1836 Act brought with it another new regime enabling a titheowner to distrain for tithe:

> '... if payment had not been made within 21 days of falling due, the titheowner could enter the defaulter's lands and distrain for the amount outstanding. If this proved impossible, the sheriff would issue a writ taking possession of the defaulter's property until the debt was discharged.' (Evans, 1993)

At the time of commutation agriculture was in one of its regular depressions. Rural conditions were deplorable in the early 1800s, and between 1820 and 1836 five Government Select Committees were appointed to report on the state of agriculture. The Napoleonic Wars led to inflated prices followed by heavy taxation and a steep fall in commodity prices, and the 1836 Tithe Act brought some measure of relief to farmers who were spared the impracticalities of paying in kind. But after the initial feeling of relief came further discontent, which rumbled on and began to gather momentum. A rift between the rural clergy and their parishioners opened up as more people questioned the authority of the State Church.

In the late 1880s the final wave of anti-tithe protest began its roll: agitation among Welsh farmers reached breaking point and in May 1887 there were anti-tithe riots in Denbighshire. Representatives of the Ecclesiastical Commissioners had tried to round up some cattle in lieu of tithe payment and the militia had to be called to restore order. The young and ambitious David Lloyd George was quick to seize the initiative and wrote to a friend, *'this tithe business is an excellent lever wherewith to raise the spirit of the people'*. He began addressing open air meetings on the subject, wrote Peter Rowland, *'touring the Lleyn area in a governess cart pulled by a small black pony'*. Such gatherings were held, where possible, in close proximity to the parish church or vicarage. For a time Lloyd George became secretary of the South Caernarvonshire branch of the newly formed Anti-Tithe League and opposition to tithe became his vehicle for political advancement. Later, in the 1930s at the height of the English tithepayers' revolt, his association with fellow Liberal MP and tithepayers' champion Roderick Kedward brought him back onto the anti-tithe platform.

In 1891 the Government passed an Act that placed responsibility for the tithe rentcharge back with the landowner instead of with the tenant, a move which took some heat out of the situation. Effectively, tenant farmers were then under pressure from their landlords, not the Bounty Commissioners, and landlords could at least be bargained with and were less likely to resort to the law.

Tithe War starts in 1918 and seeks to tell the story of how ordinary farmers and tithepayers united against the might of a reigning Establishment nominally, though not exclusively, in the form of the Church of England in the years when social revolt and civil disobedience by the middle classes was an unknown phenomenon. Set against a background of growing dissatisfaction with an archaic and peculiarly unfair tax called tithe rentcharge it is also about the clergy, some in favour of the tithe and others for reform, who in many cases found themselves at odds with their parishioners. The target for their dissatisfaction was Queen Anne's Bounty – the 'bounty' was agricultural tithe. The 'war' was between tithepayers and titheowners and the cause was the abolition of agricultural tithe in England and Wales.

Between 1914 and 1918 the nation's farmers were preoccupied with improving and increasing agricultural production to feed the population and basked momentarily in traditional war-time prosperity and public approbation. But the world thereafter was never to be the same again, and this applied in no small part to rural Britain. The large estates, where the landowner had been responsible for the rentcharge, were broken up into countless smaller farming units. Thus many of the new owner-occupiers found themselves liable for tithe, to be paid out of the slim margins from family farms. In the past the burdens of Church and State were accepted grudgingly, but nonetheless by and large without united protest in the countryside (with the obvious exception of the 1381 Peasants' Revolt and other sporadic dissent, such as the Swing Riots of the 1830s in opposition to threshing machines). But a new post-war political and social climate was starting to break down actual and unspoken barriers: amid the clamour for social justice tithepayers began the final battle of the war against tithe. Between 1930 and 1934, nearly thirty counties, from Brecon to Norfolk (see Appendix IV), formed their own tithepayers' associations with some counties such as Kent, where the burden was particularly high due to the hop tithe, having more than one local group.

I have to admit to a family involvement in the story of the tithe war. In 1938 my uncle Norman Simper attended Sir Oswald Mosley's Ipswich meeting and the following year he and my father took part in the Great Farmers' March. Mosley's 'Blackshirts' involved themselves controversially in tithe distraint sale protests at a time when farmers were looking to Mosley for a lead in agricultural politics. Later Mosley put himself beyond the pale and my ultra-Conservative maternal grandfather discovered he had unwittingly given lodging to a member of the Fascist Party in the 1940s. My paternal grandfather, Herman Edward Simper, was a great friend and admirer of the leading Methodist lay preacher of his day, H J Cordle, who came before the Woodbridge Court numerous times in the early 1930s when he refused to pay tithe as a matter of conscience. His wife, my grandmother, was a confirmed Liberal, a life-long Non-conformist and, before she married, a teaching colleague of the novelist and tithe agitator, Doreen Wallace.

The name Albert G Mobbs – 'AG' as he was affectionately known – is synonymous with tithe and when I first approached AG's son and daughter-in-law Tony and Thelma Mobbs with the idea for this book they readily agreed and without hesitation or restraint handed over what remained of AG's papers. There were books, magazines, photographs, notes and correspondence from the 1920s to the 1970s (including a slim file of carbon copies of letters and articles by Doreen Wallace). There was also the original transcript of AG's unpublished autobiography, and – amazingly – somewhere in the region of four thousand tithe-related press cuttings in scrapbooks, files and boxes. A large box contained miscellaneous notes for his endless speeches, many undated 'prompts' scribbled on the back of envelopes, others typed up for more formal delivery at various public and NFU meetings. There was also the small, leather attaché case that AG carried with him to countless meetings of so many organisations and associations, demonstrations and anti-tithe gatherings across the country for over fifty years. At the bottom of a heap of hand-written notes was his final tithe annuity payment certificate mounted on a piece of card.

Grateful thanks are also extended to the Kedward family, especially Georgia Reed and Philip Kedward, grandchildren of Roderick Kedward, who brought the story of the tithepayers' revolt up to date with information about the removal of the Westwell Monument to Ashford in 1998 at the request of their father, the late Philip Kedward.

To avoid unwieldy footnotes, references to source material are incorporated in the text, and where appropriate quotations are attributed in context. Since it has not been possible to give any more than a cursory nod toward the wider and multi-layered history of tithe, there is an abridged chronology in Appendix I. While the process by which agricultural tithe evolved was not of immediate concern to the ordinary 20th-century tithepayer, it provided ammunition for their leaders as proof of historic injustice. Appendices II-IV began life as working notebooks, but are included here for what they may be worth to local and family historians. Appendix V is a selection from the thousands of press cuttings, though unfortunately about a quarter of those in the Mobbs collection are undated and not safely attributable.

Due to the complexity of tithe, it may be that some will think that in order to achieve a simplified analysis or explanation the result is neither here nor there. Or, as Canon Brocklehurst put it in his 1911 book on the subject, *'... the author's greatest difficulty in such a book as this has been to achieve brevity without scrappiness'.*

All monetary amounts are given in pre-decimalisation figures and, unless stated otherwise, illustrations are from the author's collection or from the Mobbs archive.

ACKNOWLEDGEMENTS

In addition to my husband, Christopher (who proof-read the book and pointed out my inadequacies to me in a forthright and free manner, as is his wont!) I would like to thank the following:

Jack Boddy MBE (General Secretary, NUAAW 1978-82)

Lord Brabourne

BBC Documents Archive

Michael Brander

Bristol University

British Library of Political & Economic Science

Charles and (the late) Bridget Clarke

East Anglian Daily Times

Church Commissioners for England

Church of England Record Centre

Janet Cooper

Mrs A C Craine

Ivan Cutting, Jon Tavener and Anna Travers (Eastern Angles Theatre Company)

Susan Dalloe (Tullie House)

Andrew Deathe (Salisbury & South Wiltshire Museum)

Pip Ellaway (Abergavenny website)

(the late) Clement Gaze

Michael and Sheila Gooch

Jill Goodwin

John Harris, OBE, MC

Bridget Henderson (Rural, Agricultural & Allied Workers)

Inland Revenue Capital & Valuation Division

Leslie Jacobs (Suffolk Constabulary)

Fiona Jones (Hertfordshire NFU)

Philip Kedward

Kent Messenger Group Newspapers

Kentish Express

Robin Lightfoot, FRICS (Hobbs Parker)

Maidstone Library

Mirror Group Newspapers

Dr Andrew Mitchell

A A (Tony) and Thelma Mobbs

Nicholas Mosley

Museum of East Anglian Life

National Museum of Labour History

Jane Newton (Centre for the Study of Cartoons & Caricature)

Robert Paine, Ashford Local Studies Library

Rt Hon Lord Prior, PC (for permission to quote from correspondence)

G A L-F Pitt-Rivers, OBE DL

Moray Rash

Georgia Reed

June Shepherd

Herman Simper

Norman Simper

Robert and Pearl Simper

Richard Smith of Sax Books (who produced a copy of Percy Millard's Tithe Table with a flourish at the eleventh hour!)

Suffolk Agricultural Association

Wendy Thirkettle (Manx National Heritage)

Trinity College Library, Cambridge (for letter from A J Muirhead to 'RAB' Butler)

Gail and Andrew Wallbank

Peter H Walker

The Western Mail

Henry Williamson Society

Ann Woodward (niece of Makens Turner)

Bob Wynn

Chapter 1

ONE WAR ENDS,
ANOTHER BEGINS
1918 – 1924

*'Between the two world wars, much productive land in East Anglia was
tithed at sums ranging from 7/6d (37p) to 10/- (50p) per acre, which was,
of course, a very significant sum in those days, when many farmers were
losing money and farmworkers were paid about 25/- (£1.25) a week.'*

The Commons of Wortham and Burgate, 1999

INEVITABLY, HOME FOOD PRODUCTION is only ever profitable in
war time and so it was that in 1918 British farmers were enjoying rising prices
for their output, positive attention from government, and the appreciation of
a grateful nation. The Corn Production Act of 1917 guaranteed minimum
prices for wheat and despite the appalling lack of resources and awful weather
that prevailed over the 1918 harvest, British farmers kept the nation fed.

At the end of 1918 four million war-weary troops were demobilised and
started returning home. The last general attack on the Western Front had
begun at the end of October and on 11 November the British reached Mons
and precipitated the Allied-German Armistice. Ten days after Mons the

German Battle Fleet surrendered, and the First World War limped to its exhausted conclusion. Farmers and politicians knew that for at least two years following the cessation of hostilities home food production would still be needed and it was essential to maintain the existing arable acreage. The Women's Land Army stayed on the farms for the 1919 harvest and was not de-mobbed until November of that year.

Farm prices rose during 1919 by 25 percent above the levels of 1918 but the new programme to increase the arable acreage of England and Wales by one million acres, drawn up in the depths of the war crisis, was put on hold. The Board of Agriculture decided against enforcing the new compulsory ploughing orders and instead expressed the hope that improvements in yield might still come from the existing tillage. It was a signal that as war was ended home food production held little interest for a peace-time government or for a nation no longer looking famine in the face.

Problems held at bay during the war, such as strikes and social unrest among dockers, railwaymen, miners, and others, re-emerged together with those of rehabilitating the returning military. The decline in British industry and technology which began before 1914 had not been solved by the war and countries like South Africa and Canada had forged their own progress and were no longer dependent on products from Britain. India, which had been the traditional market for Lancashire cotton, was by then lost to home industry. Of minor interest, and relevant only to the affected few, opposition to the payment of tithe rentcharge had also been suspended for the duration and tithepayers continued to pay as usual.

Nothing was ever the same again after 1918 for the formerly ordered society of pre-war Britain and that applied especially to British farming. The Agricultural Act of 1920 laid down higher guaranteed prices for wheat and oats, based on the record high 1919 averages, but while prices stayed good the Corn Production Act did not allow landowners to raise rent levels. It soon became obvious that high prices meant increased land values and many owners saw that they would be better off selling their farms.

Thus it was that many large estate owners, weighed down under crippling inheritance tax and loss of income from outside investments, took advantage of dramatically increased land prices, thereby increasing short-term profits and in some cases saving themselves from ruin. If tenants wanted to stay and continue farming they were forced to buy their farms at current market prices or get out. Thousands of small farmers, who as sitting tenants bought land, became the new generation of landowners and found themselves for the first time in possession of mortgages. In 1919, however, with decent crop prices and a grateful nation behind them, it seemed financially possible. A farmer was in any case reluctant to leave land that he or his family had worked for generations and even those not threatened with eviction rushed to buy land.

Vast tracts of the British countryside changed hands almost overnight with a feeling amongst the new landowners of having the wind in their sails. It is estimated that between 1918 and 1920 one tenth of the agricultural land in the country was bought by occupiers or tenants. As J A Venn pointed out in *The Foundations of Agricultural Economics*, the average size of holdings by 1931 had gone down to 64.5 acres, and:

> '... [there was] an increase of some 45 percent in the number of owner-occupiers ... in all, 17 percent of the farmers were owned by their occupiers ... in 1921 this figure had become 20 percent and in 1927 ... it was actually over 36 percent; thus 9,225,000 acres were in the possession of their occupiers – whose number had been trebled during the preceding thirteen years and who now also represented more than one-third of all the farmers in England and Wales.'

Venn pointed out that the creation of small units of agricultural production was going contrary to the long recognised principle followed in all other branches of industry. By encouraging the establishment of smallholdings, the Government was not only contributing to the sentimental British desire that each should own an acre of land but was also unconsciously adding to the number of owner-occupiers affected by tithe.

Hardly were the new landowners home from the bank, mortgaged to the hilt but buoyed up by post-war euphoria, than the British Government withdrew most of the support measures which had prevailed for the duration of the war. In the time-honoured tradition of such institutions, the Government said one thing and did another. The Corn Production (Repeal) Act of 1921 removed the financial provisions and agriculture was left stranded. In *Loaves and Fishes*, Susan Foreman writes:

> 'By 1922 all that remained of war-time legislation was some ineffective machinery for regulating wages, a system of County Agricultural Committees occupied mainly with education, and a greater security of tenure for tenant farmers. The area under cultivation in Britain shrank from 12 million acres in 1918 to under 9 million by 1926. Farms were impoverished, equipment rusted, and buildings, hedges and ditches became dilapidated.'

What had turned into a very short post-war boom was soon over and left not only farmers, but also the general population, with feelings of disillusionment and resentment. The 'flu epidemic of 1918-1919 had brought a degree of misery which worsened as inflation caused prices in the shops to rise sharply and 1921 turned into a drought year.

Under the Small Holding Colonies (Amendment) Act of 1918, the Board of Agriculture made provision for up to 45,000 acres in England and 20,000 acres in Wales to be acquired for the establishment of smallholding colonies for the settlement of ex-servicemen on the land. But those ex-soldiers and sailors who were encouraged to use their gratuities to buy smallholdings and set up chicken units found that life on the farm did not live up to their expectations, based on cheery government propaganda about the joys of country living. The work was hard and unceasing and their profits were almost non-existent as the British mood followed its Government's own cooled attitude towards farmers and looked forward to the resumption of imported foodstuffs. Besides which, the new entrants were not those who had been farming during the war and who had reaped the benefit of wartime prices. They had no reserves or capital on which to draw and no experience of the rural methods of self-preservation, namely cutting their cloth according to their means.

There were rumours of 'war profiteering' charges being levelled against farmers, there being a curious premise in the British psyche that says it is somehow immoral for farmers to gain financially from the provision of that which most consider a human right.

At a meeting of the National Farmers' Union (NFU) branch at St Albans in Hertfordshire, held in February 1920, concern was expressed that because of the bad press many thought that farmers had exploited the war for their own ends:

'When the public read cases of cows yielding 2,000 gallons of milk, and being mostly fed on grass' said Mr H Cox, 'it was not difficult to understand how the general public came to regard farmers as profiteers.'

The public, apparently, thought that grass was free and took no account of the farmer's own investment in the land.

At the beginning of the 1920s farmers watched as government encouraged the resumption of food imports. In a Memorandum by the Director-General of Food Production to the Chairman of Agricultural Executive Committees, it was stated:

'The large United States maize harvest of 1917 has resulted in a production of pig meat in the United States which will supply this country with all the bacon and ham required for some months to come ... the policy of the Food Production Department is essentially an insurance policy. The task is to guard against calamity, not to provide for minor shortages which may be disagreeable but do not seriously lower the vitality of the nation.'

By 1923 farming was in such straits that the agricultural wage was forced down to 25s a week and profit margins shrunk almost to nothing. As if that was not enough, it came as something of a shock to some of the new landowners, now struggling to pay their mortgages, to find that their farms were not entirely theirs. There was something called rentcharge that was payable to some institution or distant person who had a tenth share in their land. Not all farms paid it, either, which was doubly puzzling, and it had something to do with Queen Anne. They were referred to the 1918 Tithe Act, and searched their farm particulars in vain for any mention of the Church of England, Queen Anne, or indeed tithe itself. It was not then compulsory for the vendor to mention tithe in the sale catalogue. An invoice demanding a sum of rentcharge was sometimes the first hint of their liability. In the years to come much was to be made of the fact that owner-occupiers had bought their land knowing its tithe liability, but in fact many bought from unscrupulous vendors who wanted full market price for the land, without any deductions.

At first the new tithepaying farmers had little comprehension of what it meant or why they had to pay a dividend on land they thought they owned outright; or at least their banks owned and for which they paid overdraft and mortgage interest charges. Since 1891, when a Tithe Act had transferred liability away from tenants and back to the landowners, tenants had taken little notice of something that hardly concerned them and was hidden in their rental.

Doreen Wallace wrote:

'We now have a new class of landowner, the owner-occupying-farmer, spread widely over the country. As a tenant, he had lately been doing well; as owner, he looked like doing considerably less well. He had usually pledged a good deal of his land to the bank in return for the purchase-money; he was disappointed in his promised corn-prices; in the post-war inflation the labourer's wage had risen to 46s a week; he had, besides, to

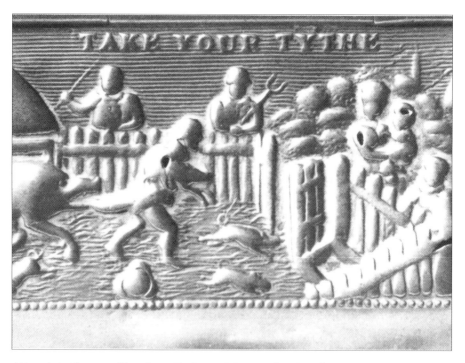

(Above) A silver snuffbox from Braintree Museum bearing the inscription
Take Your Tythe and a poem:
'Good Morning' said the Parson, 'Good Morning Sir to you'
'I've come to choose my suckling pig you know which is my due.'
The Parson went into the sty and began to pick and choose.
Whoof!
The old sow ran between his legs and whipped off both his shoes!
Although now lost, its design was used to make souvenir pewter snuffboxes
in the 1930s, one of which is
still in the Kedward family.

(Right)
Hophni and Phineas
(cartoon):
*'The only biblical authority
for compulsory tithe!
Priest Hophni: "Dig deeply
brother – but remember it's
my turn next!"'*

reckon with new liability. He must do his own repairs now, insure his own
house and buildings now, and pay the tithe. It is estimated that, since the
break-up of the large estates, fifty percent of the tithe is payable by men
who are actually farming their own land.'

R S Strachey, a titheowner as well as a tithepayer, wrote:

'The titheowners have been presented with the gift of the status of
privileged bond-holders which weighs particularly on owner-occupiers, the
very class whose increase is most desirable in the national interest.'

In October 1918, Sir Charles Hobhouse (who was on the Church Estates
Committee in 1906) said in the House of Commons:

'There is nothing whatever to be said for the titheowners who have
rendered no services to the community, but who take away from the land-
owning and land-cultivating classes an increased income at a time when
every other class has been under the necessity of facing a diminished
income and an increased expenditure.'

Writing in 1920, the principal officer of Queen Anne's Bounty (QAB)
from 1905 to 1925, W R Le Fanu said:

'It is said by the Tithe Payers Associations that tithe rentcharge is a burden
on agriculture; but it is not a burden on agriculture, it is an obligation on
land-owning, which is quite another matter. It is only when the farmer is
also a landowner that he is under any obligation to pay tithe rentcharge.
In fact the tithe bears normally only about 5 percent of the total turnover
of the occupying owner, and in some cases it is very much less. Even in the
most depressed areas, it is normally under 10 percent.'

Le Fanu did not manage to separate the practice of farming from the
necessity of owning land or explain why he thought anyone should pay any
percentage of tithe at all. Furthermore, asked tithepayers, why should
rentcharge be tied to the price of farm produce and not to the price of land if
land-owning was the first essential? It was his job to administer the Bounty,
not participate or initiate a debate on its rights or wrongs, he said. Although
the titheowner had not put any capital into the land, he claimed, the tithe
liability represented a saving in the cost price of the land for the purchaser:

'... tithe payment represents in fact interest on a sum of money which the
purchaser was not obliged to pay. In some cases he would not have been
able to buy the land at all if he had had to pay full tithe-free value, or he
might have had to borrow the increased purchase value.'

Such an assertion was extraordinary, especially when sitting tenants had been forced to buy their farms at inflated prices in order to stay in their homes and livings and there was nothing in the sale catalogue warning of the implications of tithe. There were also no prophetic indications of the profitability or otherwise of farming. Profits, unlike the inflexible rentcharge, fluctuated almost weekly. In the 1920s land re-sale was impossible even for those wanting to get out of farming since farms were worth nowhere near the purchase price of only a few years earlier and there were tracts of land lying unsold across the country. One solution was for the new landowner to redeem the tithe and then hope to sell the freed land, but even then he would end up with a negative equity.

Most new tithepayers, therefore, had no option but to go on farming, thereby continuing their tithe liability. In *Tithes and Tithe Rentcharge*, the Reverend George Brocklehurst gives instructions to his readers on 'How to Collect Tithe Rentcharge' and offers as ammunition the argument that the payments derive from the land, the tenant, tithepayer or titheowner being but variable factors.

> *'[The land] had this charge upon it from time immemorial, therefore every one who bought or sold it knew that a yearly charge must be paid to some one; and so long as the field is there so long will the charge continue.'*

He goes on to give various examples where fields (in this case Turnagates, a 10-acre field) are sold for half their tithe-free value:

> *'Turnagates, without a tithe charge, is worth £25 an acre, equals £250. Turnagates actually sells for £125 because the buyer wants the other £125 at 4 percent to supply him with the £5 yearly tithe charge. He invests this £125 in other ways, and each year, as the interest of £5 comes in, he pays his tithe with it. Because of this tithe on the field, he paid neither more nor less than if it were tithe-free. If the field had been tithe-free he would have paid the whole £250 to the auctioneer.'*

The facts of variable investment, and there being no guarantees for the provision of this £125 reduction, are brushed aside: he is absolutely certain that heavily tithed land is obtained cheaper than tithe-free land. Reverend Brocklehurst advises his readers to explain this to the tithepayer when he grumbles about paying his tithe.

Thinking he was on the first rung of the farming ladder George J Gill, author of *A Fight Against Tithes*, was one such farmer who bought a farm in 1924:

'In that year I bought a small farm of 55 acres. It had been terribly neglected ... practically waterless, it supported one cow, it produced a little third-rate wheat on its weed-choked arable of 30 acres, and it was to all intents and purposes undrained.'

George Gill criss-crossed England in a caravan looking for a farm and had seen many such holdings, derelict land with dilapidated buildings and barely worth the average rental of 15s per acre. There was no profit and Gill used his capital to restore the land, provide a water supply, and renovate the buildings. Ultimately, he would need money to stock the farm and provide working capital for the arable crops.

'Each half-year there came to me insistent demands for tithe rentcharge, one from the Church of England and a second from Merton College, Oxford ... Payment, of course, could only issue out of the capital I had reserved for restoration and equipment. I did so pay it from capital for some time, simply because it was demanded with apparent authority.'

The argument of his having got the land cheaper because of its tithe liability was put to Gill, but he disagreed:

'In 1925 ... the Government fixed a stabilised annual tithe payment on the farm of 6s 9d per acre, nearly half of the possible rent. I was told that I ought to have discounted that increase in the tithe by paying less than I did for the land ... The Government, however, had not told me beforehand what they were going to do.'

Like many new owner-occupiers, Gill offered to redeem the 'tenth share' but found the price to be nearly three times the market value he had paid on the other nine-tenths. Although the titheowner did not, in effect, have any claim on the freehold of the farm, in reality he, or they, owned much more than the actual land.

By what right, asked Gill, did the functionless titheowner stand in front of them all with his first charge upon what they produced? These and other questions had been asked for centuries. The system of tithes had been challenged almost continuously over hundreds of years but the principle was never seriously damaged as a result.

One of the first references in the popular press to what in the 1930s was to be tagged the 'Tithe War' had been in the *East Anglian Daily Times* during January 1887. A public meeting was called in Colchester, Essex to discuss the growing injustices of tithe with Members of Parliament, landowners, and farmers from Essex and Suffolk attending. The MP for Maldon, Mr C W

Grey, took the chair. Intriguingly, newspaper reports in those days recorded audience reaction:

> 'Speaking of the cruelty which was practised by the titheowners ... It would be a glorious thing if the ladies of the Primrose League [laughter and groans] would get a similar petition to Parliament, asking the legislators of this country to treat the agricultural interests with justice. [Laughter and applause.] ... The tithe war was breaking out again, and it would break out because the farmers were determined not to submit to the injustice any longer. [Loud cheers.]'

Among those present was Mr J S Gardiner, a churchwarden from Sudbury in Suffolk, who had been farming for forty years and whose family was to play a significant part in the events of 1933. The farmer, reported Mr Gardiner, was paying tithe out of his own capital, and he demanded to know where the titheowner would get his tithe from when it was exhausted. In the course of his speech, he instanced two farms:

> 'One let for a peppercorn rent, and the other farm, of 300 acres, was let for £5 a year. On the farm that was let for a peppercorn rent, the tithe was between 5s and 6s per acre, and on the other, where the rent was £5, the tithe was £150 a year and therefore 10s an acre.'

The audience greeted this with cries of 'shame'!

The growing sense of outrage that stirred up the Colchester protest mirrored new anti-tithe agitation starting again in parts of Wales, but even so England's tithe war was a hundred years behind Wales. In the 1880s Thomas Gee of Denbigh (1815-1899), a journalist, Calvinistic Minister and politician, led Wales in an organised protest in the form of the Anti-Tithe League, encouraged by a young David Lloyd George. Ten years later there were to be long and arduous discussions by the committee appointed to look into the disestablishment of the Church in Wales and its affect on tithed land. By the time of disestablishment, in 1919, £21,656 of the total Church holdings in Wales (which in 1919 stood

(Right) Minister of Munitions, David Lloyd George, with his wife Maggie and daughter Megan in 1916. Megan was among the MPs who voted against the Tithe Bill in 1936.

at £694,333) were transferred to the Welsh Church Commission. The amount consisted principally of tithe rentcharge redemption money, which was to be devoted to 'secular objects'. Other endowments worth £48,000 annually were eventually transferred to the University of Wales and the Welsh County Councils.

The National Executive of the National Farmers' Union (NFU) had tithe on its agenda almost constantly from 1918 onwards, as did most of the County Executive Committees. At a meeting of the Taxation Committee in its Bedford Square headquarters in November 1923, delegates debated the 1918 Tithe Act. It had taken a year or two for the implications to sink in, but as it did so the pace of protest quickened within the membership. The Committee agreed that joint representation between the NFU and the Central Landowners' Association (CLA) should be drafted in the hope of *'an equitable settlement on this vital matter which at present represents such a heavy burden on the industry'.*

During 1924 the Union was also in touch with a group of tithepayers who had formed an independent but informal association. Their leader was F R Allen of Canterbury in Kent. Mr Allen wrote:

> *'The reason why the association was formed was because of the alarm felt by a number of tithepayers at the manner in which the National Farmers' Union and other bodies had already, in conference with titheowners, compromised the situation to the detriment of tithepayers, and it was felt that it was unsatisfactory to leave the preparation and statement of the tithepayers' case in the hands of bodies who, however estimable, were controlled by persons who were not tithepayers.'*

Over the next year or two Union discussions concentrated on the seven-year period of stabilisation contained in the 1918 Act, which meant that the value of tithe was to remain the same until the next review in 1925. The method of valuation was that prescribed by the Tithe Commissioners in 1836, when rentcharge was set according to the amount of corn that could be purchased for £100. Towards the end of the nineteenth century the low corn prices had meant that the equivalent rentcharge had fallen below par, i.e. in 1901 rentcharge had gone down to £66 10s 9d. In 1918, however, because of the abnormally high wartime prices tithe was stabilised above the £100 figure at £109 3s 11d.

There was some discussion in Parliament as to the sacrifices being made by the Church in under-valuing payments. Some years later, in 1932, the

(Above) Letter from F R Allen to AG Mobbs, 1931.

(Left) Example of a Rectorial Tithe payment made in Suffolk during 1925, in which year collection for Ecclesiastical Tithe was passed to Queen Anne's Bounty.

Prime Minister Stanley Baldwin pointed out that in fact some £14,000,000 could be said to have been saved by the tithepayer by not setting an even higher figure than £109 3s 11d. This became a popular rallying cry among titheowners, but it never carried any logic with it: by pitching the rentcharge at a lower rate it was thought to be within the capacity of agriculture to pay and therefore to everyone's advantage.

From the beginning, it was clear that the NFU would have to tread a delicate path between support for the increasing membership who were tithepayers, solidarity with those who were titheowners, and an acknowledgement of non-tithepayers who were disinterested in the subject. The Union, founded in December 1908, soon became a part of the Establishment and worked closely with the Board of Agriculture during the First World War, running the War Agricultural Committees. After 1918 the Executive took on a consultative role and advised government at the Annual Review. The Board of Agriculture and the NFU had a shared infancy at a time when bureaucracy was developing and consolidating. The years 1914 to 1918 were formative ones for the NFU; it became accustomed to working with government and liked the *quid pro quo* that derived from the relationship. But by 1921 the NFU membership had swelled from its original 10,000 to one of 100,000, which increase brought with it a more diverse agenda.

At local level, though, the NFU membership was very anxious to raise the matter of tithe. At a meeting of the Hertfordshire County Executive in November 1923, it was stated that confidential reports between representatives of the CLA and the NFU gave instructions that a communication on tithe should be sent to Union headquarters. It expressed the hope that progress might be made in the matter of the 1918 Tithe Act and its implications for farming tithepayers. It was hoped that an equitable settlement on 'this vital matter' be made, 'which at present represented such a heavy burden on the industry'.

The CLA, having a less complicated membership, was slightly more vocal in defence of the tithepayer than was the NFU and its hierarchy was to fight on the front line. QAB spokesmen were always careful to refer to 'landowners' rather than farmers in their description of tithepayers which gave the CLA good reason to be involved. Founded in 1907 as the Central Land Association, it drew its membership from long-established landowners who were conversant with the whys and wherefores of tithe in all its forms. These were men used to the legislature and for whom the legal and statutory complexities were no bar to an understanding of the tithe system, unlike the newer, smaller farm owners. When a part of British law is as old as tithe, its roots are necessarily deeply embedded into every fibre of ancient laws relating to land ownership, rating liability, tax assessment, and a State Church that carries a dual role in civil and ecclesiastic law. To tinker with its working, therefore, was not a task to be approached lightly and it needed men conversant with the peculiarities of the British legal system to fight from within. The CLA stood for an overall prosperity for agriculture as a whole and had no trouble accommodating its new owner-occupier members while retaining the strength of the established membership. Very early on in the debate the CLA agreed that changes had to be made in the legislation; it was just a matter of which was the best course to take. However, while able and willing to take up the case of tithe, the CLA was still feeling its way and did not breathe the same air as the Board of Agriculture, as did the NFU. For the most part it played a supportive role to the NFU rather than taking any radical action. Some, however, within the ranks, such as Lord Lymington, R S Strachey and Captain George Pitt Rivers, took a high profile in the fight to end tithe and quickly gained the confidence of ordinary farmers.

One of these farmers, although by no means an ordinary man, was Albert George Mobbs, of Oulton in Suffolk. He was born into the highest ideals of Methodism, his parents and grandparents steeped in the most solid kind of political ambition there is – that born out of duty and concern for the common man and not of self-aggrandisment. The twin weapons of Non-conformity and political Liberalism combined to make Albert 'Bert' Mobbs, or 'AG' as he was affectionately and widely known, the perfect vehicle for dissent. His father had taken an active interest in local politics, and his maternal grandmother helped to entertain visiting Liberal grandees at election time, among them the Rt Honourable Herbert Asquith. When sharing a political platform, David Lloyd George told AG that he remembered his maternal grandfather standing for the Lowestoft Division, a man further distinguished by having had an audience with Queen Victoria.

AG's ingrained sense of justice, and what constituted social injustice, was aroused in the early 1920s when as a young man he discovered a book entitled *The Key to the Tithe Question* which belonged to his grandfather Mobbs. He wrote in his autobiography:

> *'It was published in 1887, the year of my birth ... there were certain passages which made a great impression on my mind. For instance,*

there was the heading in Chapter 5 "The tithe tax extorted by crushing pains and penalties" and containing a quotation from a university text book "Moral and Political Philosophy" by no less a person than Archdeacon Dr Paley.'

He discovered the irksome nature of tithe, which in essence coincided with his own feelings that the taxation of a minority, namely owners of land, for the maintenance of an Established Church was wrong. He also read about the public demonstration at the 1887 Colchester meeting and about the Tithe Act of 1891, which had shifted responsibility for the payment of tithe from the tenant to the landowner. He was astounded to find that although some measure of relief was afforded the tenant farmer there had been some sixteen more Acts all calculated to strengthen the position of titheowners but nothing that alleviated tithepayers. As pointed out later by Doreen Wallace in *The Tithe War*:

'... the Act of 1891 ... did nothing to improve matters, but weakened the voice of the tithepayers by seeming to remove the grievance from the tenant farmers. Small landowners were not numerous at that date; and the large landowners, upon whom the burden of tithe was then laid, simply raised their tenants' rents and paid the money in respectable silence.'

In June 1924, AG Mobbs took his first step along a path that he was to follow doggedly for over fifty years. He wrote to the Bishop of Norwich, the Rt Reverend Bertram Pollock:

'I am very concerned about the serious position in connection with tithe rentcharge in the County of Norfolk ... There seems to be so much misunderstanding that I feel that a real heart-to-heart talk in a spirit of genuine friendliness can do nothing but good.'

By approaching a prominent representative of the Church of England, in an apparent spirit of reconciliation, he had begun as he meant to go on. AG did not receive a personal invitation to the Bishop's Palace, but he was by then on the Suffolk NFU Executive and was one of the farmers elected from the Eastern Counties who accepted Bishop Pollock's 1924 dinner invitation to discuss with him the serious depression in the industry. Never one to miss an opportunity to raise the matter of tithe, AG wrote:

'I thought I couldn't choose a better place to air our grievances, but my fellow companions, particularly those who were non-tithepaying tenant farmers ... thought my action nothing short of scandalous, but the Bishop took it in good part.'

This was the first, but by no means the last, occasion that AG would get to his feet and launch into an exposé of the injustice of tithe. Over sixty years later the name AG Mobbs was synonymous with the word 'tithe' and those who knew him would smile affectionately, and with huge respect, at the mention. He was a forceful speaker, his message enhanced by a tall and arresting stature and the degree of painstaking research that went into the preparation for each speech. AG was never caught out when it came to facts and had an almost encyclopaedic knowledge of the history of tithe resulting from his meticulous endeavours of research. Amazingly, even after he had been delivering lengthy and detailed speeches for many years he still insisted on rehearsing beforehand.

This initial tithe meeting in Norwich can be considered to have borne some fruit, since the Bishop absorbed what was said over the dinner table and thus was informed about the issue in good time for the Parliamentary debate on the 1925 Tithe Act. In that year he rose in the House of Lords to protest at the difficulties facing farmers, and in particular landowners who found that they had to pay in tithe rentcharge almost the whole of the rental monies they received from their tenant farmers.

Although AG was to correspond with the Bishop over several years, they came to no real agreement other than to be polite to one another, the Bishop later distancing himself from the specific matter of tithe and from AG. By 1933 the Bishop was writing to the effect that he was so closely identified with the side of the Church that it would be a mistake for them to meet. In a letter written to AG on 26 June 1933, Bishop Pollock said:

> *'I do not think that there is any occasion for me to trouble you to come and see me here. Mr Middleton and I are very closely associated together in this matter of tithe at Queen Anne's Bounty, and if there is anything fresh that you have to say I think it would be better that it should be said to him in London one day when you are there and can spare the time.'*

AG replied, somewhat less politely than usual, to the effect that he thought there would be much to talk about since he had just returned from witnessing a tithe raid on Lady Eve Balfour's farm in Suffolk:

> *'I find the greatest difficulty in suppressing feelings of revenge and hatred that persistently rise within me when these raids take place in order to provide income for the carrying on of God's work. What canting humbug and hypocrisy to preach brotherly love under such circumstances!'*

But the Bishop responded, repeating that:

Painting, by J Bunting, of George Middleton JP (1922), who became First Church Estates Commissioner in 1930 and eventually assumed control of Queen Anne's Bounty. (Tullie House)

'... I am afraid that I am so closely identified with Mr Middleton in this matter that it would be a mistake for me to see you independently of him. I do not know, however, that very much will be lost because I think it is unlikely that you would be able to say anything to me that I do not know already and it may be that I could not say anything to you with which you are not already acquainted.'

'Mr Middleton' was the Labour MP for Carlisle, George Middleton, who was appointed Second Church Estates Commissioner in 1924. As Chairman of QAB he was to feature large in the tithe wars as the opposing General. AG could definitely 'spare the time' to tackle Mr Middleton and indeed did so on every conceivably possible occasion. The two men were to cross swords constantly and publicly until Middleton's untimely death in 1938. AG dismissed Middleton's role to the Bishop, writing:

'You refer me to Mr Middleton who however as an official is more or less in the position of a paid agent. Your position as Bishop I imagine carries with it far greater responsibilities than that of Mr Middleton. You say that you are closely associated with him in this matter of tithe but I should be very unhappy to think that you are in entire agreement with all that is being done. I have already had an opportunity of questioning Mr Middleton ... and am quite satisfied that the attitude he adopts towards the present position must, if continued, have very disastrous results. I have already offered to discuss the matter with Mr Middleton in public (and after all it is a National question) but until he consents to do so I cannot see that a personal interview with him would serve any useful purpose.'

By 1924, therefore, a renewed sense of urgency was growing among tithepayers as the end of the seven-year period loomed, bringing with it the possibility of influencing changes in the forthcoming 1925 Tithe Act. Representatives of the anti-tithe lobby, primarily the NFU and the CLA, began formulating organised response to the complicated tithe legislation and small groups of tithepayers met informally to see what could be done to influence the legislators. The QAB Commissioners, with W R Le Fanu at the helm and George Middleton a rising star in the ranks of the Church Estates Committee, commenced a drawbridge campaign of defence and justification.

A tithe war was about to be declared. On one side were thousands of owner-occupiers, farming on isolated holdings spread across southern England and parts of Wales, with no Establishment body to fight their minority cause and no State resources at their disposal.

The opposition was QAB, whose officers were drawn from the political and legal élite, and a formidable array of lay impropriators such as Oxford and Cambridge Universities. QAB had unseverable links with the Government and the Established Church and its arguments, whether right or wrong, were put forward from a position of authority. It was to take a very special band of men indeed to even consider the possibility of civil disobedience at a time when the middle classes were seen to be the upholders of the law and a force for stability.

A new feel for actual, rather than rhetorical, democracy was to come from the trade unions in 1926, when discontent manifested itself in the General Strike. But dissent was already in the air of rural Britain – the very last place it could be expected to exist, let alone thrive. When ordinary men and women are pushed beyond endurance in a matter they consider unfair they are empowered to rise up against what they see as oppression. The tithe war was one of the first examples of how post-war Britain was to develop. That note of defiance which accompanied the almost constant anti-tithe

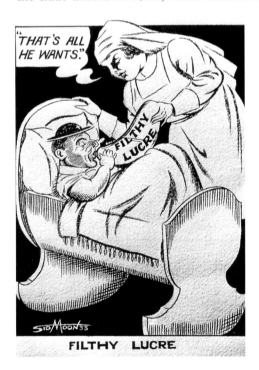

'Filthy Lucre' by the cartoonist Sid Moon.

Kentish hop garden. Between 1904 and 1907 the price of hops per hundredweight plummeted from 160 shillings to 50 shillings, brought about by the increase in cheap American imports, but tithe rates stayed the same.

agitation in Wales found a voice among the new generation of English tithepayers as they perused the details of the 1918 Act and considered its implications for 1925 and thereafter. Unlike previous generations, they were not so inhibited by, or in awe of, authority or the Establishment. They were embittered and disillusioned as revelations seeped out to a horrified public about the ghastly realities of trench warfare and the Government's wartime role, and angry at the way home food production was abandoned in favour of resumed imports. The new class of landowner wanted to know why titheowners had a claim on their farms, on some farms and not others, and what they could do about it.

The common man had found his voice and it would take a second World War to stop him using it. Between 1918 and 1939 large parts of the countryside were in revolt, physical demonstrations of anger and resentment emanating from the depths of rural England and Wales. Vocal dissent would be heard in ever higher places on the subject of agricultural tithe.

~ 0 ~

BARSHAM TITHE RENT-CHARGE.

Beccles,

1 Oct 1909

Dear Sir,

We shall be obliged if you will kindly pay to us the HALF-year's Tithe Rent-charge due from you on the

1 Oct 1909 , particulars

of which are given below.

Yours faithfully,

RIX & SON,

For the Incumbent.

Colonel Churchman

No. on List.	APPORTIONED TITHE RENT-CHARGE.	AMOUNT PAYABLE.
2ᵃ	6 15 . .	2 7 2¼
Recd. 7th Oct 1909		

ONE PENNY

A demand for tithe rentcharge sent to Colonel Churchman in October 1909 by Rix & Son on behalf of the Incumbent.

Chapter 2

THE 1925 TITHE ACT

'In the early 1920s, rather more than £3 million was still being paid in England and Wales to owners of tithe, both church and lay; for this archaic tax, designed to support the established Church and its Ministry, had often been converted into income for lay persons. The Tithe Act, 1925, abandoned the idea of linking tithe to the price of grain; the value of the rentcharge was fixed in perpetuity at £105 per £100 of nominal value, with a further £4.5 to be paid annually to ecclesiastical persons or corporations as a sinking fund for the eventual redemption of tithe after the year 2000.'

Edith H Whetham
The Agrarian History of England and Wales, Vol VIII

THE 1925 TITHE ACT was introduced in Parliament on 22 May. The seven years laid down in the 1918 Tithe Act had expired and the new Act was read and passed. Its main objects were (a) to stabilise the annual value of tithe rentcharge for the next eighty-five years; (b) to provide for the gradual extinguishment of ecclesiastical tithe rentcharge by means of an annual sum, payable by the landowner in addition to the stabilised annual value of the rentcharge; and (c) pending extinguishment, to vest all ecclesiastical tithe rentcharge in Queen Anne's Bounty in trust for the incumbent of the benefice or corporation entitled to the rentcharge income.

The principle that the rentcharge was eventually to be extinguished had been acknowledged, but only in the year 2009 would tithepayers and their successors be free of tithe. For eighty-five years farmers and landowners would have to pay ecclesiastic tithe at a rate of £105 per annum plus £4 10s to pay for a capital endowment.

For the lay impropriators, roughly a third of all titheowners, there was to be no £4 10s sinking fund addition, tithe being established at £105, thereby creating yet another anomaly for those involved in the tithe war.

By far the most controversial of the enormously complicated 1925 Tithe Act was that QAB would be responsible for collecting ecclesiastical tithe rentcharge. As far as the clergy were concerned this was a huge advantage: it meant that they no longer had to collect tithe for themselves (although they had the option to continue). The nasty business of collection would be removed from them and henceforth be done under the protective cloak of QAB, a powerful body that had Parliament's full authority to recover and enforce the recovery of any arrears. The tithe vested in QAB would be held in trust for the incumbent who was entitled to receive the rentcharge monies. Those clergy who had employed lawyers to recover their tithe would not only be saved the expense but would, they thought, increase their popularity in the parishes if they were one step removed from the rentcharge.

It was the contention of the titheowners that all interested parties agreed to the Bill, but the National Tithepayers' Association (NTA), which provided a voice for one half of the tithe debate, had not been officially recognised by Government and was therefore not consulted. The only representation from the tithepayers' side had been through the NFU, which membership still consisted chiefly of tenant farmers who had, since 1891, paid tithe only indirectly as part of their rent. Many direct tithepayers thought the tenant NFU members did not fully understand how far the rentcharge influenced their farm rents. These, and owner-occupiers in the grass areas where tithe payments were only a meagre amount per acre, dominated the NFU Council. Answering the criticism in retrospect, a paragraph in a later *NFU Record* said:

> 'Quite inaccurate reports have appeared in the Press recently announcing a "revolt" in the ranks of the National Farmers' Union because of alleged opposition to the Union's "official attitude to the tithe problem". [In 1924] when the NFU, in collaboration with the Central Landowners' Association and the Land Union, was doing everything humanly possible to secure fair treatment for the tithepayers' interests, the same type of

*guerrilla warfare was employed to embarrass the efforts of the farmers'
leaders, and the direct result was that the Government of the day was
encouraged to embody in the Tithe Act of 1925 provisions which were
manifestly inequitable from the standpoint of tithepayers.'*

After the Act was passed, in 1925, there was yet more criticism. The *NFU
Record* defensively instanced 'two prominent politicians' who were reported to
have repeated the allegation that the NFU had agreed to the Tithe Act of
1925 as a settlement of the tithe issue. Part of the statement issued by the
Union to the press on the completion of the House of Commons Report
Stage in November 1925 was quoted:

*'... In spite of the vehement opposition to the Bill reinforced by the
admission of the principal Church newspaper that the Bill "loads the dice"
in the titheowners' favour, the measure remains as flagrantly inequitable
as it was on the day it was introduced ... the Bill cannot and will not be
accepted by [tithepayers] as a final settlement of the tithe problem.'*

Nevertheless, in 1930, when more attacks were being made on the NFU,
M C McCreagh of the Tithe League, wrote to AG Mobbs:

*'It is their Joint Report of 1925 which renders the NFU practically useless
in the present tithe campaign. If the NFU Council had not committed
itself to anything in 1925, one would be quite right in saying that if the
Council was ill-informed in 1925 that is no reason why it should not be
well-informed now. But in view of their Joint Report it is impossible to
take that view, because having in the face of the Church Assembly, the
CLA and the Land Union, openly accepted all the false theories of the
titheowners, it dare not eat its words and proclaim that it was ignorant
and negligent in 1925.*

   *'That is the explanation of the Council's refusal to take any serious
action. It is naturally unwilling to put itself in a position which will cause
the titheowners to say "You are going back on everything you agreed to in
1925" and the tithepayers to say "Now you see how badly you let us down
in 1925?".'*

M C McCreagh, who later became Treasurer of the NTA, was not alone
in his assessment of the Union's line. In 1921 he had inherited property in
Hampshire and, in protest at the high tithe charge on his 3,000 acres, let the
estate go to rack and ruin. He was an habitual writer of letters to newspaper
editors. One of many he wrote during the 1920s and 1930s was to the
Farmers Express in June 1929:

'In your issue of May 20th there is an account of a meeting of the Council of the National Farmers Unions where "it was decided to reiterate the view that it was impossible to countenance the suggestion that the State had a right to confiscate property in tithe". That seems to be an inverted view of the matter. Whoever approves of the Tithe Acts approves of the confiscation of property by the legislature, for the object of the Tithe Acts was to confiscate a tenth of the subject's annual increase. Tithe is a tax imposed by Parliament, consequently tithe belongs to the tithepayers ... At a recent political meeting one speaker said to a number of tithepayers: "People approve of tithe only because you pay it and they don't." It would be interesting to know how many members of the above-mentioned Council are tithepayers.'

Throughout the early 1930s the NFU came under constant fire from factions not just from within its membership but in the national press. However, very early on in the campaign, AG Mobbs decided that for better or worse the main thrust of opposition should be channelled through the NFU, which body was widely acknowledged to be the 'respectable' voice of agriculture. His argument that a split within the interested parties was of no use to anyone was one he had to defend stoutly on more than one occasion over many years. Had it not been for AG's consistent and uncompromising view on the matter, and his indisputable influence on the thousands of irate tithepayers, the house would undoubtedly have divided against itself.

Eleven days before the 1925 Act was introduced into Parliament, the Council of the NTA met to discuss the situation. Shortly before his death, NTA Chairman Sir Henry Rew published a report of a resolution passed by the Association in *The Times*.

'Tithe £3,000,000 annually' – one of a number of cartoons commissioned by the NTA for use on placards and banners at public demonstrations.

'... in view of the uncertainty of the future of agriculture, there is in the opinion of this meeting no certainty that stabilisation of tithe rentcharge will be fair or satisfactory, but that if tithe rentcharge is stabilised the figure should be £90 with an adequate and effective remission clause to operate as a safely valve wherever and whenever tithe rentcharge becomes an excessive proportion of the annual value of the land charged therewith.'

In 1920 Sir Henry had been on the same Government Committee as Mr Le Fanu, Treasurer to QAB, which looked into the prospects of future corn prices. After what R S Strachey described as a 'strong difference of opinion' between the two men, Sir Henry changed sides and became Chairman of the NTA. The third member of the Committee was Sir Charles Longmore, who in the end was the single voice in the recommendations of likely cereal prices, Sir Henry and Le Fanu having both died in 1925. Sir Charles had a less than adequate grasp on the situation and made a recommendation for rentcharge above that which was finally set, having over-estimated prices.

Formal opposition to the 1925 Act was still mainly in the hands of the fairly toothless NFU, but in the two or three years which followed it became clear that the issue was far from settled. Headlines began to appear in the press; the *Daily Herald* said 'Nation's Farmers Unite to Banish Tithes':

'The tithe war is developing swiftly. Tithepaying farmers all over the country have now banded together into one big body, determined to fight to the last the demands on them to pay tithes which often make the difference between the success and failure of their farms ... The tithe war is one of the fiercest battles the farmers of Britain have waged for years. All over the country there have been demonstrations.'

At one such meeting held in Ipswich during January 1928 the Minister of Agriculture, Walter Guinness braved a storm of criticism over the Government's agricultural policy. Before the Minister's address a resolution was carried unanimously that the Suffolk branch of the NFU recorded its emphatic dissatisfaction with the Government's 'so-called' agricultural policy. Inevitably the question of tithe was raised, but the Minister appeared unmoved. In response to questions about the Tithe Acts he said that if the Act had not been passed farmers would be paying the rate of £135 instead of £109 10s. The 1925 Act, he said, was passed in a demand for a permanent settlement and contended that *'... the result must have been fair because I received just as much criticism from the titheowners as from the tithepayers'.*

The quarrel was not, however, so much about the levels of rentcharge but more about the fact that it was an anachronistic, unfair and random tax. Even had there been enough money to pay tithe, it was still resented in principle and was seen as another disadvantage English and Welsh farmers had when it came to competing on a world stage where no foreign farmer paid tithe. It was no longer a question of negotiating low payments merely to keep the lid on tithepayers' resentment.

The acceptance of final abolition in the 1925 Act led tithepayers to believe that the Church would revise its operations in line with that thinking. Not only did this not happen, but the decision of the Church Assembly not to pursue the question of an inquiry into the working conditions of the 1925 Act was the impetus for tithepayers' accelerated fight for an earlier abolition of tithe. The attitude of the Church Assembly was seen as apathetic and complacent by tithepayers who were increasingly unhappy at the way the situation was viewed by the Church. Whenever he addressed a public meeting, F R Allen, Secretary of the NTA, was quoted as saying: *'We are thousands strong now, and we are going to fight to the last.'*

Walter Guinness was wrong: although opposition to the 1925 Act was universal no one thought it fair. Tithepayers were incensed at the new powers conferred on QAB, while the Church thought itself cheated out of both short-term income and the long-term value of its assets. Officers of QAB found that collection was becoming both more difficult and expensive and the tithe issue was beginning to attract newspaper headlines unfavourable to the Church with ever-increasing column inches devoted to turbulent anti-tithe demonstrations.

The rural clergy saw their authority, and the respect of their parishioners, evaporating daily as they waited for a new lead from their Archbishop in the matter of Church finances. The Archbishop's advisers, in their turn, appeared to be making no effort to make up the shortfall in money to pay the rural clergy when tithe ceased. Lay impropriators disliked the fact that the ecclesiastical owners had a sinking fund and they did not, while the NFU was attacked publicly by members for not having fought hard enough for their interests.

Government regarded with increasing unease the volatile nature of anti-tithe protests springing up all over the country, and the courts started to struggle with the mounting numbers of rentcharge defaulters. Each April, when the half-yearly tithe demands were received by tithepayers, a new crop of defaulters emerged. By May even those courts which had caught up with distraint orders were then faced with a new lot.

In the wake of the 1925 Tithe Act the NTA, with the hard-working F R Allen as Secretary, gained strength. The situation was dire amongst the Kent farmers who paid high hop tithe and pressure was building in the newly formed Kent TPA. Well-attended meetings took place in Kent and registered a united dissatisfaction with the tardiness of the NFU in opening any kind of forum, not just there but in the other hop-growing counties of Hereford, Sussex, Worcester, Hampshire and Surrey. They thought that the Union should have begun serious discussions in the year following the 1925 Act and saw the delay as leaving the way open for the foundation of tithepayers' associations which could set their own agenda.

Aware of the groundswell of opinion in Kent, AG decided to make contact. In January 1929, a Mr Blomfield of Halstead in Essex wrote to F R Allen to say that a Suffolk farmer, Mr A G Mobbs, had expressed an interest in the NTA and would like to know more. F R Allen wrote the first of a great many letters to AG:

'Mr Blomfield of Halstead has informed me that you are enquiring about the [Tithepayers'] Association ... as you see the subscription is only 5/-. Funds are needed, of course. But numbers are of more importance, and we should like to form Branches all over the country especially where the land is heavily tithed as in Essex. I shall be pleased to hear from you, and to give you any further information that you may require .... PS Could you attend the Annual Meeting to be held at No 20 Hanover Square London on Thursday the 31st inst. at 2.30pm?'

Suspicious that the NTA was by no means as effective as it should be, given the number of demonstrations by tithepaying farmers being reported across the country, AG took up the invitation. At first he was not greatly impressed:

'I joined [the NTA] in the early stages and attended two or three annual meetings but it didn't seem to make much headway, although the state of the industry was compelling more and more farmers to become owners of their farms with the landlord and tenant system rapidly disappearing. I think most farmers were looking to the NFU to accept responsibility for fighting the wretched [tithe] system, but if so, they looked in vain.'

F R Allen and AG were to correspond and meet regularly over very many years. Between 1930 and 1936 they worked intimately for the same cause, yet, as was usual for the time, they continued to address each other formally both on paper and in person. Even by the late 1950s, F R Allen was still beginning his letters 'Dear Mr Mobbs', the only concession to familiarity

TITHE NOTICE for 1930.

I DO HEREBY GIVE NOTICE that under the authority vested in me and by the Tithe Commutation Acts, 1839 to 1905, I will attend on the days, and at the times and places hereinafter named, for the purpose of

Receiving All Rent Charges,

MODUSES and PRESCRIPTIVE PAYMENTS that will then be due and owing under and by virtue of the said Acts of Tynwald, and I do require the several persons liable to the payment thereof, to attend at the times and places appointed, and pay the same:—

LONAN.—Monday, 20th January, 1930, at THE INSTITUTE, LAXEY, at 11 a.m. to 11-30 a.m.

MAUGHOLD. Monday, 20th January, 1930, at the COURT HOUSE, RAMSEY, at 2-15 p.m. to 3-15 p.m.

BRADDAN.—Tuesday, 21st January, 1930, at MESSRS QUALTROUGH and CO's. OFFICES, THE BRIDGE, DOUGLAS, at 2 p.m. to 2-10 p.m.

MAROWN.—Wednesday, 22nd January, 1930, at CROSBY STATION, at 8-40 a.m. to 8-50 a.m.

PATRICK.—Wednesday, 22nd January, 1930, at the PAROCHIAL SCHOOLHOUSE, at 9-10 a.m. to 9-30 a.m.

GERMAN.—Wednesday, 22nd January, 1930, at the COURT HOUSE, PEEL, at 9-45 a.m. to 10-30 a.m.

MICHAEL. — Wednesday, 22nd January, 1930, at the COURT HOUSE, MICHAEL, at 11 a.m. to 11-45 a.m.

BALLAUGH.—Wednesday, 22nd January, 1930, at the NEW CHURCH HALL, BALLAUGH, at 1-30 p.m. to 2-15 p.m.

LEZAYRE. — Wednesday, 22nd January, 1930, at the CHURCH ROOM, SULBY, at 2-45 p.m. to 3-45 p.m.

JURBY.—Thursday, 23rd January, 1930, at The PAROCHIAL SCHOOLHOUSE, at 9-10 a.m. to 10-15 a.m.

ANDREAS—Thursday, 23rd January, 1930, at The PAROCHIAL SCHOOLHOUSE, at 10-45 a.m. to 12-15 p.m.

BRIDE.—Thursday, 23rd January, 1930, at The PAROCHIAL SCHOOLHOUSE, at 1-45 p.m. to 2-45 p.m.

ONCHAN.—Saturday, 25th January, 1930, at THE TITHE OFFICE.

SANTON.—Friday, 31st January, 1930, at SANTON STATION, at 8-30 a.m. to 8-40 a.m.

MALEW.—Friday, 31st January, 1930, at BALLASALLA STATION, at 8-50 a.m. to 9-10 a.m.

ARBORY.—Friday, 31st January, 1930, at COLBY STATION, at 9-30 a.m. to 10-20 a.m.

RUSHEN.—Friday, 31st January, 1930, at PORT ST. MARY STATION, at 10-30 a.m. to 11 a.m.

The TITHE CHARGE IS DUE ON THE 30th SEPTEMBER IN EACH YEAR, and is payable between the 20th January, and the 20th February following, and the same having to be accounted for on the 20th February, I hereby give NOTICE that PROCEEDINGS will be taken against DEFAULTERS immediately after the 20th February, 1930.

RAMSEY JOHNSON,
Agent and Receiver of Tithes.

Tithe Office: 23, Athol Street,
Douglas, December, 1929.

NOTE.--When paying Tithe, please bring or send the enclosed Tithe Account, to be receipted.

Tithe Notice for 1930 – in the Isle of Man, the Tithe Agent would collect payments on appointed days at each of the seventeen parishes. (Mrs A C Craine)

being a change from 'Yours faithfully' to 'Yours truly' to an eventual 'Yours sincerely'. He was a formal and precise man who brought order to the umbrella Association, which undoubtedly contributed to its success. He was not only highly efficient, but was totally committed to the cause, and as Secretary of the NTA his name (always F R Allen or Mr Allen, never his Christian name) appeared in countless newspaper cuttings. He was always ready with a 'Letter to the Editor', to issue a statement when required, or be interviewed over the telephone, and invariably accompanied the NTA President to public meetings across the country. He was also a fair man, and in July 1929 he wrote to AG Mobbs:

'... had a letter from Mr McCreagh stating that he was preparing for the Association a "Short History of Tithe". I have no doubt that this will contain references to Authorities, etc. It is extremely difficult to get a non-partisan account of tithes. If you wrote to the Liberation Society they would send you some publication setting forth the "Liberationist" point of view, which by the way is by no means necessarily favourable to the tithepayers as such. If you wrote to the Church Defence Society you would get a publication setting forth another point of view.'

F R Allen also took the opportunity to warn AG:

'You want a good deal of courage and patience, however, if you are really going into the subject of Tithe. It is and always has been a source of endless controversy. I have been at it for nearly 30 years, and can assure you that when I try to envisage its hopeless entanglements I sometimes am tempted to doubt whether man is a rational being.'

Both men were blessed with courage and patience, to which can be added persistence and dedication. Even in the 1940s when the heat had died down, F R Allen never entirely gave up his compulsive and generous capacity to help tithepayers, while fifty years later AG Mobbs was still appearing before the Lowestoft County Court for non-payment of tithe. Although not a lawyer, F R Allen was described by both AG Mobbs and Doreen Wallace as having a 'legal mind' and a highly developed grasp of tithe law.

In the Guildhall at Sandwich, on 19 December 1930, a decision was taken by angry tithepayers to form a committee to consider all means for bringing pressure to bear on the Government and titheowners to secure relief from the excessive burden of tithe on agricultural land. Tactics had to be agreed and it was unanimous that the protest must be passive. The only choice they had, as tithepayers, had been demonstrated by the Welsh dissenters in the

1880s, namely non-payment. The direction of the movement was decided – it would be one of 'passive resistance' – and it remained, on the whole, the tactic for the entire 'war'.

The Ashford MP Roderick Kedward, swiftly gaining a reputation as a champion of the tithepayers, succeeded in getting the Minister of Agriculture, Dr Christopher Addison to call a joint conference of titheowners and tithepayers. Early in 1931, an NFU deputation to the Minister was organised. According to a private account of the meeting by A G Mobbs:

'I am bound to say that Dr Addison treated us with every consideration. Each delegate in turn was given an opportunity to address the Minister, and I as a delegate was able to read a statement setting out as far as possible the situation in Suffolk ... Whilst sympathising with our position he could hold out no hope of any tithe legislation being introduced by the present Government. Moreover the Government had not the time to deal with it as they had a very full programme. It was a question bristling with difficulties and if they attempted to open up the Tithe Acts they would have the Church coming down on them.'

AG's status as delegate had at first been in some doubt. When he had arrived at Bedford Square with the seven other delegates, objections were made to his being there at all. He had, said the Union hierarchy, attacked the NFU at a meeting in Ipswich and had joined 'another association'. AG wrote:

'When I was given an opportunity to reply I informed Mr Robbins that I was not aware that my position in the Union confined me to membership of that particular organisation. I assured him that it was with considerable reluctance that I accepted the invitation to be one of the deputation, but that so far as I was aware it was at the unanimous wish of my County Executive and that I was expecting to go to the House of Commons.'

However, all the delegates felt beleaguered, as the Union President refused to take part in the proceedings other than to introduce the delegates. It was made clear that so far as the delegates were concerned, they were not officially supported by the Union in any definite demands for immediate action in the matter of tithe; in fact, the last pronouncement to come from the Council was that the time was not 'opportune' for taking action. The Union had *'not yet formulated a policy based on the opinion of the rank and file of its members'*, which seemed strange considering the strength of feeling among the membership. All the delegates felt that the exercise would have been more worthwhile if they had been there as representatives of an organisation with a definite active tithe policy.

The Reverend Roderick Kedward, who became President of the NTA in 1932 and fought vociferously for the tithepayers' cause until his untimely death in 1938. (Philip Kedward)

But the fall of the Labour Government almost immediately meant that any rapport established with Dr Addison was wasted, as the new Minister, Sir John Gilmour refused to continue the discussion. Sir John followed the Government line that they had a full programme of legislation to get through and that if Parliament attempted to *'open up the Tithe Acts they would have the Church coming down on them'*.

Following the Ministerial Deputation early in 1931, AG and F R Allen agreed that were the tithepayers to have been represented by an organisation with a definite active policy, expressing the united voice of those in the agricultural industry who were tithepayers, it would not have been 'such a waste of time'. It was essential that the new NTA had the right President and later that year the NTA found one in the Reverend Roderick Kedward, MP and a farmer at Westwell in Kent. Strong, cohesive leadership became a reality and the team that was to lead the tithepayers began to assemble.

Roderick Kedward was born in Westwell and in 1923 had been elected MP for Bermondsey West. His religion and his politics matched those of AG, as did his loathing of agricultural tithe. In his autobiography AG wrote: *'He was a valiant fighter and a very loveable man.'* The two were to remain close friends and allies until the Rev Kedward's early death in 1937. Doreen Wallace said in *The Tithe War*:

> *'Rev R M Kedward, a Non-conformist minister, ex-Member of Parliament, and a farmer too. His training for pulpit and politics has given him verbal power and quickness in argument, while his experience as a practical farmer ensures that he always speaks to the point.'*

In February 1930, F R Allen mentioned Roderick Kedward for the first time in a letter to AG:

> *'Mr Kedward is, I understand, a Primitive Methodist minister, but I believe he prefers not to be called Rev. I must find this out, as it is a bit*

awkward not knowing. He and his brothers are farmers in rather a large way near Ashford.'

When the Government fell in 1931, election fever in the Kentish Ashford Division was fierce and Kedward's opponents used his connections with the activities of the NTA to their advantage. Kedward stood as the National Liberal candidate against Captain the Honourable Michael Knatchbull, Conservative. The *Kent Messenger* called it 'Hard hitting in Ashford Division!' and said *'although the candidates have observed the utmost cordiality towards each other, the contest has been characterised by bitter controversy and warm personal feeling on the part of certain supporters'.*

Kedward's most outspoken critics were Sir Auckland Geddes and Edward Hardy, Chairman of the Conservative Association. Sir Auckland had written to *The Times* making references to the 'lawless' attempts by tithepayers to defeat the payment of tithe which he said had been encouraged by Mr Kedward and which had humiliated many of the Ashford electors. Sir Auckland was invited to justify his accusations in debate, which he sportingly did and attended a Liberal meeting at Rolvenden in Kent.

By urging people to refuse to pay tithe, justified Kedward, he was not encouraging lawlessness but passive resistance. However, Sir Auckland saw it differently: he said he knew about the tithe difficulty, and that something had got to be done, but no one, if he was a law-maker of England, should associate himself with law-breaking in his constituency as Mr Kedward had done.

In reply, Kedward spoke at a meeting in Hawkhurst, where he again responded publicly to Sir Auckland. He said that the Conservatives were trying to poison the minds of people by suggesting that he was a 'low down' individual, not worthy of the public confidence. In regard to tithe, he fully admitted taking part in a campaign to incite people to rid agriculture of the burden of excessive tithe, pointing out that Kentish hop farmers were paying a tithe of around £1 per acre on land that had not grown hops for years.

But the press compounded the accusation of lawlessness by reporting: *'A prominent feature of [Kedward's] Parliamentary activities has been the introduction of the Tithe Remission Bill. As is known, he followed up this constitutional method of redress by giving personal support to the farmers of East Kent in their demonstrations against payment of what they consider excessive tithe.'*

He had introduced his unsuccessful Bill for Tithe Remission early in 1931 but it fell foul of the NFU's Parliamentary Committee who recommended that it should not be supported.

In spite of claiming to appeal to 'honest voters', Kedward lost his seat in 1931 to the Conservative candidate Captain Knatchbull (later Lord Brabourne) and the following year threw his lot wholeheartedly in with the tithepayers. He took over the Presidency of the NTA from Viscount Lymington, a post he held for the rest of his life. It was hardly surprising that voters should have been persuaded against Kedward since he openly admitted supporting the tithepayers in their refusal to pay. Opinions echoed the suggestions by M C McCreagh that people actually approved of tithe so long as they didn't pay it. However, even if he had continued as an MP, Kedward would certainly have had to compromise his absolute and, some might say, single-minded ideals at some point if he was not to be seen as a one-issue and unrepresentative MP. By the same token, if he had won the seat, the tithepayers would have lost a champion, and much of the newspaper coverage devoted to the tithepayers' problems throughout the 1930s derived from Kedward's personal fight with Merton College, Oxford.

With the main protagonists in place, the NTA immediately became the mother ship for the small emerging tithepayers' associations (TPAs) and the tithe war had begun. The Village Square in the village of Elham in Kent became the meeting place for farming protestors, or the 'Farmers' Army' as they were dubbed by the *Folkestone Echo*. Merton College was in receipt of an annual sum of about £1,400 for tithe from the Elham Parish, and for many years at least ten farms in the valley would be in arrears with their payment. Whenever any of the scouts, with cars and motor bikes at their disposal, spotted the County Court Bailiff in the district, the protestors would gather to see which farm was to be distrained upon that day. During the day impromptu speeches would be made to the waiting 'army'. Alderman Christopher Solley, of Sandwich, would often use a lorry as a platform, and was sometimes joined by Mr H Roseveare JP of Ashford, who told his audience that the payment of tithe had become intolerable and encouraged them to stand together. Tithepayers from Berwick-on-Tweed to Land's End were having their say and, he reminded them, tithe was a deep-rooted institution and those who had been receiving millions of pounds from tithe would not give in lightly. They would make tremendous efforts to retain the money they had been getting for nothing.

One farmer, H G Cullen of Mount Farm, Elham had a particular grievance, in that distraint had been levied on nearly all his stock for a tithe debt amounting to £13 4s 1d, but stock taken included five cows in milk, a heifer and forty sheep, the market value of which was over £100. There was no rebate for Mr Cullen.

The *Farmer & Stockbreeder* recorded numerous instances where Kentish farmers had seen their stock sold for more than their debt, as did all the national dailies, including the *News Chronicle, The Times,* the *Guardian* and scores of local papers across England and Wales. The *Daily Telegraph* informed its readers in November 1932 that the Reverend Kedward had said he was *'... going to paper a room with all the Court orders he had received in connection with unpaid tithe'.*

If the fires were hotting up in Kent, those in East Anglia were not much cooler. The major source of malcontent was in the Saffron Walden Division of Essex, not just with the lay impropriator New College, Oxford but with the Church of England. Here the tithepayers met with support from two unlikely sources – the local clergy and the Conservative MP, Richard 'RAB' Butler. In November 1932 the *Essex Chronicle* reported that a conference between the clergy of Saffron Walden Rural Deanery and a committee of Saffron Walden Tithepayers' Association had taken place in the Radwinter Village Hall. They had passed the following resolution:

> *'We are strongly of the opinion that under the present conditions of agriculture, when produce has reached a price lower than ever previously recorded, both Queen Anne's Bounty and the Ecclesiastical Commissioners should do something to help the farmers to meet the arrears of tithes that have accumulated during the last two years. It is, therefore, suggested that both Queen Anne's Bounty and the Ecclesiastical Commissioners should make a fund available and use it for the relief of necessitous cases in the present deadlock. In the event of neither of these bodies taking such action, the outlook will, in our opinion, be extremely serious.'*

The Rector of Radwinter and Rural Dean, G E Whitworth and the Chairman of the TPA. David J Smith signed it. The resolution attracted the attention of 'RAB' Butler, who suggested a deputation to the Chairman of QAB Tithe Committee, George Middleton, and he offered to chair the meeting. This was to be the first ever deputation that the Bounty had received from farmers on the question of the payment of tithe. Not once during its 200-plus year history had the QAB Tithe Committee heard directly from tithepayers. The *Ipswich Evening Star* recorded the event on 17 November 1932:

'Members of the deputation stated their difficulties and asked for greater consideration than had been given in the past, particularly having regard to the even greater difficulties which the agricultural industry had been faced with during the last few months.

'A full and frank discussion took place and assurances were given that the Governors of Queen Anne's Bounty would sympathetically consider the representations which had been made to them, and would continue their policy of investigation with a view to concessions in hard cases.'

QAB's principal objection to any concession was that, as trustees to thousands of titheowners, they were unable to be lenient even if they wanted to. Just two days after the Deputation, the trustees of QAB sued J E Holliday for £10 3s 4d in Penrith County Court under the 1925 Tithe Act. The defendant was not in court since, he said, the particulars of the property concerned did not correspond with those on the Ordnance Survey map.

Meanwhile, in neighbouring Suffolk, AG was consolidating his political profile in the county by becoming Chairman of the Beccles Branch of the NFU, which meant that he could attend County Executive meetings. He became more than ever convinced that while the NFU was fairly good at voicing members' opinions on purely agricultural matters, it was a very long way from getting to grips with the tithe issue. It was at these endless Union meetings that AG first began to make his mark:

'Although not a member of the NFU Council I had by [1930] some experience of NFU committees in London on the Cereals, Milk and also the Parliamentary Committees, to which any representations regarding tithe were forwarded. If this subject came up it was usually the last item on the agenda when I had to catch my last train home. I found however that this difficulty could be overcome if I motored to Ipswich which enabled me to travel by a later train. The first time I did this I noticed the Secretary continuously looking up at the clock as if to remind me that I should lose my train, but he had a shock when he found me remaining to see the Agenda through.'

He had already established a certain reputation as a protagonist when, a few years earlier, in December 1929, he had been invited to an NFU Preliminary Tithe Conference in London. Only a few weeks later he was castigated by the Chairman of the NFU's Suffolk County Branch, who wrote:

'I was surprised to see the remarks that you made about the NFU Headquarters in your letter on tithe to the East Anglian Daily Times.

Apart from the merits of the Tithe question, I think it was rather indiscreet of you to make the reference to the NFU Headquarters which you did, seeing that you are the Chairman of a local Branch. There are always enough people ready to criticise the NFU Headquarters without the Chairman of a local Branch doing it. Quite an effective reply to your criticism of Headquarters could be made, but I do not consider it would be a very edifying spectacle for the two of us to quarrel in the press.'

This did not have the sobering effect that the Chairman hoped for, but AG did modify his outright criticism of the NFU. His relationship and loyalty to the NFU was going to be as important over the next few years as it was for him to be seen in a good light by the press.

AG was also busy cultivating various journalists and numbered among his friends the Agricultural Correspondent of the *News Chronicle*, a Liberal newspaper formed in 1930 by the merger of the *Daily News* and the *Daily Chronicle*. Controlled by the Cadbury family, the *News Chronicle* was both anti-Conservative and anti-Fascist. Its stable-mate the *London Evening Star* could also be counted on to report tithepayers' activities. The unnamed 'agricultural correspondent' in AG's autobiography is believed to have been the well-known and highly esteemed L F Easterbrook, who was awarded a by-line in the *News Chronicle* during the 1940s. By-lines were not common practice in the 1930s and Lawrence Easterbrook was known only as 'Agricultural Correspondent'. He came from Ipswich and farmers often took the *News Chronicle* in order to read his articles. During the Second World War, Easterbrook was part of MAFF's Information Department. In 1945 he was appointed to lecture on behalf of the Royal Agricultural Society of England and was the first editor of *Quarterly Review* which was launched in 1945.

Legal representation was also going to be important and the NTA had on board a member of the Steed family, J O Steed of Long Melford, whose firm of solicitors represented tithepayers in court. His brother was Henry Steed, a former Editor of *The Times*, and the family was both well known and highly respected in the two worlds of journalism and the law.

Newspapers would occasionally take up a particular cause on behalf of a newsworthy tithepayer. In 1931 the *Daily Telegraph* championed 70-year-old pensioner Arthur Groves of Canvey Island who was being made an example of by QAB. Officials at Southend's County Court had been instructed by QAB's Tithe Committee No 10 (which was responsible for that area) to auction

Mr Groves' furniture which had been seized for tithe arrears of £130. The bailiffs had taken all his furniture except the beds and a few pieces of crockery. In the end QAB agreed to withdraw the furniture from sale if Mr Groves agreed to pay the £6 court costs, and the *Daily Telegraph* took full credit:

> *'Mr Groves is to apply for the redemption of his property ... After the* Daily Telegraph*'s exposure of his case it seems unlikely that the Queen Anne's Bounty collectors will again attempt to single out any individual owners of property for payment of tithes due on a whole area.'*

This was not, of course, the case. QAB continued to make some quite eccentric demands on individual tithepayers, often deriving from land sold for development. Anonymous donors saved an elderly couple in Salisbury from distraint after QAB demanded tithe on their cottage garden, and there was more than one court case where QAB demanded tithe on coastal land that had long since been lost to the sea. Sometimes, as in the case of Mr Groves, individual plot-holders were liable for only part of the tithe, but were asked to pay the total that applied to the entire former holding.

During 1933, when the tithepayers turned up the heat of protest, cartoonists were happy to include the tithepayers' cause in their work, among them Australian-born William Dyson who worked on and off for the Labour Party paper, the *Daily Herald* and contributed regularly to the *Daily Chronicle* and *Daily Sketch*. Dyson was noted for his radical outlook and his 'Sky-pilot – a farmer's nightmare' sketch was widely acclaimed and used on the tithe-payers' banners at demonstrations. Sid Moon, cartoonist for the *Cambridge Daily News*, did many pro-tithepayer cartoons for use as posters, banners and propaganda leaflets put out by the TPAs. Another, who signed himself 'HB' was also commissioned and a series of cartoons were photographed and used at auctions and tithe sales for the benefit of the press.

While the TPAs were assembling, AG's farming contacts were not ignored. In addition to being a prominent anti-tithe protestor and organiser he was also a working farmer and judged livestock at the local county and other shows, plus competing in national livestock competitions. Although the years 1931 to 1933 were among the busiest of the tithe years, AG was still competing for and winning national trophies:

> *'A glance at my National Bull Cup on the sideboard reveals the fact that it came my way each year of those three years, and in the first of those years I secured second place in the National Herd Competition open to all breeds.'*

As part of the campaign to establish the authority of the NTA, AG was asked to go to Wales, where the tithe war had first started in the 1880s, to see what could be done there. Disestablishment in 1919 had taken the sting out of the Welsh tithe war, but under the Welsh Church Acts the Commissioners of Church Temporalities were still entitled to collect tithe. Although the money did not, therefore, go directly to the Church, it was nevertheless still a burden on tithepaying farmers. AG was contacted by John Davies of Ruthin in North Wales, who wrote in one of his several letters to him (none of them less than four pages and written as he would have spoken):

'Well, the fight has (s)tarted in Wales and I would have been delited if you could have come down to see how Wales started the battle. It's very hard to say how many was present, some say 4 to 5 thousand, but one paper puts it at 2,000. At any rate, I think it was an excellent start and I hope to keep it up, the bulk of the organising is on my shoulders. But we have the best men in the world at our disposal, the spirit that prevailed at Gwersyllt Hall was one of the best possible, the whole crowd was at Mr Edwards' disposal and I am very glad everything passed off very well.'

Spirits were indeed high in Wales, as Mr Davies went on:

'I was told today that they had close by in Wrexham, a battalion of the Royal Welsh Fusiliers ready for any need. There is hundreds of Welshmen ready to die any day for this cause, but what good would that be now at the start. If it comes to that in the end, it cannot be helped.'

AG, Roderick Kedward, F R Allen and the other tithepayers' leaders very much hoped that it would not come to anything of the sort. Mr Kedward was able to keep an eye on things, however, as the Ruthin MP, Dr Morris Jones, was a close friend and often invited him to speak at their tithepayers' meetings. There is no doubt that the Welsh farmers were more militant in their opposition than the English, in spite of John Davies' occasional complaints of bad publicity due to farmers' behaviour at the English distraints.

In Llannefydd, Conway, John Davies addressed his audience in Welsh, explaining the different clauses of the various Tithe Acts, and the *North Wales Times* reported:

'... Mr John Davies occupied most of his time in expounding the proposals of the Tithe Scheme ... and in his own inimitable way kept the audience's interest to the very end.'

He gave the same talk at Llanarmon, where his remarks were greeted with 'recurring cheers'.

Richard Edwards of Gwersyllt Hall Farm, Wrexham was the most high-profile of the Welsh tithepayers and supported in his stand by neighbouring counties. Whenever there was a raid on his farm hundreds of farmers from Lancashire, Cheshire and Shropshire would converge on Wrexham. Edwards was fighting the Commissioners of Church Temporalities in Wales and his farm was distrained on repeatedly. In March 1933 the *Manchester Evening News* reported:

> *'Scenes at a tithe sale on a Welsh farm were related to a King's Bench Division Court ... when the court granted an order nisi against Mr Richard Edwards ... on the grounds of alleged contempt of court ... on February 22 an attempted auction sale of cattle took place at Mr Edwards's farm, distraining for tithes due under an order of the County Court. No sale, in fact, could be held because of disturbances which occurred. Mr Singleton mentioned that the money raised by tithes did not go to the Church.'*

Counsel read an affidavit of Thomas Huw Davies, secretary to the Commissioners of Church Temporalities, who said that within the last few years agitation against tithe had sprung up in England, had spread into Wales, and was at its height in Denbighshire. In fighting mood, Richard Edwards told the court:

> *'I should not care if they brought an army. I am prepared to die in defence of my rights, and I should not die alone.'*

(Below) **Tithe barns which still survive are reminders of the days when tithes taken 'in kind' were stored by the titheowners.**

Possibly alarmed by all the talk of dying for the cause, the Welsh Church Commissioners invited the tithepayers' leaders to meet them in London. John Davies was in two minds: he wanted to turn down the offer, but his Committee had accepted and he felt

Old Tythe Barn, Maidstone.

obliged to go since he himself had pressed for such a deputation some twelve months earlier. He wrote to AG:

'Well, Mr Mobbs, in a way I am not quite sure we are doing justice to you in England ... if we find that this (offer) is only an endeavour to nip our movement in the bud, Wales will be a terrible place before the end of this year.'

The *Manchester Guardian* reported Counsel's attempt to refute the suggestion that in spite of claims to the contrary the tithe still went to the Church:

'Not one farthing of tithe went to any ecclesiastical personage. In the next twenty years it would go for the repayment of interest on money lent by the Loan Commissioners, which would otherwise fall upon the taxpayers, and beyond that the money would be used for education in Wales and for other obligations under the scheme.'

Roderick Kedward addresses farmers in Ashford Market during 1933. (Georgia Reed)

Relations between farmers and the NFU were no better in North Wales than they were in England. The tithe war spread from Denbighshire to Montgomeryshire and at a meeting of the NFU in Welshpool, a letter was read from the Llanidloes branch urging that the Union's headquarters should take stronger measures to press for a revision of the tithe system. In March 1933 the question of tithe was discussed at a meeting of the Welsh Committee of the NFU. The *Western Mail* said:

> '... a conference of Welsh MPs on the question was again considered. The committee decided that no useful purpose would be served at this juncture by such a conference, as the whole position was under consideration by the tithe committee of the Union. Denbigh's suggestion that Wales was not adequately represented on the tithe committee, and that the Welsh Committee should be allowed to nominate another representative, led to the committee deciding to recommend the desirability of appointing a representative from Denbigh.'

Certainly John Davies was sceptical of their taking any positive action:

> 'I think we can claim that we have started this movement in Wales, and also we know more about tithe by now than the two men who are on the Committee representing Wales. Mervyn Davies is of no good, a little time ago he said that we might as well try and jump over the moon than to try and do away with tithe.'

However, the *NFU Record* confirms the resolution to write to the Welsh MPs asking them to give support to the Union's request for an inquiry into the 1925 Tithe Act. John Davies underestimated Mervyn Davies, as he was to give solid, enduring service to the cause of the tithepayers. Together with Makens Turner of Suffolk, he was to press the Union in 1933 to set up a Tithe Committee, as recorded by AG Mobbs:

> 'With the help of the NFU members in the other heavily tithed counties we used every available opportunity to hammer away at the NFU in London. At one of the Annual Meetings in 1933 our Association Vice-Chairman, Mr Makens Turner, scored a wonderful victory. He was a delegate that year and responsible for moving a resolution from Suffolk requesting the forming of a separate tithe committee to be comprised mainly of tithepayers. The Council represented by the President were in opposition but he gained overwhelming support from the other delegates and accomplished a feat that has, I imagine, seldom happened in the history of the NFU. He beat the Council by a two to one majority. He was

ably seconded by one of the Welsh delegates who accused members of the Council of acting like ostriches by burying their heads in the sand.'

Mervyn Davies was also a member of a 1933 Deputation to the Minister of Agriculture spearheaded by the new NFU Tithe Committee and served on the Committee for many years, becoming Chairman in 1935.

In August 1932, John Davies wrote to AG:

'I am very glad to say that we in Wales are making good progress with the tithe movement but as you are well aware the Headquarters of the NFU are very reluctant to move in the matter. No doubt this is a political stunt more than the feeling of the farmers in the country at present but I can assure you if Headquarters will not give its members a better hearing on this vital question, and that immediately, Wales will go on its own ... they in London will be faced with one or two things, namely the Welsh Farmers will have a Union of our own called the Welsh Farmers Union.'

He was right – there was to be a Farmers' Union of Wales, but not until 1955. In the meantime, the Welsh Committee continued to press the NFU on those issues that affected them, including tithe.

After the formation of the National Government in 1931 the new executive of the NTA were already firmly established and the gathering momentum of the tithepayers revolt started to take effect. Politicians began to take sides, and tithe became a high-profile topic of the time. In England, churchmen began to break out of their straitjacket of humble silence and some spoke out publicly against the tithe system. As the rural clergy watched, helplessly wringing their hands in despair and contemplation of the disintegrating relationship between Church and farm – a new figure emerged as the object of revolt. At Elham in Kent the burning discontent moved from rhetoric to reality as the mood turned nasty. The proximity of Canterbury to the highly tithed hop lands meant that many of the livings were in the direct control of its Archbishop. Effigies of Queen Anne were burned by protestors, along with those of the rotund, be-hatted Archbishop of Canterbury, the Rt Reverend Cosmo Lang.

~ o ~

Chapter 3

THE RURAL CLERGY

"God save us from these raiding priests,
Who seize our crops and steal our beasts,
Who pray 'Give us our daily bread!'
And take it from our mouths instead."

Sung to the tune of *All People That*
on Earth do Dwell (Old Hundredth)

IT WAS NOT THE FAULT of the rural clergy that in 1704 Bishop Burnet persuaded Queen Anne to assemble the 'first fruits' and 'annates' and use them to augment their livings. Nor was it their fault that throughout the early 1930s *These Raiding Priests*, first sung in Ruthin, Denbighshire, resounded throughout the countryside to a hymn more traditionally heard in the East Anglian fenlands as thanksgiving for the end of flooding and high tides. That, and other such verses expressing contempt for their office, came not from atheists or anarchists, but from the yeomen of England and Wales whose instincts and traditions should have made them friends of the Church. Their ancestors had been the mainstay of its history, yet tithe had made it their enemy.

In fact, the tithe problem seemed to be no one's fault. In 1928 the newly enthroned Archbishop Cosmo Lang merely inherited the responsibility from his predecessors and was more interested in millionaires and duchesses. QAB Chairman George Middleton said that the Bounty officers were legally obliged to collect and they themselves had neither the means nor the inclination to lobby for change. Tithepayers derived responsibility from the land they owned and the rural clergy had little choice in how they were paid. In 1933, the Essex tithepayers' leader F C Krailing wrote:

> 'To such a pass have the latest phases in the tithe war brought us, making enemies of those two friends, the Church and the Land, sowing ill-will, contempt of the law, and devastating huge tracts of once fertile farm land.'

Government, the only body that could solve the problem, was under pressure from both the Church of England and the powerful lay impropriators to protect their income which derived from that which they considered a 'property' (a point hotly disputed by the payers).

Rt Reverend Cosmo Lang became Archbishop of Canterbury in 1928.

In 1925, the voices of neither the rural clergy nor the farmers had been listened to, but as the 'war' went on it was not only tithepayers who appeared regularly in the press, but also individual clergy members.

Wherever groups of anti-tithe protestors gathered, on village greens as they waited for the bailiffs to arrive at a farm, outside County Courts, at markets, and at public meetings across the rural communities, the 'raiding priests' refrain resounded with increasing bitterness and recrimination. Bishop Burnet could never have envisaged a time when those who led their parishioners in prayer would be so reviled. The incumbent's pastoral role was severely embarrassed by parishioners' antagonism towards the source of his living and in many ways the rector was even worse off than the farmer. He had nothing to sell, produced nothing tangible and lived in tied accommodation which brought with it heavy and costly obligations. In *The Church of England,* Guy Mayfield comments:

> 'The doctor is paid by the State and by his private patients. A solicitor looks to his clients for fees. But the payment of the parochial clergy is not

so simple. The Church has no paymaster-general and the clergy no single source of stipend.'

Tithe was but one of the sources of income, however:

'Even in its simplest form the tithe system was suitable only for an undeveloped community. From the eighth century onwards canon law, and later statute law, appeared in a steady stream in the attempt to adjust the tithing system to a society to which it was never suited. The legislation failed and made matters worse by perpetuating an anachronism. By the nineteen century tithe had become a serious cause of friction between the Church and agriculture.'

In the 1930s, as individual members of the clergy came under direct attack, they began to break their silence. Some had disposable incomes of only £350 to £400 a year, out of which they had to pay rates and annual dilapidation payments relating to the parsonage house, as well as all other everyday expenses. The Reverend Parsons, from Salle Rectory in Norfolk, told the *Eastern Daily Press*:

'I am in favour of agitation for the removal of real grievances, but by lawful means, not by refusing to pay legal dues ... though a parson I claim to know something about land for my father was a farmer ... I think I may say for my brother clergy that we are not out to make money, but unless the tithepayers pay us we cannot pay our way.'

Another Norfolk rector, the Reverend William Llewellyn of Brandon Parva, appeared before the Wymondham Police court for non-payment of rates. He was £25 in arrears, but said he had no income to pay owing to the non-payment of tithe. Although he claimed to have almost £700 outstanding in owed tithe, one tithepayer not having paid for almost four years, the annual living was worth only £300 of which £43 went for dilapidations and £11 for pensions. The Court could do nothing more than make an order and suspend it for a month.

The problem was that although tithe arrears seriously affected his stipend it was the man at parish level who felt the force of parishioner dissent. The Reverend George Brocklehurst, author of *A Text Book of Tithes and Tithe Rent-Charge*, was not afraid to speak out and made a public statement in February 1935 repudiating the claim of QAB that they always consulted the incumbent before legal action was implemented on his tithepayer:

'... a witness for QAB made the profound statement that the Clergy of his diocese could not sustain a loss of 10 percent, or even 5 percent of this

*income ... this would cut more ice if it were not the policy of the Governors
of the Bounty to re-imburse themselves even up to 33 percent of the total
income of a living in one year. Cases are before me where the Governors
during 1930 and 1932 failed to collect, but paid the incumbent without
warning him that he would have to refund. During 1934 in one case,
they took out of the current income of the living £259 which is more than
40 percent of the man's living. I am told that widows have had to repay
money spent by their husbands more than two years before.'*

The Reverend Howard Dobson told his Suffolk parish of Huntingfield-
with-Cookley in February 1932:

*'Because tithepayments are due half-yearly and payable within six months
after the due dates, QAB makes payments to the Rectors and Vicars
quarterly in advance: this was meant to be a blessing but it is a curse when
an incumbent is called upon unexpectedly, perhaps two years later, to
make repayments to QAB in respect of uncollected tithe.'*

In the benefice of Huntingfield-with-Cookley no less a sum than £403
was taken out of the Rector's income under the Ecclesiastical Dilapidations
Measure and in pension contributions before he had anything for his own
use. He then had to pay income and land tax, and rates on house and land.
On top of that there was the obligatory upkeep of a large house and garden
to the standard expected by parishioners. Mr Dobson concluded:

*'QAB has warned the Rector that arrears of tithe up to April 1 1931
amount to £343 and that there may be further arrears up to October 1st
1931. It is an impossible situation. How can anything like £343 be
repaid to QAB without insolvency? The tithe must be collected somehow
... It is unfair and useless for the Tithepayers' Association to slang the clergy,
for we cannot do anything about the tithe, as they ought to know.
Disestablishment of the Church would not bring relief: the Church in
Wales is both disestablished and disendowed, but tithe is not abolished; it
is paid to the State instead of the Church.'*

The Church authorities appeared to think the rural clergy could live on
fresh air and the tithe issue had the effect of reducing traditional farming
parishioners' support. Guy Mayfield defined the clergy role:

*'For both town and country parson alike, the paramount function is to
teach people about God ... Baptisms, marriages, funerals, sermons, eating
with Rotarians, serving on committees, producing plays, discussing crops
with a farmer – all these and many other secular occasions are for the*

parson, skilled in his job, opportunities of getting to know people so that they may be taught.'

Conversations with farmer parishioners were, however, more likely to end in acrimonious conflict over tithe than in a discussion about crops.

At a public meeting held by the Norfolk TPA in 1932 the Reverend F A Chase, Vicar of North Walsham, braved what the *Eastern Daily Press* dubbed 'the lions den' to say:

> *'... we clergy do not want to feel when we eat our bread and butter that you farmers grudge us having anything more than dry bread. It is a very difficult thing for you to pay tithe, it is a nasty thing for us to have to live on tithe and feel that you are grudging it. If I could live without tithe I would gladly give it up, because I know it is a burden on people who cannot pay, but because of my official position I cannot give away what I want to because of my successors.'*

Writing in the *Daily Mail* in 1934, F G Prince-White quoted the Bishop of Exeter, Lord William Cecil as saying that a vicar cannot afford to marry on £7 a week and a vicarage, and gave several instances of abject poverty among the rural clergy:

> *'... consider this: the rector of a rural parish in the diocese of York collapsed and was taken, unconscious, to hospital. Investigation revealed these facts: The total income from the living was not more than £350 a year ... For years life had been a bitter struggle for the rector, and he had got deeply into debt.'*

In Devon during 1932 the Reverend H P Scott, Rector of Atherlington, addressed a luncheon at the Umberleigh Christmas Fat Stock Show, saying:

> *'... the day is not far off when some means, other than tithes, will be devised whereby clergy can early their daily bread without having to pick the pockets of farmers.'*

Mr Scott admitted that he was one of those people who took away farmers' money as tithes but realised it was hard that they should have to support a church to which perhaps some of them did not go and in which they took little interest. He hoped, one day, that they would see a better system and that the time would never come when a farmer and a parson refused to shake hands.

As Chairman of the Suffolk TPA, AG Mobbs corresponded with several churchmen, including the Reverend George Holborow of Ringsfield, who wrote in March 1933:

'I am very far from being unsympathetic to the difficulties of Tithe Payers, but in view of the attitude of the Association as reported in the Press that all concessions on the part of Tithe Owners are to be refused, I do not feel that any good can result from local Tithe Owners discussing the matter of Tithe with your Committee, for until and unless further legislation governing Tithe takes place all that we can do is to offer concessions to hard cases among Tithe Payers and this of course you are rejecting. The discussions of any possible changes in the Tithe Acts is principally a matter for QAB (our trustees) and the Ministry of Agriculture and not for us local clergy who do not possess the available facts and are governed by conditions, such as Rates and Land Tax on Tithe, over which they have no control. The question of concessions would be pertinent for us to discuss but this I understand you are barring.

'As I daresay you know, I have attempted as a personal contribution to meet Ringsfield Tithe Payers by offering a number of them a concession of 18% where I feel that the circumstances are at present especially hard, and I arrived at the figure of 18% on the advice of your brother Mr Percy Mobbs who while I believe him to be perfectly fairminded could not be regarded as being biased in favour of the Tithe Owner as he is a Tithe Payer himself and a Non Conformist Churchman.'

The NTA had always seen the acceptance of concessions as an admission that tithe was property and was, therefore, unacceptable as any kind of solution. The Reverend Youlden Johnson of St Mary Elms in Ipswich wrote to P J Butler, Secretary of the Suffolk TPA and a Quaker, at the beginning of January 1932 criticising the tone of the tithepayers' propaganda:

'... you talk about the clergy themselves or other bullying agents. Had you said some of the clergy there might be truth in your statement, but it can do your cause no good to send out bitter and inflammatory leaflets grossly slandering all the clergy, or leading the unthinking to believe you are stating a fact concerning all the clergy. This is not English fair-play.'

Mr Johnson reiterated his belief that tithe was a property which tithepayers acquired when they bought and owned the land that carried the liability. The much-vaunted argument that tithed farms had been purchased more cheaply in the first place was put forward endlessly by Mr Johnson and others but never carried much weight since it was not true and easily disproved. Many farmers had unwittingly bought tithe along with their properties in the 1920s, often forced to buy when the large estates were split up, whilst others inherited their farms from fathers and grandfathers. Just as the new owner-occupiers had not been warned of the implications of tithe, so no one had warned the clergy of the need for private means in order to survive if they had to pay back their QAB income. In 1934 QAB's Principal Assistant Secretary W G Hannah attempted to justify this in *The Churchman's Handbook*:

'It may be desirable to correct a popular fallacy that Queen Anne's Bounty have vast funds available for disbursement. They are trustees of large funds, but most of their income is ear-marked for payment to incumbents entitled under the trusts.'

Articles critical of the clergy began to appear in the press, criticism that would have been better directed at the Chairman of QAB, Archbishop Lang, or the Government. John Sussex was typical of many commentators when he wrote in the *Daily Herald* in April 1930:

'... it is not often that a member of our family is seen at the village church these days, much as we love the place ... we are losing our respect for the parson.'

Doreen Wallace wrote in one of her many letters to the press:

'One must sympathise with those clerical titheowners who are seriously impoverished by the tithe crisis; but is it not a disgrace to that wealthy organisation, the Church, that such a situation can come about? It is absurd, surely, for the Church to place a parson in a parish and tell him, in effect – "You will live or starve according to the success or failure of a handful of farmers in your parish". This great organisation calls itself the National Church, not the Farmers' Church, yet in hundreds of years it has made no attempt to move with the times, to alter its constitution to fit national development; to face, in short, the fact that farming can no longer support it.'

The next step up from the ordinary clergy were the Bishops who after 1925 had a difficult time having to defend tithe, knowing, by then, that the Church would have to make up the shortfall when it was eventually abolished. The Bishop of St Edmundsbury and Ipswich drew the fire of the Suffolk and Essex tithepayers when he addressed the 1931 Diocesan Conference at Bury St Edmunds. There could be no question, he said, but that property in tithe was one of the oldest forms of property and that the Church just 'happened' to hold a very large investment in land in the form of tithe. The following year, at the spring session of the Church

Assembly in Westminster, Canon George Brocklehurst sought to secure a private debate on tithe as he thought a public debate was almost a 'dangerous proceeding'.

Canon Partridge, on behalf of the Central Board of Finance, agreed:

'I am convinced that it would be disastrous if we embarked on a public debate on tithe rentcharge at this session – disastrous from a political and from a business point of view.'

George Brocklehurst, Rector and Vicar of Newchurch, Kent had included in his book a very specific and detailed guide on how the clergy might best collect their tithes. He thought that the matter had never been explored from the parson's point of view and that his brother clergy should have better knowledge of the chief source of their income. He endeavoured to show how the parson might collect tithe with a minimum of expense:

'The tithe rentcharge payable to clerical owners is rather more than £3,000,000 per annum, and the fees and salaries for collecting this must amount to quite £100,000 a year ... it behoves every clergyman to have his facts on tithe clear and certain.'

Though twenty years out of date, Canon Brocklehurst's book was still on many rectory desks in the 1930s and for much of the rural clergy it was all they had in the way of guidance. (Although collection was done for them by QAB after 1925 there were several that maintained the right to collect their own tithe.) His attempt to start a debate was spurred on by what was happening in Kent at the time by way of public demonstration and was a brave move. However, his suggestion of debate, in private or otherwise, was dismissed by Conference. A few days later, in February 1932, a Suffolk tithepayer wrote to a newspaper:

'[Canon Brocklehurst's] motion was dropped at the instigation of our local Bishop ... the Bishop suggests that tithe should be redeemed. I, in common with many small landowners, am not a rich man. To redeem my tithe would cost £740. Can he suggest why I should pay that to the Church for nothing? ... Surely it would have been better to have supported Canon Brocklehurst's motion. I have known him (Canon Brocklehurst) well for many years, and a fairer, more just and broader-minded cleric never lived.'

At the Church Assembly's autumn session in the same year, the Archbishop was again asked to appoint a commission to go into the question of QAB and the Ecclesiastical Commission. A small group did meet, but as far as the tithepayers were concerned it achieved nothing more than to assert that the Royal Charter of 1704, which had brought the Bounty onto the statute books, should remain. It seemed a poor response to the tithe question that daily became more urgent. There was a risk of yet more clergy losing a large part of their income through non-payment and the general public seemed to have strong sympathies with the tithepayers. Unlike the Bishops and Archbishops, the rural clergy were in the front line.

Occasionally, a tithepayer ventured into the Trollope-like halls of Lambeth Palace. Mrs J E Oliphant of Bromley in Kent told AG Mobbs in 1933:

> 'I paid a visit to the Palace on the Embankment, and was ushered into the presence of a representative sitting in state in a lofty room. I was asked my business, and when I had stated how impossible it was to meet the heavy tithe expenses, was most politely dismissed with a shake of the hand and "Oh, I am afraid there are ways and means of procuring the tithe – good bye" ... and to think all that I have in life to live on is £800 and yet these dignitaries of the church live in comfort taking our little earnings.'

In 1933 an article, one of many on the subject, appeared in the *Church Times* and included the comment:

> '... the Anglican rector or vicar, who draws the whole or a portion of his professional income from tithe, draws it as a minister of a Church to which this tithe in some form or other has been payable for more than a thousand years. This tithe has been treated as property by the law, and when it was owned by a layman passed, on his death, to his heir as hereditable property.'

The contentious point as to whether tithe should or should not be regarded as 'property' was almost the only argument put forward by the Church and the one most often repeated by the man charged with the responsibility of collection, the Labour MP George Middleton. It was Middleton who, as Chairman of QAB and First Church Commissioner, became the mouthpiece for the defence of tithe, arguing consistently from the viewpoint of its unassailable legality. It was his answer to almost any question, regardless of what the question was, although he invariably managed to spin out the essence of his argument into very long speeches. At a crowded meeting of tithepayers at Canterbury he addressed his audience for nearly three hours. He only had one line of defence, and it was enough to keep him permanently on the 'right' side. It was simply unlawful for tithepayers not to pay their tithe. No amount of reasoning would move him on this single,

THE PARASITE

(This and page 73)
Cartoons showing the depth
of animosity felt by tithepayers
towards the Church.

' I'LL GET BLOOD OUT OF YOU – OR SMASH YOU ! '

irrefutable point: those who distrained on the farmer were maintaining the law and those who found themselves in the County Courts were breaking the law. He never competed for the morality of tithe but always accepted it as an inalienable right of the Church.

Middleton went to great lengths to stop the clerical debate instigated by Canon Brocklehurst. He told the Diocesan Conference in 1933 that they must leave the matter of tithe to QAB and keep the Church 'out of it'. Such was the strength of his persuasion that when the Bishop of Chelmsford called on Canon Brown to move a formal adjournment to the Conference discussion, those present took it as a direction from the chair that they were not to engage in public debate of any kind. The Bishop ordered that a proposed discussion on tithe in his own diocese be halted immediately, causing the newspapers to declare that a muzzle had been put on the clergy. The Bishop's adjunct for silence was not universally obeyed, however, and the debate continued.

Middleton was even criticised by the *Church of England Newspaper* who saw his refusal to take part in a conference to discuss the 1925 Act as 'regrettable'. A more sympathetic and less legalistic policy was looked for which could have avoided misunderstanding and bitterness. It was the unfortunate parsons who suffered, pointed out the editorial, not QAB.

Having served his formative years among those able to use language in a pedantic and obscure way, designed to give the impression of substance while in reality saying nothing, Middleton was always able to respond to the tithepayers with a stream of 'bureau-speak'. He used words such as 'burlesque' and 'subversive' to describe the tithepayers' cause, and referred to the TPAs as 'the quack remedy of tithe resistance'. He deliberately tempered his comments about AG with such dismissals as '... *I am afraid that Mr Mobbs has succumbed to the temptation of indulging in what, for politeness, I must term picturesque exaggeration...*'.

At a meeting in the Ipswich Co-operative Hall, the *East Anglian Daily Times* reported:

> '*Mr AG Mobbs, who is chairman of the Suffolk Tithepayers' Association, was loudly applauded when he got up to question. He said he merely wanted to know whether Mr Middleton considered that the titheowner was a partner in the land? ... Mr Middleton replied: "What on earth does it matter to me how and when the property represented by the tithe rent-charge was created by the other party? If I borrow money from another person in order to help me over a difficulty I am then under a legal obligation to repay it – but I don't lie awake wondering where he got it from".*'

Middleton saw non-payers as taking advantage of the situation. '*There is no need,*' he told the *East Anglian Daily Times* in 1934, '*for the Church to stand in a white sheet over this tithe rentcharge. I do not want the clergy to feel they have anything to be ashamed of. Tithe rentcharge is just as much the property of the Church as land owned by the Ecclesiastical Commissioners; and the tithepayer has no more right to refuse to discharge this liability than has the tenant farmer to refuse to pay his rent.*'

There appeared to be no place for ethics in Middleton's brief. J A Venn, however, wrote in his commentary on the subject:

> '*This is not the place in which to discuss the ethics of tithe payment; it is simply the duty of the historian or of the economist to give an unbiased account of its development and of its incidence. One is bound to record, however, that exception has, during the last century, been taken to it on the grounds that, even in England, it often causes*

the payment of money by members of one religious body to the support of the personnel of another denomination. On these grounds, it is urged, that neither commutation in the past nor redemption at the present meets the case; that only its immediate and complete extinction or its forcible secularisation by the State to such purposes as education can assuage the claims of conscience.'

Venn might have been better advised to stick to his original instincts as to his duty as historian, since he also wrote:

'Surely the answer to this is that, for upwards of fifteen hundred years, custom has ordained its payment, not idly to any sectarian party, but to the partial support of the established and national Church – that Church which the vast majority of even its non-members call to their assistance on all the most important occasions of their passage through life?'

That was exactly the point, so far as tithepayers were concerned. Tithe could not be justified merely because it had existed for 'upwards of fifteen hundred years', which very time-span made it an anachronism.

Various objections to the use of tithe for the national Church are too numerous to list, but one example cited by the Non-conformist brethren was that, until the Burial Law Reform Act of 1880, their members could not be buried in Anglican churchyards.

In Oxfordshire a Baptist Church owned a one-acre plot of land and had to pay tithe to the local vicar. The Baptist Minister had a stipend of £250 a year and charge of six village chapels, while the vicar had a gross income of £766 and charge of two churches. When the Baptists refused to pay the tithe the bailiff tried to seize a portion of the plot of land and sell it for unpaid arrears, but the treasurer refused to tell the Court the whereabouts of the land. The Tithe Commissioners, however, discovered that the chapel was in receipt of a mere £3 from Abraham Atkins Charities, which they somehow took from the charity fund.

English Catholics merely pointed to the Reformation and what they felt to be lingering discrimination against them, not to mention the theft of their church buildings.

Quakers had a long and honourable tradition of resisting tithe and cited the special legislation that once applied to land in Quaker occupation. Until 1891 their goods, chattels and effects, not only on the premises but also elsewhere, could be distrained on for the recovery of rentcharge. One of the first 1930s tithepayers to call for passive resistance in Suffolk was the Quaker

SHARKS.

P J Butler, who walked the streets of Ipswich with a sandwich board denouncing tithe. He suffered six enforced sales at his farm.

Objections to paying tithe were not based solely on opposition to the Church, since there was just as much resentment aimed at lay impropriators, although in Wales the 'Church' problem had been mitigated, if not solved, by the secularisation of tithe under the Church Acts of 1914 and 1919. No obligation devolved on QAB to collect in Wales – a point George Middleton often used to illustrate how reasonable QAB was in negotiating with hard-pressed English tithepayers. At a public meeting in Dorset in April 1933 he asked whether any owner-occupier in Wales was likely to get the sort of remission from the Government that he would get from QAB. The Bounty, he pointed out, was not responsible to Parliament and could make remission if it pleased. He said that there were a thousand cases currently where discounts had been negotiated with tithepayers who had been able to prove they were unable to pay. Tithepayers' answer to that was that they were not in the business of asking for charity or for discounts. They wanted justice and justice meant abolition.

The task facing QAB investigators was outlined in the Journal of the Chamber of Agriculture:

'Mr Middleton, when speaking in the West of England, said that QAB was out to help hard cases. There are about 80,000 to 100,000 tithepayers in England, and if Sir George Courthope's figures of 70 to 80 per cent of the farmers are on the verge of bankruptcy are correct, QAB, with only four investigators, who had only so far gone into 2000 cases, still have many thousands of cases to investigate, and a long way to go before any real relief is given.'

Under the 1925 Tithe Act, QAB was entitled to collect some £2,165,000 of ecclesiastical tithe annually and hand it over to around 6,000 beneficed clergy. To justify this collection to the thousands of small tithepayers, Middleton's tactic was to set out what the Church had lost in potential income by allowing a more flexible system of setting the average annual payments. A sum exceeding £14,000,000 had been 'saved' by stabilising tithe in 1925 at a lower figure than it had been in 1918. In May 1933, the Bishop of Chelmsford wrote in the *Chelmsford Diocesan Chronicle*:

'The Tithe Acts of 1918 and 1925, the latter of which has particularly come under denunciation, have saved the tithepayer fourteen million pounds: the greater part of which would have been received by the Church. As was pointed out in the debate on April 17th, in the House of Lords, in 1925 the tithe was mounting to unprecedented levels, and the stabilisation of tithe meant a tremendous loss to the titheowner.'

Unsurprisingly, the argument that while tithe might be hurting it could be hurting a lot more was not one which found any favour among those who thought it should not hurt at all.

The lack of moral justification on the part of George Middleton was, no doubt, a deliberate move to distance him from the emotional aspects of the job. But in the end it came down to money. When tithe was abolished, where would the money come from to pay the rural clergy? There could surely have been no doubt in either Middleton's, or indeed Archbishop Lang's, mind that tithe would go, since provision for compulsory extinguishment of ecclesiastical tithe had been made in 1925, to be paid for by annuity payments until the year 2009. From the tithepayers' point of view this was a very long drawn-out process, but the Church could hardly claim that it was not given enough time to make alternative arrangements. Yet in 1936, when the Church was finally compelled to surrender its income from tithe in exchange for £70,000,000 of government stock, the Commissioners were still wondering how to make up the shortfall. Inevitably, this caused many rural incumbents severe economic hardship and, writes Guy Mayfield:

'The Governors of Queen Anne's Bounty lost an annual income of about £50,000 and the cathedrals about £15,000 annually of a total income of £95,000. In effect the State expropriated capital funds of the benefices amounting to £11 and a half million, and the ultimate capital loss was about £18 million.'

Tithepayers thought ecclesiastical and lay impropriators were exceedingly lucky to get anything at all, since they disputed the fundamental concept of tithe being either property or an inalienable right. In France tithe had been abolished in 1789 without compensation or a sinking fund, and in 1837 it had been abolished in Switzerland and Spain.

By 1935, when confrontation between the tithepayers and the Church came to a dramatic head, it was difficult for the Church of England to pretend nothing was happening. The new Tithe Bill introduced into Parliament in 1934 was met with such open hostility that a Royal Commission was appointed. While the Commission took evidence, the pressure mounted: throughout the early 1930s public protest at the seizure of farm stock by the bailiffs and the County Courts occupied vast areas of the national press. Oswald Mosley's 'Blackshirts' were involved in high-profile distraint raids and payment arrears became serious, if not disastrous, for the rural clergy who depended on tithe.

In April 1935 tithepayers' anger overflowed in Kent. They mounted a ferocious attack on Church and State, the focus being the Archbishop of Canterbury and the Bounty's founder, Queen Anne. It took place at Beechbrook Farm at Westwell in Kent, where nine cows were to be seized by order against the Reverend Kedward's tenant, his brother-in-law Mr A T Chapman, for tithe worth £69. Demonstrators blew trumpets and whistles throughout the proceedings, and fireworks were thrown into the auction ring. Wives and daughters of the protesters lay down in the road in front of lorries loaded with oats that had been seized from the farm. The bailiff's job was made impossible as the strings binding the sheaves were cut; lorries attempting to escape the barricades drove across a potato field, leaving a trail of oats behind them.

Donkeys wearing placards declaring 'Even I Know Tithe is Nothing to Bray About' led a line of banner-waving protesters who carried effigies of Archbishop Lang and Queen Anne shoulder-high. The banners read 'Queen Anne is Dead', 'Tithe a Disgrace to the Church' and 'Crematorium for Ecclesiastical Commissioners', and were aimed in the direction of the press

Roderick Kedward (right) leads the protest at Westwell, Kent in 1935, after which an effigy of the Archbishop was ritually burned.

cameramen as they followed the procession round the farm. Roderick Kedward addressed the crowd:

'These cows are being offered for sale – we are not bidding ourselves for them. We are not buying them in or arranging for anybody to bid.'

Neither the owner of the farm, nor the farmer, could bid for their own stock, but the auctioneer, Mr Harry Judge of Tenterden, appealed in vain for other bids. Lot after lot was led out of the ring, each time to the explosion of fireworks and a rendering of 'Rule Britannia' from the crowd, which consisted of farmers, representatives of several TPAs, around sixty local farmworkers, and a gathering of well-wishers.

They were successful in stopping the auction of the farm stock, which had been seized on orders of the County Court for arrears of £38 3s 9d and £21 2s made at Ashford in favour of the Ecclesiastical Commissioners. Mr Judge appealed again for bids until eventually the last lot, a piglet that was the property of Mr A C Birch of Eastry, was offered for sale in aid of TPA funds. It was sold forty times, realising a total of £20 2s 6d. The report in the *Kentish Express* remarked on the fact that '... several ladies made bids'. Then:

> *A procession was formed, headed by the effigies, which were carried shoulder-high from the farmyard to a bonfire, which had been built in an adjoining field. The effigy of the Primate bore a placard which read, "The Arch of Cant" and "Church on Sunday but hands on the farmer", whilst that of Queen Anne carried the words: "Parsons' feet have been under our table too long" ... amidst the firing of maroons, exploding fireworks and the blowing of squeakers, the procession moved to the bonfire, upon which the effigies were placed.'*

Mr Chapman lit the twelve-foot high bonfire and the cameras of the national press clicked gleefully as the crowd sang 'Keep the Home Fires Burning' and clods of earth were thrown at the effigy of the Archbishop.

The *Daily Sketch* headline 'Primate's Effigy in a Bonfire – Fireworks at an amazing Tithe Sale Protest' was accompanied by graphic images of banner-carrying protestors.

Lurid reports in the *Daily Mirror* told of the mock inquest held after the burning of the effigies, when the Reverend Kedward found that '*... these people died a just death for robbery with violence on various farms and small holdings of England*'.

The *East Anglian Daily Times* reported Mr Kedward as saying that he intended to serve a subpoena on the Archbishop of Canterbury, as the first Ecclesiastical Commissioner. The Archbishop would be required to appear at Ashford County Court and produce the accounts, pass book and correspondence relating to previous distraints made on his property. In particular there was the matter of some ducks that had been removed from the pond at Beechbrook Farm to a pond on the Ecclesiastical Commission's farm at West Court, Shepherdswell. (Mysteriously, though, some of these ducks found their way back to Beechbrook Farm and Mr Kedward was quoted as saying he thought they must be 'homing ducks'!)

In the cold light of day, questions were asked in the House of Commons about the Westwell incident and about a report that had been sent to the Minister of Agriculture by the Reverend Kedward. The Minister was asked if he was in a position to give any information about the proceedings of the Royal Commission. The *Kentish Express* was unable to reassure its readers:

Roderick Kedward (centre) poses with his youngest daughter Brenda, brother-in-law Mr Chapman and effigies of Queen Anne and the Archbishop at the 1935 distraint sale at Beechbrook Farm, Westwell, Kent. Cattle were seized against tithe arrears of £69 due in 1929. (June Shepherd)

'Major G Davies, for the Minister, said that while the Minister had not received the report referred to, he had seen the references in the Press to the sale. As the hon. Member was informed ... the collection and recovery of tithe was not within the jurisdiction of the Ministry. The answer to the last part of the question was in the negative.'

The MP for Canterbury, Sir William Wayland said he thought it was 'most discreditable' to any farmer or body of farmers that they should have insulted the head of the Church. He told the *Kentish Express:*

'We all have the greatest respect for the Archbishop of Canterbury. He has no more to do with the tithe you and I pay – than that stove. He could no more have cancelled that sale than anyone in this room.'

Sir William appeared to be correct; the Archbishop of Canterbury was, indeed, no more effective in the matter than a stove.

In the face of such inertia from both the Church and the Government, the tithepayers could only plough their chosen furrow. Over the next few months more bonfires were lit and the 'Archbishop' and 'Queen Anne' reduced to ashes, while in the countryside the Bishops were on the receiving end of angry lobbyists. Soon after the Westwell incident, a huge demonstration threatened to greet the Bishop of Dover when he attended the village of Ruckinge, Kent to induct a new rector. A group of men found hanging around the church porch on the night before told a reporter from the *Daily Mirror:*

'We know the farmers are up to something ... but our new rector (the Rev H Hammond) will win them over when he gets here. It will be a pity if they do anything that will make this impossible. He is a first-rate sportsman.'

It was to be hoped, presumably, that the Rev Hammond was going to have more to offer than his prowess as a sportsman. In the event, when the Bishop arrived there was a Superintendent of Police on hand, together with an inspector, two sergeants and a large number of constables, but there was no demonstration. Instead a gate opposite the church had been painted with the words 'Thou shalt not covet thy neighbour's ox' and posters put up on boards in a neighbouring field bearing anti-tithe slogans.

Some years later the tithepayers were heavily criticised for the 'terrible and appalling habit of burning effigies', thus singling out the Church for ridicule. Lay impropriators were not ridiculed, said the critics, and therefore proved the agitation to be one of religious prejudice. The reply was that the majority of

**Queen Anne burned in effigy on the gallows at Fordingbridge,
Hampshire during a tithe sale.**

tithe was paid to the Church and that the Government had also given QAB
authority to collect on behalf of lay rectors. Doreen Wallace said:

> *'We have got to burn effigies ... if the English character had not been
> constituted as it is there might have been bloodshed by now ... but we are
> a cool and humorous lot of people and a little foolery liquidates a lot of
> ill-feeling. Effigy-burning has always been done to express dislike and
> resentment instead of committing bodily violence. If anybody can see
> anything disgusting about it I suggest they should go away and get their
> sense of humour brightened up a bit.'*

Bishop Shedden, in a sermon preached in the Oxfordshire parish of Cuddesdon,
called tithe '... *a stumbling block in the way of the Church's spiritual mission'* and added:

> *'... the scandal of the tithe is still with us ... as so many country parsons
> know well, it is doing much to poison the relationship between priest and
> people. Is it not an intolerable situation when a parish priest can only save
> himself and his family from death or starvation by forcing his principal
> parishioner into bankruptcy?'*

During the years 1931 to 1935 tithepayers' mood generally was one of
angry defiance against the Church such as had not been witnessed in rural

"SCANDAL OF THE TITHE IS STILL WITH US"

Bishop Shedden's Remarkable Sermon at Cuddesdon College Festival

A REMARKABLE comment on the question of tithes was made by Bishop Roscow Shedden, Vicar of Wantage, in a sermon at the service in connection with Cuddesdon College festival at Cuddesdon Parish Church to-day.

" It is a far cry," he said, " from the day when Bishop Barlow could sell the lead from the roof of the old palace at St. David's to provide a marriage portion for his daughter, and we do not hear nowadays of Bishops of Durham building princely houses in Berkshire out of the revenues of the Northern See.

" But the scandal of the tithe is still with us. I use the word scandal in its strictest sense. However clear the rights and justifiable the position of the clergy in regard to tithe, it is in fact a stumbling block in the way of the Church's spiritual mission.

INTOLERABLE SITUATION

" As so many country parsons know well, it is doing much to poison the relationship between priest and people. Is it not an intolerable situation when a parish priest can only save himself and his family from death or starvation by forcing his principal parishioner into bankruptcy ?

" Even though we learn with a sigh of relief that Queen Anne's Bounty has been more successful in collections of tithe during the past year, there are deep undercurrents of resentment which are not always voiced.

" Can you wonder that farmers who bought their land on a mortgage, at a time of inflated prices, should, in a period of depression, feel bitter about paying the tithe that was stabilised during the time of those inflated prices ?

MOST DEPRESSED INDUSTRY

"Also they feel it inequitable, or shall I say iniquitous, that in these changed conditions of English life, agriculture, the most depressed of English indus-

tries, should still be compelled to bear the cost of the maintenance of the clergy through the length and breadth of England, while the non-land-owning classes get their religious privileges for nothing.

" I speak to you as one who depends for his living on tithe. I do not know what my position would be without it, and I dare say that for some of you the position is rendered even more difficult from the fact that you have given hostages to fortune in children and wives.

" The whole question is enormously complicated, but I am certain there is something we ought at least to do, and which I am convinced for myself that I have hardly attempted.

BLIGHT ON SPIRITUAL INFLUENCE

" We ought to show we are not simply acquiescent in the regular receipt of whatever Queen Anne is able to collect for us, preferring to know nothing of the hardships inflicted thereby.

" We ought from Archbishops and Diocesans downwards to cultivate a fuller understanding of—and manifest a much larger sympathy with—the genuine difficulties of the tithepayer.

" It is the lack of this which is doing much to blight the spiritual influence of the Church at the present time and, following on this, we ought not, I am certain, to yield to the temptation of asking them to acquiesce in the sacrifice of their own prospects and their children's on the grounds of the arrangements whereby all tithe will have been redeemed by the end of 80 years.

READY TO WELCOME SACRIFICE

" If we are to be truly faithful to our divine mission, we ought to be ready to welcome some sacrifice for ourselves as a means of bringing the present state of things to an end at the earliest possible date.

" Therefore I plead, in the name of Jesus Christ, that whatever the recommendations of the Tithe Commission, the attitude of the clergy shall not be one of intransigeant opposition."

Britain for a very long time. The Royal Commission inaugurated in 1934 seemed to be taking forever. Thousands of pounds were being extracted from desperate tithepayers suffering from one of the worst agricultural depressions for fifty years, and the battles raged back and forth as they refused to pay and were distrained upon by QAB.

The press could hardly contain itself as it ran anti-Church headlines and splashed sensational photographs of rural England in chaos and open revolt across its front pages. At public meetings the NTA used their cartoon posters, showing the parson as the villain of the piece, though in truth it was not the parson but the institution that was the enemy. The Royal Commission's report was going to be crucial, not just to the tithepayers, but to the embattled rural clergy who were suffering badly at parish level. The protesters were not, as the press pointed out, anarchists or atheists: they were ordinary, usually law-abiding, farmers who were aggrieved at the injustice wrought on them and whose patience was as exhausted as their financial resources.

Towards the end of 1935, however, the tithepayers' cause was in danger of drifting into the muddy waters of political extremism, with several in the ranks giving support to right-wing factions of the main parties. As will be seen in later chapters, the Fascist leader Oswald Mosley had only a short flirtation with British agriculturists, but his 'Blackshirt' supporters were identified in the national press as being on the side of the tithepayers in several high-profile distraints. AG and his supporters knew it was essential to retain public goodwill and to be seen to be linked with the respectability of the NFU and CLA. Some in the TPA ranks were alarmed at what was happening in Kent and were frankly shocked at the tactics of their President, but they had little choice other than to give their support. Publicity was their only weapon, although in order for it to be effective it had to be good publicity, not violent or associated with Fascism or extremism. They needed to raise awareness of the cause, not alienate either their supporters or the public at large, and most especially they needed to keep 'on side' those MPs who supported them and who owed their allegiance to the Head of the Established Church.

Many tithepayers had an understanding for the plight of the rural parsons, many of whom suffered greatly, not just financially but in their status as clergymen. But the tithepayers could not afford sentiment, however much it was merited. It would not help either party if they let the institutions of

(Opposite) 'Scandal of the tithe is still with ss' – leaflet distributed in 1935.

Church and State off the hook. An inquiry into the degrading and degenerating state of the rural clergy was long overdue, but would never be accomplished so long as tithe remained their source of income. A wide body of opinion, including most of the Bishops, generally agreed that something had to change and the sooner the better.

There was, though, a problem in that some of the rural clergy had private means. They lived in comparative luxury and kept quiet about it. In the tithe-rich Eastern Counties some parsons had incomes of around £1,000 from tithe, as did the Rector of Wortham in Suffolk, which drew attention away from the worse-off clergy.

In *The Tithe War*, Doreen Wallace launched a fierce attack on clergymen whose incomes were well over £1,000 per annum, in parishes that had populations of only around 800 souls, not all of whom attended regular services. Several incumbents had incomes of between £500 and £600 in parishes of less than 1,000 head of population. She gave specific amounts and named the parishes, evidence she was later to submit in exhaustive detail to the Royal Commission. Yet although she raged indignantly against ecclesiastical tithe, her portrayal of a country parson in Barnham Rectory shows compassion for those at the mercy of 'a great body like the Church', whose Archbishop ought to make better arrangements for the paying of its men and not leave them dependent on farmers for a living. In the novel, the Reverend Austin Mapperly is portrayed as an innocent victim of the tithe and his Church.

Tithepayers would often make an effort to bargain with the clergy where they could and in what became a famous raid on Delvyn's Farm, Gestingthorpe in Essex, the tithepayer Mrs Gardiner (whose husband's family had been vocal in the tithe uprisings in the 1880s) offered the rector half the amount due. She thought it was fair enough, since the rector's net stipend from the parish was £580 per annum, and much of his tithe holding was not linked to his office but tithe he had acquired. Mrs Gardiner's offer was refused and an auctioneer from Wales was brought to Essex to tender for the goods. Three hundred farmers assembled on the farm to hinder the auctioneer, Mr James of Swansea, a solicitor and the bailiff in their task.

In his evidence to the Royal Commission the Norfolk tithepayers' leader F Kidner said that he was a churchwarden but criticised the efforts of many clergymen who, he said, obtained good stipends from the poverty-stricken countryside. He declared that one incumbent who received £1,000 a year went to Monte Carlo for eight months of the year, while his curate received 55 shillings a week to do his job in the parish.

Naturally there were differences of opinion within agriculture about tithe and its relationship to the Church. Farms were not run entirely by their owners and anything that reduced agriculture's profitability necessarily affected farm workers. With the prevailing objective of land nationalisation in mind, the 1932 Biennial Conference of the National Union of Agricultural Workers held a long debate on the tithe question. Brother E Brice (Wiltshire), a Wesleyan local preacher, moved a resolution for the abolition of tithe, to which Brother W Martin (Dorset) replied

George Edwards with his political agent, Edwin Gooch outside the Labour Institute at Wymondham, Norfolk in 1923. (Michael Gooch)

that he was seconding the resolution, although as far as he was concerned he did not 'care twopence' about the farmer or the landlord. The man who concerned him most was the one who was earning 30s a week. Even those incumbents with assured incomes of a modest £400 a year knew it was several times that of a farm worker, he said.

Sir George Edwards, a legend in his own lifetime among farm workers, took part in the debate and thought the Union should keep out of it and

Brother H E Durham (Norfolk) agreed. He said that if they left tithe alone *'it was likely to split the holy trinity of the landlord, the parson, and the farmer'*. He thought that one of the finest things they could do was to increase the burdens on land and make it impossible for farmers to carry on. Land would become cheaper and it would lead to land nationalisation, a much-cherished ambition of many delegates. If they left the matter alone it would allow the 'parsons and the farmers to fight it out between themselves' and, as agricultural workers, they would be much better off.

For his part, the Lord Archbishop of Canterbury was unconcerned about the plight or otherwise of farm workers. In a parliamentary debate on the Tithe Bill going through the House of Lords in 1936 he said:

'... I am not going to follow the noble Lord who has just sat down in his discourse about the Old Testament, nor do I propose to discuss whether or not the agricultural labourer has been left out. If he has been left out, it is for the good reason that in this matter he does not come in.'

The noble Lord Marley had said that the land could not bear both tithe payments and wages; it was clear that if tithe payment was too high the agricultural labourer would have to be dismissed, or it would be used as an argument to keep down farm workers' wages.

Archbishop Cosmo Lang, though, was aloof from the masses and sought the company of royalty and prominent persons. He had a romantic attachment to the office of the Royal Person and his deference to the aristocracy occasioned him to be called a snob; he was definitely not a man who enjoyed mixing with ordinary people, and certainly not with farm workers. There is just one, eighteen-line paragraph about tithe in J G Lockhart's biography of Lang in which he says: *'... The Archbishop was inevitably prominent in the Parliamentary debates. He took the line that the Church would not oppose commutation in principle, but was entitled to a more generous rate of compensation than either of the Bills allowed.'*

How much difference it would have made to the failure of the Church to grasp the nettle of tithe if the more left-wing Archbishop of York, William Temple had become Archbishop of Canterbury in 1928 is debatable. Dr Temple, a former Labour Party member who openly supported Socialism, was scathing about the process by which the proposal for eventual abolition was reached, maintaining that it was an infringement of the rights of the Church. As Archbishop of York, he spoke in the eventual debate of the 1936 Tithe Act, saying:

'... at least one thing can be affirmed with satisfaction. The Church is receiving nothing from the State except security for part of its own property. Whatever else may be said of the reduction of our resources by some £11,000,000, it cannot be represented as an act of endowment. In years to come it may be important to make this clear. Because the Government, in taking away some of our property, is giving a renewed guarantee for what remains, that remaining part may one day be falsely described as a gift from the Government. Let us then take care to make it plain that what is now to be again secured to us is our own property, and only part of that.'

In the run-up to the 1936 Act it appeared strange to many that two of the most ardent defenders of tithe – Dr Temple and George Middleton – were Labour supporters. As a declared Socialist, Dr Temple might have been expected to take a more hands-on approach when, in his turn, he became Archbishop of Canterbury in 1942. During his term of office he corresponded with tithepayers' leaders and shortly before his death two years later he acknowledged the on-going grievance. He initiated consultation on the matter but died before anything came of his intervention. (In 1945 his successor, Dr Fisher refused a tithepayers' deputation, saying it was no longer a matter for the Church but for Government.)

As spokesman for the ecclesiastical titheowners, and a remote figure, Archbishop Lang was blamed for much of the anti-Church feeling from both sides. Lay impropriators looked to him in vain for a more aggressive stand on their behalf as well as for the ecclesiastical titheowners. In a caption under a photograph of the Archbishop's effigy, A E Waddell, a former member of the East Kent Yeomanry and a Kentish hop farmer, warned readers of the *Daily Mirror* that 'Britain will be seeing more of this soon'. He wrote:

'I am being persecuted by the Church. You have read, no doubt, of men who have been harried, imprisoned, even tortured in the name of religion. And you think that all passed with the Dark Ages. Yet the shade of Church oppression still falls on me and mine. This month, for a matter of £2, I am to be the latest victim of that powerful body, Queen Anne's Bounty. Twenty ewes and a haystack which belong to me are to be seized.'

Mr Waddell owned only half of his farm; the other half belonged to the Ecclesiastical Commissioners. Mr Waddell had taken out a mortgage to buy his half of the land from the Commissioners for £4,950. He was particularly bitter when the QAB agent tackled him over his arrears as he had suffered the indignity of having to open his books to them in order to prove his inability to pay. He told the *Daily Mirror*:

> *'These Church people are dreadful: money is their God. They persecute you like this ... the adjoining parish of Mersham is worth over £600 a year to the clergyman, and Aldington, nearby, is worth £1,050 a year.'*

The agent demanded that he pay out of capital, though Mr Waddell explained that besides an overdraft of £400 and an annual loss on the farm of £169, he had only a small amount of capital, money left to his children by his late wife:

> *'... and I will see you in hell before I rob my three motherless children to pay tithes.'*

As the Royal Commission languidly and ponderously took evidence from the interested parties during 1935, the sensational press coverage was bound to have an effect on those who would weigh and evaluate the considerations over eighteen months. For that reason the tithepayers kept up the pressure, and everyone's eyes turned to the Archbishop and Parliament for the final solution. As Bishop Roscow Shedden, Vicar of Wantage said in his Cuddesdon sermon:

> *'... We ought to show we are not simply acquiescent in the regular receipt of whatever Queen Anne is able to collect for us, preferring to know nothing of the hardships inflicted thereby ... we ought from Archbishops and Diocesans downwards to cultivate a fuller understanding of – and manifest a much larger sympathy with – the genuine difficulties of the tithepayer ... I plead, in the name of Jesus Christ, that whatever the recommendations of the Tithe Commission, the attitude of the clergy shall not be one of intransigent opposition.'*

~ o ~

Chapter 4

BATTLE LINES ARE DRAWN

'A meeting was arranged at the Crown and Anchor Hotel, Ipswich, in February 1931 and advertised as being for the purpose of forming a Suffolk Tithepayers' Association. We were crowded out, a large number of farmers being unable to obtain admission. We soon agreed to set up an organisation with myself as Chairman and Mr Makens Turner, another member of the Suffolk NFU Executive, as Vice Chairman.'

AG Mobbs
Eighty Years on Suffolk Soil

IN HIS AUTOBIOGRAPHY, AG Mobbs recorded that the years 1931 to 1934 had been the busiest for the Tithepayers' Associations. By 1930 the effects of the 1925 Tithe Act had begun to bite: QAB was using the facility of distraint and in reply a deliberate policy of non-payment became the tithepayers' first weapon of defence. Distraint raids were taking place on farms – animals, crops, machinery and household furniture taken in lieu of tithe rentcharge. Tempers were frayed as rural parishes saw local men and women hauled before the County Courts to be made criminals by the Church and lay impropriators. Those who did pay, terrified into submission by their first confrontation with law and authority, did so out of fast-dwindling capital, or bank overdrafts; others saw what small profits there were creamed off by the titheowners, often leaving left them destitute. Owner-occupiers with mortgages found tithe demands an intolerable burden and harboured resentment against the titheowner, invariably the Church of England. With agriculture in the doldrums there was little chance that they could sell their farms, and even if they did it would be at a price well below that which they had paid.

Judges were also concerned that the increasing intensity of the tithe war was bringing the legal process into disrepute. Sir Boyd Merriman, the Solicitor-General appeared in the High Court when a ruling was sought against Judge Clements, the County Court judge of Hythe in Kent. QAB was applying for a rule as a sequel to Judge Clements's refusal to make an order against a farmer for £81 tithe rentcharge. The Judge had announced that he would not make further tithe orders against farmers at a time when there were over 1,000 unexecuted orders outstanding in Kent alone. The *News Chronicle* reported:

> *'Many attempts at levying tithe execution are also accompanied by fighting between farm workers on the one hand and hired minions on the other. A number of cases in which the fighting has assumed such proportions that men on both sides have been badly bludgeoned are being considered by officials from the office of the Director of Public Prosecutions, who, on this matter is in close touch with the law officers.*
>
> *'On one of these tithe raids, the "defenders" in an attempt to keep back a number of men, who had arrived in lorries, "electrified" a wire fencing round the farm by connecting it with the coil of a motor-car and running the engine at full speed.'*

On another occasion two hundred farmers who had not paid their tithes were summoned before Judge Clements at Ashford County Court. Fifty attended and sustained five hours of legal argument. After 180 cases had been dealt with, mainly by the appointment of a Receiver, the Judge expressed the opinion that it was a pity that in those days of conferences and truces, the tithe would not cease. He thought it would be better settled in a spirit of conciliation, and went on to rule that the titheowners could not recover more than two years' arrears at one time.

Judge Hildesley, at Sudbury County Court in Suffolk, told defaulters that he found himself in something of a quandary. He had no fewer than 273 cases of non-payment before him and had no option but to enforce the payments as there were farmers who had agreed to pay and he could not prejudice them by allowing some to pay and not others. Judge Hildesley was also called upon to make a judgement at Stowmarket where QAB was claiming eleven shillings rentcharge from the Needham Market Gas Company on a certain portion of their land at Needham Market. The Gas Company had not paid the tithe for over eighty years and produced title deeds to confirm that at least part of the land had been conveyed tithe-free. An adjoining piece of land, owned by Quinton & Sons, was liable to the same tithe and the judge decided that although the amount was small and the liability dubious, there was no Statute of Limitations that ran in the Gas Company's favour, and he made an order for payment.

In 1933 AG Mobbs was invited to a Lowestoft Chamber of Commerce dinner where the principal speaker was the Minister of Agriculture, Walter Elliot. Judge Herbert Smith, at the time responsible for the Lowestoft County Court where he had dealt with a large number of tithe cases, was also a guest. When called on to speak the Judge, who was shortly to retire, told the Minister publicly:

'I have honest straightforward men coming before me, who are suffering from a great injustice and you have just got to do something about it.'

The post-war downturn in agriculture's fortunes, set against the backdrop of the financial and political crisis which ended with the formation of a National Government in 1931, mirrored the mood of gloom and despondency among tithepayers. Those affected by tithe began to feel that they had very little to lose by protesting. With their backs against the wall and with the courage of their convictions they began to act as men and women do in such circumstances – they fought back against an unfair system.

The opening rounds of the intensifying tithe war coincided with a change in the way newspapers did their business and AG Mobbs' ground-work with journalists in 1929 and 1930 began to pay dividends. During the First World War the role of the press had been heightened and during the inter-war years newspapers became big business. The cover price of most had to be subsidised by advertising, which meant that for the first time they had to entertain as well as inform their readers. The age of the 'Press Baron' had arrived and the national dailies reflected the politics of their owners. The journalist attending public gatherings and laboriously recording events point by point (including audience reaction) was losing column inches to photographs that showed what dull blocks of print could not.

The day of the photo-journalist had also dawned, for whom the sight of protesting farmers, burning images of the Archbishop of Canterbury, bailiffs carrying goods and stock away from destitute farmers and confrontations between the Blackshirts and the Police could hardly have been bettered.

The on-going and clever use of press, and later newsreel, publicity was an important component in the arsenal of the organised Tithepayers' Associations, though it was clear from the start that such publicity would depend on clear co-ordination with a specific and unambiguous objective. Tithepayers would need to speak, as far as possible, with one voice and to be seen reading as near as possible from the same hymn sheet as the NFU. It was also vital to maintain momentum and crucial that it did not turn sour. AG had guidance on this from Lawrence Easterbrook, the Agricultural Correspondent on the 'progressive' Liberal daily, the *News Chronicle*, who helped guide the NTA in the ways and means of the developing press jungle. There were others in the organisation who understood the nature of press coverage, such as J O Steed and Lady Eve Balfour, which was useful when in 1934 tithepayers had to disassociate themselves from Fascism while using the publicity advantages of the intervention of the Blackshirts in distraint sales.

From 1930 onwards small, independent tithepayers' associations began to form and AG received letters from all over the country asking for help in formalising protest and for legal advice. From the growing number of farmers expressing their willingness to face the might of the Establishment, he realised that it was a fight that could end with a real and lasting solution. He found himself much in demand as a speaker, since it was necessary that the TPAs call on the support of good and practised public orators to put their case. As one of Doreen Wallace's fictional characters pointed out:

> 'Our people are not educated on lines to fit them for public speaking or propaganda, and an even worse obstacle has been the scattered-ness of farmers. You can get people in towns to bunch together easily, but each farm is a little kingdom unto itself … You can't make farmers come to meetings, but if you bill a meeting on Tithe they'll roll along of their own free will because they hate the thing; and men who've never spoken a word in public before will get up and tell you their plain thoughts on the subject.'

The NTA grew in importance as a focus for branch associations springing up all over the country. Since 1929 the NTA had been under the leadership of Viscount Lymington (later the Earl of Portsmouth) and although he and AG Mobbs were on the same side they did not have the same rapport as did AG and the Reverend Kedward when he took over the Presidency in 1932.

Nevertheless Viscount Lymington had many influential friends and acquaintances, many of which agreed with his views, including Lord Elmley who became for a time NTA Vice President. It was important that titled or influential men and women, who were not afraid of the Establishment because they were part of it, should lend support to ordinary, law-abiding farmers who were prepared to brave the County Courts for the first time in their lives.

Like many other large landowners, Viscount Lymington was both titheowner and tithepayer and took the view that it was necessary to make the voice of agriculture heard among his fellow MPs. As the Member for the Basingstoke Division of Hampshire (1929-1934), and a strong supporter of the Church of England, he came to the protest movement on a platform of opposing tithe held as 'property by right but without responsibility'. Lymington and George Middleton met for the first time on a public platform in April 1933 at a meeting held in the Tithe Barn Theatre at Hinton St Mary, Dorset. It was organised by Captain George Pitt Rivers, whose family farmed in Dorset and Wiltshire and who took a characteristically high-profile position in the tithe debate. Like Lymington, he was both titheowner and tithepayer, and lost no opportunity to speak out against the system. Viscount Lymington, Captain Pitt Rivers, the Duke of Somerset, Lord Seymour, together with local MPs, representatives from the CLA, QAB, the Agricultural Workers' Union, F R Allen for the NTA, and others from local Tithepayers' Associations debated the issue in front of an audience who considered it their right to join in. The *Salisbury and Winchester Journal* reported a sample of the lively heckling:

> '*Mr Middleton said ... as far as Queen Anne's Bounty was concerned, it was selected by Parliament as the central authority to administer the Act. It was the duty of the Bounty and of the governors of the Bounty to administer the Act as passed. (A voice: "Go on strike".) ... The ecclesiastical tithe throughout the whole of England brought in about two million pounds a year. (A voice: "Shame".)*'

When Middleton told his audience that he could see no justification at all for many of their claims, a heckler told him '*... then you need an extra pair of glasses!*'. The audience was, though, as ready to applaud as to heckle:

> '*Viscount Lymington said that it was a meeting organised by Captain Pitt Rivers to see how they could get to the root of the tithe question, which was now causing a very real agitation throughout the country*

(Above) The interior of the Tithe Barn Theatre, Hinton St Mary, 1933.
(Below) Captain and Mrs George Pitt Rivers with Titus, a sheepdog of uncertain
temper! (G A Pitt-Rivers)

(Applause) ... and there was the vast, ignorant public who knew nothing about it whatever. (Hear, hear.) He ventured to say that in a democratic country [those present] were the real reason why this agitation had arrived at all, because there was a vast public upon whose votes Members of Parliament depended – (laughter) – who were neither interested in it nor cared about it.'

It was this point – about tithe being of interest to a small minority of voters – which persuaded those in the movement to use the publicity weapon: it was virtually the only one they had, and another reason why the NTA executive had to be drawn from those with standing in the wider community whose leadership in other areas of life qualified them for public respect.

Captain Pitt Rivers was something of a rogue element in this respect. He was Chairman of the Wessex and Southern Counties Tithepayers' and Common Law Defence Association, a somewhat different organisation to most other TPAs. On more than one occasion he annoyed his Secretary, Allan Lemon by putting out notices and posters without due consultation with the Association. In October 1933, Mr Lemon wrote to AG Mobbs who had just regretfully turned down an invitation to speak in Winchester:

'I quite appreciated from the first that it might be difficult for you to attend at the meeting, in one way I am glad that you did not come ... I think you will appreciate the reason when I enclose you a postcard issued by Captain Pitt Rivers, subsequent to the official bill which I sent previously, from which you will see that he put your name and Mr H Roseveare on the foot of his fresh posters, and placed himself as chief speaker, quite contrary to the arrangements approved by my Committee 10 days ago.'

Captain Pitt Rivers used the Tithe Barn Theatre for many public meetings and it was an eminently suitable venue for anti-tithe protest. In February 1933, the *Western Gazette* waxed poetically:

'The magnificent old tithe barn at Hinton St Mary was a not inappropriate setting for the gathering of landowners, farmers, and other tithepayers which assembled there on Saturday night at the invitation of Captain George Pitt Rivers to discuss the tithe question. The atmosphere of bye-gone centuries mingled with a sense of modern comfort in a striking way in this elaborately restored and decorated hall, and among the valuable pictures which adorn its walls was one which had a definite bearing on the purpose of the gathering, a painting by Pieter Breughel in

*about 1550. This was illustrative of the peasants bringing their produce
in eggs and poultry to the tithe barn, the compulsory offerings being
checked by a Rectorial proctor. Scenes such as this must have been common
in this building before the Reformation, and the rents from the Abbey
tenants, paid in kind, were also stored in the Manorial barns.'*

Backing for the meeting came from nearly all the local MPs, including
Lord Cranborne and Major W P Colfox. Cecil Hanbury, MP for North
Dorset, attended and Hall Caine, MP for East Dorset, wrote giving his
support. Major Despencer-Robertson wrote to say that he had had rather bad
luck in the ballot for Private Members' Bills that week. His name was read out
as successful and he had given notice to call attention to the tithe question,
but the Speaker discovered that he had read the wrong name.

Later on in the campaign, Rowland Rash was to voice concern over
Captain Pitt Rivers' linking of the 'struggle of common law' with the anti-
tithe movement and over his complicated, if valid, arguments against tithe
based on the Statute Laws of property. He wrote to AG Mobbs:

*'My wife goes down to Devonshire or Somerset, I forget which, to address
a Mass Meeting next week at the behest of Pitt Rivers; she will make her
usual fighting speech but you may rest assured she will say nothing to
prejudice the Policy of the Association which she supports. Pitt Rivers, I'm
afraid, is doing more harm than good in some quarters with his
confiscation 'tactics'. After all, we must face facts and realise that we
cannot expect to abolish Tithe without some compensation, however much
we may wish to.'*

F R Allen was also concerned that confusion over the issues was clouding
the public's perception of the tithepayers' objectives. Pitt Rivers' recommendations that tithe should be confiscated forthwith from the titheowners,
much as it had been in France during the Revolution, was considered a step
too far by many. In August 1933 F R Allen wrote to AG:

*'There has been a good deal that is encouraging in recent events. On the
other hand, the confusion among tithepayers as to objectives is worse than
ever. Mr Kedward and I returned quite dispirited from London on
Wednesday after an interview with Captain Pitt Rivers.'*

In October 1933, Pitt Rivers was mentioned in court by the Reverend
F Etheridge, Rector of Okeford Fitzpaine, one of a small number of rectors
who had elected to collect their own tithe rather than employ QAB. The 72-
year-old Rev Etheridge was summonsed by the Sturminster Council for not

paying his rates, and he told the magistrates that he was 'a victim of the tithe agitation'. QAB, he said, had told him that if he relinquished the task to them he could not resume it, and he estimated that it saved him between £15 and £20 a year to collect the tithe himself. Captain Pitt Rivers owed him a year's tithe rentcharge, he said, and he had written to the Captain pointing out the invidious position in which he found himself. The reply came that while he sympathised with him, he suggested the Reverend Etheridge apply for his wages to those who employed him, namely the Church of England. He also pointed out that, in fact, incumbents were exempted from the major portion of rates that other rate-payers had to bear.

When, a year later, Captain Pitt Rivers addressed a meeting of the Norfolk TPA, under the Chairmanship of Mr S Kidner, he was in danger of becoming obsessive in the

Wessex and Southern Counties Tithepayers' and Common Law Defence Association

T I T H E S !!

A P U B L I C M E E T I N G

under the auspices of the above Association will be held in the

BANQUETING HALL, GUILDHALL
WINCHESTER
ON
MONDAY, 2nd OCTOBER, 1933

The Chair will be taken at 3 p.m., by
COLONEL SIR VERE HOBART, Bart.
D.S.O., O.B.E., D.L., J.P.

ADDRESSES WILL BE DELIVERED BY
CAPTAIN PITT-RIVERS
Chairman of the Wessex Association
STANLEY KIDNER, Esq.
Chairman of the Norfolk Tithepayers' Association
SUPPORTED BY
Capt. E. M. Ford, H. W. Thomas, Esq., J.P., E. C. Lovell, Esq., J.P., H. Walton, Esq., representing Hampshire Branch, National Farmers' Union ; A. G. Mobbs, Esq., Suffolk Tithepayers' Association ; and H. Roseveare, Esq., J.P., East Kent Tithepayers' Association.

Resolutions will be submitted, calling for effective legislation to relieve Agriculture of the burden of Tithes.

Tithepayers' meeting postcard.

matter. He was said in the *Eastern Daily Press* to have proceeded to 'exhaustively' review the effects of the various Tithe Acts from 1838 to 1925. He then exhibited diagrams showing land use and farm employment statistics, and then *'went on to quote some of the speeches made in Parliament at the time the 1918 and 1925 Acts were passed'.*

In *Who's Who*, Captain Pitt Rivers gave one of his recreations as 'refuting politicians' and no doubt he was one of those on Cosmo Lang's mind when, during the parliamentary debate on a Tithe Bill in 1934, the Archbishop said:

> *'I have in mind certain comparatively well-to-do landowners – I dare say some of them are known to some of your Lordships – who are perfectly able to pay their tithe rentcharge but not only decline to do it themselves but foment agitation in the area in which they live, advising all other owners or owner-occupiers to refuse to pay it. It is really intolerable that there should be no way of dealing with that class of person, who is obviously entitled to no kind of consideration.'*

Over the next few years cross-party support was given for a debate on the tithe question. In East Anglia, four leading MPs – Conservatives Richard 'RAB' Butler (who had led the first-ever tithepayers' deputation to QAB in

1932), Sir Gervais Rentoul and P C Loftus, plus the Liberal Edgar Granville – were consistent in their support for the tithepayers. 'RAB' Butler 'joined hands' politically (as he put it in his autobiography *The Art of the Possible*) with Lord Lymington and in 1935 tried to persuade the Prime Minister, Stanley Baldwin to address a constituency meeting on tithe. The PM declined, saying that the issue was 'too controversial'. As the Constituency MP 'RAB' Butler was closely associated with his local TPA in Saffron Walden and in February 1932 A J Muirhead had written to him on the progress of the Deputation to the Minister by Essex tithepayers:

> '*The members of the deputation were Mr Krailing, Colonel Guy Blewitt, the Secretary of the Essex Tithepayers' Association, Harvey, Mr Keeble, and I think a fellow called Bowyer ... Unfortunately I have lost the list of names. They put their case on the whole moderately, and I think were out to show me what reasonable people they were and not stormy petrels like Kedward and his crew, but I must say their statement of the case was very disjointed. One man said that all they wanted was a re-casting of the 1925 settlement and there was no necessity to go back to anything before that. The next speaker, on the other hand, stuck fast at 1836 and could not be moved beyond it. There was really nothing in their case, and as pleasantly as I could I gave them no comfort. But they were friendly, and I think genuinely grateful that I had come; and I hope I have not done you or your political cause any harm.*'

Not to be outdone, the Saffron Walden Division of the Liberal Party put out anti-tithe publicity, including a special issue of *Liberal Messenger* in 1934 including an exposé of the system by Alderman E W Tanner, JP, CC entitled *Tithe: 'Ye Devour Widows' Houses'.*

Through the emerging Suffolk Federation of Labour Parties, AG Mobbs began lobbying for tithe to be put on the agenda of the Annual Labour Party Conference. The Secretary of the Eye Divisional Labour Party wrote to AG in 1931:

ANGLIAN DAILY TIMES

PUBLIC NOTICES.

A

TITHE PIG SALE

In aid of the funds of the
SUFFOLK TITHEPAYERS' ASSOCIATION
will be held on

TUESDAY, 19th JUNE, at 2 p.m.

IN THE

SWINE SALE YARD

OF

MESSRS. R. BOND & SON,

IPSWICH.

A number of pigs have already been promised.
Promises of further pigs will be gratefully received by the Hon. Secretary, P. J. Butler, Barking Road, Needham Market.

'Tithe Pig Sale' held in June 1934, when pigs of all sorts, sizes and colours were sold to raise funds for the Suffolk TPA.

'... I will try to get a resolution on the agenda of the Annual Labour Party Conference which is to be held at Scarborough, Oct 5th, and four following days. We should then see what support we have in the Labour Party. I shall be very pleased if my support can give you encouragement ... I want to learn the case for the Association – have you any handy leaflets or books?'

At a Labour meeting held at Diss Corn Hall in 1934, the Labour candidate for South Norfolk, Colin Clark said he had a farming business of his own in Devon. He was both a tithepayer and a churchman and agreed that the burden of tithe was too high. He thought the amount should be reduced and bear more relation to agricultural profits, but said nothing about abolition. Miss Ellen Wilkinson, however, said that as a Socialist she believed that people should pay for their politics, and as a Non-conformist she believed that people should pay for their own religion. They should not have burdens placed on their land whether they agreed with that form of religion or not.

With the highly efficient and totally committed F R Allen on board as Secretary, the NTA had a first-rate team and, together with first Viscount Lymington and then Roderick Kedward, he travelled widely to attend public meetings whenever he could. In March 1933 he wrote to AG:

'The tithepayers at Welshpool appear to be very anxious to have a meeting on the 7th of April. Mr Kedward has definitely said he cannot go, and I am already booked for Dorset for the 7th and 8th. I do not know whether you could see your way to go there. I scarcely like to suggest it, knowing what a lot you have done, but it would be an advantage to have someone buck those Welsh people up ... I was unable to book the Committee Room at Livingstone Hall for the 29th so I have booked it for the 5th and hope that will suit you.'

Allen, together with Roderick Kedward, AG, Doreen Wallace, P J Butler, Makens Turner and others formed what became known as a 'flying squad' of support, although George Middleton referred to them as 'peripatetic agitators'. One or other member of the 'flying squad' would attend any tithepayers' association needing help of any kind. April was the month when the half-yearly bills came in, so it was usually at the end of April or the beginning of May that the annual crop of calls for help began to arrive. The willingness of working farmers to address meetings up and down the country can only be admired and says much for the support team which they had at home, mostly in the form of wives and family. Spring on any farm is a busy and demanding time, and it was often difficult to get about the country by train. The dawning age of increased mobility helped. Doreen Wallace acquired a Rover coupé and on one famous occasion Lady Eve Balfour and Beryl Hearnden were summoned to attend a distraint raid and drove their Buick the twenty-six miles from Haughley to Gestingthorpe in thirty-five minutes.

When in 1934 AG's elderly car began to buckle under the unaccustomed strain of long journeys, the tithepayers contributed towards a new one. Nearly 350 names of those who had contributed were inscribed on a beautifully illustrated scroll and presented to AG along with the car. As well as the Suffolk tithepayers there were contributions from Norfolk with the inscription:

> 'To AG Mobbs
> Chairman of the Suffolk Tithepayers' Association
> We, the undersigned ask you to accept the accompanying gift subscribed in grateful recognition of your untiring and self-sacrificing efforts on behalf of Tithepayers to obtain relief from the burden of Tithe and its final removal as a charge upon the land.'

AG was invariably 'chauffeured' on local trips by fellow NFU member Jack Oldrin of Rushmere, whose sister was married to AG's elder brother. F R Allen, however, invariably travelled by train, and in *The Tithe War* Doreen Wallace remarked:

> 'The secretary, Mr Allen, has a legal mind, and is invaluable in directing policy; to tithepayers, he is almost a legend – allowing the barest minimum of time for food and sleep, he works night and day for the pittance which is all the farmers can afford him ... Mr Allen, it may be assumed, makes up some of his lost sleep in trains.'

On one occasion, in October 1931, F R Allen and Viscount Lymington addressed a meeting of the Wiltshire Agricultural Association, which had just announced that, due to the present economic situation and the financial state of the country, there would be no show held in 1932. Instances of local farmers having been brought before the County Courts were discussed and the case of Mr E C Lovell of Andover in Hampshire was highlighted. Mr Lovell was on the point of bankruptcy, having paid tithe of £40 with another instalment due imminently, but he had almost no income:

> 'I am 80 years of age and very deaf, and could only come to Salisbury by bus, and have to walk a mile to come that way. I have an old car, but have not been able to take out a licence this last twelvemonth. Two years ago when we had that gale I had over £500 damage done to my property,

*from which I shall never recover. I have been obliged to pay off most of my
labourers as I have no money to pay them. My tithe amounts to £75 on
a 300-acre farm.'*

Mr Lovell did have some hay to sell, but the depression meant that it was
worth almost nothing. It seemed that whatever it was worth, the money did
not belong to him but to QAB. Mr Lovell had been in correspondence with
AG Mobbs and his case had been taken up by the NTA.

In the Eastern Counties the story was much the same. Local farmers were
organising themselves into Tithepayers' Associations, in turn allying
themselves firstly with a County TPA and secondly with the NTA.

The establishment of the Suffolk TPA was typical, and is recorded by AG
Mobbs. At the inaugural meeting in February 1931:

*'We soon agreed to set up an organisation with myself as Chairman and
Mr Makens Turner, another member of the Suffolk NFU Executive, as
Vice Chairman. We had already contacted a Mr Philip Butler, who had
been seen in Ipswich carrying sandwich boards which called public
attention to the unjust tithe demands. He belonged to the Quakers, a
religious body for whose members special laws were at one time enacted
enabling authorities to fine and imprison those who defaulted tithe
demands. He was a man of outstanding integrity and became a very
popular and efficient secretary. It was here that Mrs Rash first made
herself known to an agricultural audience, making a fighting speech and
promising to use her pen to expose a serious state of affairs. She was
certainly true to her word, and with her husband also became a member
of the Association Committee.'*

The team which led from the front in the Suffolk tithe war had
assembled: AG Mobbs, Makens Turner, Philip Butler, Rowland Rash and
Mrs Rash – soon to be better known as the novelist Doreen Wallace (whose
first novel was published the same year). Viscount Lymington had not been
able to attend the meeting but wrote to AG a few days later:

*'Alas, I have been in the country since the 13th and your letter was
forwarded to the wrong address … I am glad to hear that the movement
to impress upon the people the disability from which tithepayers suffer is
growing in proportion as it becomes more intolerable to the depressed state
of farming. Whatever the good intentions of its original imposition, it has
utterly changed its character and now represents a property divorced of
responsibility. It is a tax directly on the land much of the advantage of*

which goes to the towns. Owing to its incidence on arable land, it has grown to be a food tax which no foreign country has to pay. And today I doubt if there is a single case of land which pays tithe, which pays it as a tenth of income earned from it, or indeed out of income at all. Nothing is so much needed as a redistribution of this burden and an inquiry into the total inequality of the way in which it acts together with the passing of the Tithe Remission Bill to meet the most urgent of our difficulties ...you may rest assured of my continual support, in Parliament and out, for every constitutional effort towards a just settlement of the tithe.'

In the course of the Ipswich meeting it emerged that a West Suffolk farmer by the name of James Melbourne Jones, living at Stoke-by-Clare near Bury St Edmunds, had received a court order for distraint on his goods. Mr Jones was prepared 'to allow the law to take its course' if the new association would support him. It would.

This was the start of accelerated tithe protest in the Eastern Counties and was to follow the pattern of the first distraint sale at Pluckley in Kent, where the farmer E J Haffenden had refused to pay the tithe. These two cases set the scene for distraint sales that over the course of the next two years would grow in number and fury, culminating in the desperate Kent demonstrations led by the 'stormy petrel', Roderick Kedward.

The case of Jones versus Mrs I M Sullivan dragged on for years and was one of the many high-profile wrangles that involved a lay impropriator. The reason why Mrs Sullivan held out so determinedly remains a mystery, and considering the amounts of money she must have paid her solicitor, knowing that her tithepayer was practically destitute, points to a titheowner making her point.

James Jones had emigrated to Australia but returned to England in 1929 with his Australian-born wife and bought a 750-acre unit of land, comprising separate farms, from the Stoke College Estate near Sudbury, Suffolk, which he re-named 'Australia Farms'. Mr Jones paid his first tithe rentcharge (a six-monthly payment at 6s per acre) buoyed up by the process of setting up what he thought was going to be a profitable farming enterprise. Instead he was part of the 1930 'slump'; his income fell dramatically, and the price of wheat went down from 46s a quarter in 1929 to 22s a quarter the following year. The farm was worth less than he had paid for it, and someone called Mrs Sullivan who lived in Bournemouth was not only demanding over £200 a year but could legally distrain farm stock for non-payment. Mr Jones thought it unfair and refused to pay, but then decided that to be rid of the debt he would take what he understood to be an alternative route. He offered Mrs Sullivan farmland in partial payment, which she refused. Mr Jones withdrew the offer and the battle lines were drawn.

A few months later auctioneers prepared to seize property belonging to Mr Jones and offer it for sale, the resulting funds to be paid to Mrs Sullivan who was suing for £105, being the second yearly instalment. The sale took place on 8 June 1931 and the newly formed Suffolk Tithepayers' Association was on hand to give support, AG in charge supported by the Halstead TPA (under the direction of F C Krailing, who had been a member of 'RAB' Butler's 1932 Deputation). The TPA members wore white carnations and an estimated 500 people attended, not all of them good-tempered.

Events took what was to become a familiar turn: when the auctioneer, Stanley Moger from Halstead, arrived to start the bidding he was heckled and some in the crowd threatened to throw him into the pond. When no bids came Mr Moger berated the crowd, which booed him in return. The mood turned angry and AG intervened:

> 'I stood on a lorry next to the Auctioneer and told him he was being very stupid. I said I was Chairman of the Tithepayers' Association and prepared to assist him if he carried out his duties properly, but that if not I could not be responsible for what might happen and pointed to a large horse pond nearby. Eventually I persuaded him to try, which he did, and I made a bid of two shillings for a lorry. When he knocked it down to me the cheering was deafening.'

The plan was that AG would buy the stock for a paltry sum, with money raised by the TPA, and it (the stock) would then be 'lent' back to the farmer. The small amount paid for the goods might or might not offset the tithe owing. On that particular occasion the auction proceeds went no way towards the required total – two lorries, a set of harrows, two Smythe corn drills, two bay geldings, a dressing machine and a horse rake were knocked down to AG for £1 16s.

Afterwards Stanley Moger thanked AG for assisting him to do his job, but thought they had not helped Mr Jones by giving him his goods back since he would be destrained on again in due course, but:

> '... I told him I had no intention of giving them back. They were now mine and I intended to lend them to Mr Jones for the rest of his life. I then appealed to the farmers to let the auctioneer leave quietly and we proceeded with our protest meeting.'

Farmers from Norfolk, Suffolk and Essex at a tithe sale at Rushmere, Suffolk watch as a pig (decorated with red, white and blue ribbons) is auctioned for NTA funds. (Charles Clarke)

A cow from the herd of Mr J Baxter goes under the hammer for tithe distraint at Rushmere in Suffolk. There were no bidders, and the assembled crowds sang *Rule Britannia.* (Charles Clarke)

Among the assembled farmers at the Rushmere tithe sale was a woman farmer who had cycled from Bury St Edmunds to be present, leaving home at 5 am. There had been a distraint raid on her own farm which had been resolved by the NTA. (Charles Clarke)

Auctioneers did their duty by the courts, but often found themselves under fire from their more usual customers. the farmers. (Charles Clarke)

The auctioneer's clerk (centre) consults with AG Mobbs (on his right) at one of several distraint sales to take place at the Wortham farms of Rowland and Doreen Rash. (Charles Clarke)

AG Mobbs addresses the crowds at Wortham, assisted by Doreen Wallace (seated first left). (Charles Clarke)

The NTA leaders addressed their audience from farm carts, invariably after the auctioneer had finished the business of selling distrained goods. (Charles Clarke)

Line-up of landowners and auctioneers including Doreen Wallace (3rd from left) and AG Mobbs (right). (Charles Clarke)

Auctioneers at this time found themselves in a difficult position since tithe sales were conducted against their usual clients, the farmers. This was highlighted in North Wales at the start of 1933 when a Welsh farmer brought his children to a tithe distress auction at Wrexham and offered them for sale. The auctioneer, Mr Aston afterwards signed a pledge that he would never conduct another tithe sale.

In Norfolk John Stevenson, barrister and General Secretary of the Incorporated Society of Auctioneers and Landed Property Agents, was to tell the Royal Commission in 1935 that distraint sales were 'distasteful to the auctioneers' and brought them into bad repute with their clients. *'He hates to his bones the carrying out of tithe sales,'* he said.

At an auction of cattle seized for tithe in Worcestershire, auctioneer A E Baldwin was accorded 'musical honours' and cheered by onlookers as he told them he was a farmer himself, paying between £140 and £150 each year in tithe. He considered it absolutely and entirely wrong that the land should be made to support the National Church.

A Plymouth auctioneer, Peter Hambley also came under fire from hundreds of angry farmers at a farm near Liskeard in Cornwall where he attempted to hold a distraint sale. He was first jeered at and then hustled out of the field by the police, who suggested he get into his car and return to Plymouth for his own safety.

Invariably, though, the auctions would be conducted in good humour. At Rushmere in Suffolk C W Durrant held an auction sale on instruction from the County Court Judge for two years' tithe demanded from J Baxter. Two cows from Mr Baxter's herd were put up – Bubbles and Gaycoat – but the only offer Mr Durrant got was 'three ha'pence' amid much good-natured heckling. The auctioneer suggested that perhaps buyers did not like the colour of Bubbles and Gaycoat and called for two more – red ones this time – Sally and Strawberry. After several more abortive attempts AG asked how much was needed to clear the debt. Mr Durrant told him £75 and AG asked if that would stop the sale. Assured that it would, he bid £75 for one cow and the sale was over.

Not all disputes were so easily settled: the fight between Mr Jones and Mrs Sullivan was to go on for years with the bailiffs eventually seizing 600 acres of the farm. To muddy the legal waters Stannard's Farm was made over to Mrs Jones, which meant that it was separately apportioned, and neither Jones showed any sign of giving in. The following March (1932) Mr Jones wrote to AG:

'The bailiff came along on Thursday and levied on everything on the farm. 5 corn stacks, all the horses, and implements again, on all the farms. 15 cows, furniture and poultry. Today his letter tells us a sale by tender is to take place ... What is our position now? ... Are they going to walk over us, or are we going to fight?'

The vindictive and immovable Mrs Sullivan instructed her solicitors accordingly and although in November 1933 an offer was made for a meeting with Jones' representatives, Steed & Steed of Haverhill, it was not considered in any way constructive. In the midst of all this Mr Jones kept his head and even called a mini-conference among local farmers to try to solve the unemployment problems among farm workers. Many years later, in November 1970, Mrs Jones wrote to AG, who had been in the news again for non-payment of tithe:

'Today I had a press cutting sent to me by a friend ... regarding the tithe problem. So it is still alive. In 1933 you were very brave and battling against this evil and the demands being made on the farmers then. You purchased horses, carts, and ploughs, when we were sold up ... I do hope you will not let this wicked old business worry you. You have the fighting spirit as my late husband. He passed away to be with his Lord 33 years ago last month. I do send you my best wishes ... Widow of James Melbourne Jones, late of Australia Farms.'

The Jones family and the events at Australia Farms had a special place in AG's memory. He put Mrs Jones' letter with those from her husband written in the 1930s, plus the receipt from Stanley Moger in the sum of £1 16s, and kept them together in his archive.

So the pattern was repeated across England and Wales. Goods were sold, auctioned and returned. No bids other than those of the TPA were made, and while there were suggestions of intimidation towards other non-TPA bidders, it did not amount to much. Feelings within agriculture ran very high against the titheowners and even those unaffected by tithe gave their wholesale support to the way in which the distraint sales were conducted. Tithe sale reports began to appear in almost every national and local newspaper, journal and magazine in the land. Farmers and farming on their own are not news, but banner-waving farmers capable of pelting court officials with rotten eggs and tarring and feathering auctioneers' cars were!

Events at the Waspe farm at Ringshall in Suffolk were the next to make the headlines when a seventy-year-old widow, Mrs Waspe had her farm implements put up for sale by tender on behalf of the titheowner, King's College, Cambridge. Even more helpless without the means to cultivate her farm, which had been collected in seven lorries with fourteen men and fifty policeman in attendance, the widowed Mrs Waspe had to lay off her two farm workers. Wheat was taken from the Waspe farm and sent to one of the King's College properties in Lincolnshire.

Shortly afterwards, in May 1932, an Elmsett farmer, Charles Westren had eight stacks seized for a tithe of £132 6s 4d, plus costs. A haulage contractor was sent to remove the stacks but the alarm was rung on the church bells and a large crowd of hostile farmers blocked the way. After four hours the gang withdrew, having removed only about a third of the barley stack. There is a lasting memorial to the Elmsett distraint, erected by Charles Westren before he left Suffolk for New Zealand. It is an eight-foot tall concrete block, erected in the field immediately opposite the Parish Church, which bears the inscription:

1934

TO COMMERATE [sic] THE TITHE SEIZURE AT ELMSETT HALL
OF FURNITURE INCLUDING
BABY'S BED & BLANKETS
HERD OF DAIRY COWS
EIGHT CORN & SEED STACKS
VALUED AT £1200 FOR
TITHE VALUED AT £385.

Not all the publicity had good results, however, as F R Allen wrote to AG after attending a public meeting in Bury St Edmunds:

'I think it was a mistake, exhibiting a poster about the amount of stuff
seized at Westren's. One woman in the audience said "if this sort of thing
is done, we must give in". Mr Turner did his best to put matters right, but
I do not see what good purpose is served by parading what the titheowners
may do or have done.'

It was clear, however, that distraint by the courts would not intimidate tithepayers and QAB's collection rate was falling. To counteract this, the Bounty decided to introduce sale by tender, and at the start of 1932 F R Allen wrote to AG saying that QAB was 'very pleased with the way things were going':

'... they boast that sale by tender is highly successful, that the tithepayers
are frightened and are paying. There is a good deal of anxiety among our
people in Kent ... there is a great deal of the 1930 tithe still outstanding
and of course we expect an onslaught at any moment.'

The Gestingthorpe raid, to which Lady Eve had driven her Buick at break-neck speed, ended in the High Court when the Rector, who had either bought or been given the tithe rather than 'inheriting' it with a living, instanced contempt of court. Three farmers had been charged over the incident and brought to Sudbury County Court where Norman Birkett KC, speaking for the three defendants, pointed out that there were currently no fewer than a thousand warrants in Suffolk and Essex in regard to non-payment of tithe.

Since, of course, the TPA had to pay for the goods bought at auction, they were always short of funds, so Gift Sales were held to raise money. The first in Suffolk was at Ipswich Market in April 1933 and followed in similar fashion those already held in Norwich and Colchester. Buyers attended from all parts of the county, and four auctioneers were occupied almost continuously for four hours selling live and dead farming stock, poultry, dairy and other produce for the benefit of the Suffolk TPA. The *Suffolk Chronicle* reported:

> 'Tuesday's unique event brought together well over a thousand agriculturists in a large or small way of business, whose interest in the auction sales organised by the County Tithepayers' Association and carried out by Messrs Robt Bond and Sons and Messrs Spurlings and Hempson, without any cost to the promoters, was of a spontaneous character, and, therefore, all the more successful, from whichever standpoint this remarkable demonstration against the inequalities of the tithe system was viewed.'

Roderick Kedward was present, and joked that although he was speaking from an insecure platform on the bonnet of a lorry, tithe was just as insecure. *'Agriculture alone,'* he said *'is carrying this burden.'*

Stock for the great sale had started to arrive overnight and a long procession of vehicles drove continuously into the market from seven o'clock in the morning. Corn came from Halesworth, Beccles and Bungay districts, pigs arrived from Framlingham and Eye, and cattle and sheep came from around Ipswich and North Essex. Over six hundred lots went under the hammer, the first lot being a Dartmoor pony named 'Tithekicker'. Before the sale commenced Doreen Wallace presented the auctioneer with a copy of her novel *The Portion of the Levites*, a fictional account of the plight of East Anglian tithepayers. After the event a letter appeared in the *Eastern Daily Press* from AG Mobbs:

'... *our heart-felt thanks to our friends in Norfolk who came forward so
generously with gifts and cash and assisted in making the sale such a
success ... It is not yet possible to announce the total amount realised, as,
apart from the payments received by the auctioneers amounting to
approximately £750, there have been a number of gifts in cash, and these
are still coming in, but I think I can safely say that the total will be not
less than £800.*'

The *East Anglian Daily Times*, however, refused to carry a similar letter of
thanks, the editor saying he considered the event to be 'of a purely secular nature'.

Invariably newspaper editors would have to call a halt, albeit temporarily,
to on-going tithe correspondence. The editor of the *Western Gazette* had the
same problem whenever Captain Pitt Rivers wrote to his paper, and more
than once told his correspondents:

*'We have continued this correspondence with the idea that all interested
in this controversy should have an opportunity of discussing varying points
of view, and that readers not so closely interested might form their own
opinions. In our judgement the opportunity given has been ample, and
the correspondence is now closed. – Ed.'*

Nevertheless, in addition to the daily news reports of skirmishes on the
front line, F R Allen, AG, Doreen Wallace, M C McCreagh and others kept
up the pressure in the 'Letters' columns of the national dailies. Almost
without exception where a letter from a tithepayer appeared there would
follow one in answer from George Middleton. It was said that Middleton had
a ready wit, was gifted with quick debating skills and had shrewd common
sense, but for the most part an appreciation of these attributes, plus his
renowned honesty of purpose and flawless administrative skills, passed the
tithepayers by. If any fact was expressed in less than accurate terms Middleton
homed in on it and no doubt made full use of his experience as a Justice of
the Peace. During his years at the Post Office he had been a member of the
committee that advised on the appointment of magistrates in the Knutsford
Division of Cheshire and he also had a fair working knowledge of journalism,
having been editor of the *Postal Clerks' Herald*.

When AG had a letter published in the *Yorkshire Post* warning tithepayers
about accepting concessions from QAB, Middleton responded that it wasn't
QAB they were fighting, but the law:

*'I may remind Mr Mobbs that titheowners do not collect tithe by distraint.
The remedy of the titheowners in the case of an occupying-owner is to ask*

the Court to appoint an officer to distrain, and Mr Mobbs is taking upon himself a grave responsibility in suggesting that the law is not strong enough to vindicate the rights of the titheowners.'

A press report of another public meeting in Shrewsbury illustrates a typical Middleton response:

'... I refer first to some remarks by a Mr J R Gornall, who, judging from his published speech, has but little knowledge of the nature of tithe rentcharge. After a display of humour, not in the best of taste, he suggested that the man who pays the tithe should have "some chance of calling the tune"... He overlooks the fact that a landowner who acquires land subject to tithe rentcharge does not acquire the whole interest in the land ... the land is one form of property and tithe rentcharge another.'

Although always basically the same letter, George Middleton must have been writing to the newspapers several times a week from his office in Dean's Yard, Westminster. Until the public meeting in the Hinton tithe barn, however, he had not addressed tithepayers face to face. Nor did he confront AG Mobbs in person until 1934. They fought many duels via the 'Letters' pages, and had taken part in a radio discussion, but in spite of several challenges from Mobbs they had not met on a public platform.

In 1934, however, a farmers' meeting took place in the small Cornish market town of Stratton, where George Middleton was speaking. He was heckled on all sides for having thus far refused to meet AG openly. AG wrote:

'They were twitting him because of his refusal to meet me when he suddenly remarked that if I cared to come to Cornwall he wouldn't mind taking me on. The Secretary of the local tithepayers' association immediately sent me a prepaid telegram saying, "Middleton will accept your challenge if you meet him here". I replied with three words, "Fix it up".'

There was no building large enough in Stratton so a meeting was arranged at the nearby Bude Picture Theatre. AG, together with his wife and the Agricultural Correspondent of the *News Chronicle* drove the 650 miles to Bude. The *News Chronicle* reported:

'Six hundred farmers from all parts of Devon and Cornwall crowded Bude Picture Theatre today to hear a debate between Mr George Middleton, chairman of the Tithe Committee of Queen Anne's Bounty, and Mr A G Mobbs, vice-chairman of the National Tithepayers' Association. It was the fulfilment of a four-year-old challenge by Mr Mobbs. It had, too, particular local interest, for yesterday there had been

a heavy distraint on the farm of Mr H Dunn, a member of the Executive Committee of the Cornwall Tithepayers' Association. Live stock, household furniture, farm implements – even the electric generating plant – to a total value of £1,415 had been impounded for £233 tithe arrears.'

The argument went roughly as expected and AG considered it a triumph: *'I thoroughly enjoyed it. Later [Middleton] received a knighthood which tithepayers cheekily described as a consolation prize!'*

The *Cornish and Devon Post* said of Middleton's contribution:

'It was too much of a history lecture ... but no answer to the question which the farmers are putting.'

After the meeting, hundreds of farmers left for Bodmin where another demonstration was held at which, in their own words, 'they could get their real feelings off their chest'. Writing afterwards, the Cornish TPA Secretary, Edwin J Honey confirmed AG's expenses and thanked him for a successful meeting:

'A year ago there was nothing doing in this district, and in fact very little in the county, but I thought we were shirking our duty by standing by and doing nothing, while you in the Eastern Counties were fighting so well ... now we have in Stratton a larger membership than any other district in Cornwall. I am glad to say that the public generally are now with us in our demand for a fair settlement ... Mr Middleton complimented me on our Stratton organisation and said it was the most orderly tithe meeting he had ever addressed ... Well, you gave him just the flogging he deserved.'

One argument that became something of a grey area was the question of the abolition of tithe. It seems from AG's early speeches and letters that he did not hold out any hope that this would happen. The *Post and Weekly News* report of the Bude meeting quoted AG as telling George Middleton:

'I have never in my four years' campaign – and I have given up a great deal more time than I could afford to this particular question, asking no reward and expecting none, making the operations on my farm a secondary consideration – gone on a platform and advocated the immediate abolition of tithe.'

At the beginning of 1930, F R Allen wrote to AG:

'I think that most of the members want abolition ... but after prolonged discussion it was decided that abolition at present at any rate was not "practical politics" ... I must say that the Kent executive had definitely turned down abolition.'

HUMAN BARRIER IN KENT TITHE RAI

DRAMA AT A
TITHE RAID

Demonstrators Prone on the Ground

FREE FIGHTS

FROM OUR OWN CORRESPONDENT
ASHFORD, Thursday.

Farmers and their wives and daughters lying prone on the ground while lorries charged at them. . . .

This was the amazing scene witnessed this afternoon at Beechbrook Farm, Westwell, near Ashford, Kent.

Men had been sent to the farm with three lorries to collect a load of oats which had been seized for tithe, and farmers came from all parts of the county while the lorries were being loaded.

The police refused the request of Mr. R. M. Kedward, owner of the farm and president of the National Tithe-Payers' Association, that they should arrest the men removing the oats.

Then Mr. Kedward and the tithe-payers lay down in the roadway. There were cries of "Everybody down," and farmers, their wives and their daughters, to the number of between thirty and forty, lay on their backs across the cart-track.

The lorries charged at them and swung round into a potato field to avoid them.

The farmers then rushed at the lorries in an attempt to stop them, but were unsuccessful.

WAGON BLOCKADE

Further along, the track was blocked by a number of wagons.

Young farmers attempted to hold this barrier and several free fights occurred.

The police had to intervene, and a number of warnings for obstruction were given. The four lorries were able eventually to get away over a rough field.

This is the fourth time that Beechbrook Farm has been raided on one order for £67 worth of tithe. More than £600 worth of goods, it is stated, has been taken away.

When the bailiff's men proceeded to load the oats into the lorries they were hampered by the fact that on pitch-forking, each sheaf fell to pieces, as the strings binding them had been removed.

Young farmers trying to prevent the removal of the oats by lorry.

Cutting from the *Daily Mirror,*
7 September 1934

Tithepayers gradually moved from instinctive protest against a perceived injustice, exacerbated by financial depression, to a demand for a just solution. During the inter-war years there began a revision in society's expectation of justice and as the revolt against tithe matured it required something more than recognition. It demanded change and an answer to its outrage in much the same way as Socialism drew strength from the increasing power of 'the common man'.

At Bude AG challenged Middleton to say why he did not pay tithe while farmers did, and went on to answer the question for himself: those outside farming did not pay tithe, he said, because they had long since renounced their obligation because it was unfair. It had lapsed simply because lawyers, politicians and others in a position to repudiate it had done so. AG told his audience that farming had not repudiated its obligations, but wanted it to be a fair charge. This was a very different message to that proclaimed a few years later and there were certainly many forward-thinkers in the TPAs who preached a cessation of tithe from the very beginning, among them Captain Pitt Rivers. In fact it was AG's use of the word 'abolition' that later drew fire from those in the NFU who stopped short of demands for outright abolition.

Wales had the same problem. The Welsh Committee of the NFU toed the line, while John Davies wrote to AG:

'Our goal is total abolition. If you once admit even the one tenth to be justice then two thirds might, be, also. We oppose the tithe on principle as an unjust burden on the land by confiscating what was once a free will offering into compulsory.'

Another slight hitch in AG's campaign was the fact that he did not, in fact, pay tithe himself. This had been used by some in the NFU who saw AG as a troublemaker and a threat to the organisation. A two-page article in the Union's monthly publication early in 1931 deplored the setting up of 'rival organisations', i.e. tithepayers' associations, to represent the owner-occupiers in the NFU. He referred to *glib writers who have not even the qualifications to speak for tithepayers that comes from being tithepayers themselves'*. Stung by this, but quick to see a gap in his defences, AG then took on a farm in his home parish that did carry the tithe burden and on which he experienced distraint on numerous occasions over many years.

But if Cornwall was a personal success for AG, so was the BBC radio broadcast that took place in November 1933. In a half-hour programme he and George Middleton discussed The Tithe Question to the delight of tithepayers listening in across the country. The *Listener* carried a transcript of the discussion between AG and Middleton and it went well for the tithepayers' cause, though Middleton did his duty by QAB:

'Agricultural land is not the only land which pays tithe. In hundreds of parishes tithe is payable upon land that has become urbanised and built upon. Tithe rentcharge is payable also by railways. Let me make it clear that tithe rentcharge is not a burden on agriculture. It is an obligation on those who own land.'

At one point AG interrupted Middleton with an exclamation of 'Rubbish!' in response to the allegation that tithe was a 'blessing' for agriculture since it prevented landowners from having to pay the full purchase price of the land. Middleton also asserted that in fact QAB was 'lending agriculture £70 million' by not demanding compulsory redemption which would have to come from the industry. Towards the end, however, he admitted:

'... tithe rentcharge has nothing to do with values or profits. That was laid down definitely a hundred years ago.'

Following the broadcast AG's postbag was full of congratulatory cards and letters from across the country, including one from a supporter in Guernsey who wrote: *'You were more than a match for your pedantic and most unconvincing opponent'*. George Solley wrote from Kent to say that *'it was a real treat to hear the familiar voice on the wireless, and it was so good we heard every word'*. Several of the letters were sent by anonymous well-wishers, and a correspondent from Salisbury wrote: *'It gives me considerable pleasure to note that all your arguments were sound in fact and exceedingly well put forward'*, while H A Smith from North Tuddenham in Norfolk said he thought Middleton must have been very glad when the half-hour was up.

If, however, this opinion was shared by anyone else, they seriously misjudged George Middleton. It was his duty to defend the tithe and he would not countenance any viewpoint that differed from his stand as QAB Chairman. He was immune from rancour and criticism from such as AG Mobbs, possibly because he did not take it personally. This appears at odds with his upbringing. His obituary in *The Times* read:

'George Middleton was country-bred, and came of yeoman stock. He was born at Ramsey, in Huntingdonshire, in 1876, and retained through his career an unassuming naturalness typical of the best in English character.'

Hand-drawn cartoon postcard of AG Mobbs at BBC microphone, George Middleton depicted as a rag doll – one of many cards and letters sent to AG after his radio broadcast in 1933.

He should, then, have recognised that part of the English character which is in all yeoman farmers, namely that once they had the bit between their collective teeth it was a fight to the death.

It was in his job at the Post Office that Middleton first become aware of the oppressive and unfair conditions of service prevalent in the 1920s which had eventually led him towards Socialism and the burgeoning Labour Party. While in Crewe, to where he was transferred as a telegraphist, he became a member of the United Kingdom Postal Clerks' Association, afterwards moving down to the new headquarters of the Union of Postal Workers in London. But in the matter of tithe he was not the protector of the rights of the working man as he had been in his early years, perhaps because he saw titheowners as landowners, not individual family farmers.

In 1931 Middleton came under a hail of constituency criticism over his acceptance of the post of First Church Estates Commissioner, which brought him an extra salary of £1,200 a year and a pension. Supporters found it odd that a Socialist MP should accept such a large sum for having a foot in the Establishment camp. The *Morning Post* said that it was not to the liking of certain members of his party, who maintained that a workers' representative should not accept such a position. A meeting was held, without his knowledge, and rumour spread that he was to resign as MP for Carlisle over the issue. Middleton immediately put out a disclaimer, in a style which was to become his trademark in his dealings with the tithepayers, to the effect that he was not only refusing to resign but that he intended to stand at the next election. George Middleton began to enjoy moving in high places and was learning how to flex the muscles of power.

QUEEN ANNE'S BOUNTY.

AREA COLLECTION COMMITTEE No. 9.

Mr. F. S. Fisk,

Two Gates,

Eyke, Woodbridge.

1, Old Butter Market,

IPSWICH.

April 1933

Dear Sir (or Madam),

TITHE ACTS, 1836 to 1925.

Benefice of   RENDLESHAM

We shall be obliged by payment of the Rentcharge due from you to Queen Anne's Bounty (as Trustees for the above Benefice), as stated below.

Cheques or Post Office Orders should be made payable to " Q.A.B. Tithe Committee No. 9," and crossed " Garrod, Turner & Son, A/c Payee."

Please return this Application with your remittance.

Your obedient servants,

GARROD, TURNER & SO

Agents for the Committee.

Lands or Premises		Half Year's Tithe Rentcharge due	Amount			
			£	s.	d.	
YEAR	1st October 1927		2	4	4	C.C.
½ Yr.	1st April 1928		1	2	2	" "
"	1st October 1930		1	2	2	" "
YEAR	1st October 1931		2	4	4	" "
"	1st October 1932		2	4	4	
½ Yr.	1st April 1933		1	2	2	
	Court Fees			5	—	
	ditto			1	6	
			£10	6	—	

NOTE.—By the Tithe Act, 1925, all ecclesiastical tithe rentcharge, corn rents, etc., became vested in the Governors of Queen Anne's Bounty on 31st March, 1927. The value of ordinary ecclesiastical tithe rentcharge is now at the rate of £109 10s. 0d. per £100 commuted value, out of which £4 10s. 0d. per cent. is to be set aside as sinking fund for redemption and extinguishment of the tithe rentcharge within 85 years from 31st March, 1927.

The Governors would be obliged if, whenever there is a sale of the property charged with tithe rentcharge, the tithe payer would immediately inform the collector of the purchaser's name and address.

Tithes. **Form No. 1.** W. S. Cowell, Ltd., Ipswich. 10M. 1/9/32.

Order from QAB for tithe at Rendlesham, 1933.

At a rally held in Norwich during 1934, AG told members of the Norfolk TPA that they would be interested to hear that George Middleton was at one time a Labour MP. *'I once heard the manager of a co-operative society say "It is wonderful how autocratic democracy can become",'* AG quipped, amid much laughter and applause.

Middleton also became Parliamentary Private Secretary to the Secretary of State for India, and a councillor of the Corporation of Church House, but it was his job as Commissioner that enabled him to justify the fruits of his ambition. There was no guilt attached to these rewards when the cause he fought for was the Church. He put considerably more energy into the defence of QAB against the tithepayers than he had in earlier years put in on behalf of the Post Office workers against the State. His first acquaintance with real politics had been as leader of the Union of Post Office Workers, a post he took out of sympathy with the workers, yet as Chairman of QAB he chose the Establishment over the underdog.

~ o ~

FEAR OF A CONFLICT IN TITHE WAR

FASCISTS CAMP BESIDE
TWO BAILIFFS

Taking Up "Strategic Position" To-day

POLICE THERE, TOO

FROM OUR SPECIAL CORRESPONDENT

RINGSHALL, Suffolk, Tuesday.

A crisis is developing in the tithe war here, where bailiffs—guarded continuously by five policemen—and Fascists are camping in adjoining fields and keeping a watchful eye on each other.

To-day tenders were received for cutting eleven acres of wheat and seven of barley, impounded on the farm of Mrs. Waspe, aged seventy, who is the centre of local excitement owing to debt for tithes.

As soon as the winning tender is accepted, cutting is expected to begin.

The crops were impounded by bailiffs, two of whom have been camping in one of the fields

A party of Fascists is camping in a neighbouring field on the farm.

They are stated to have declared they intend to resist attempts to cut the wheat and barley, "by force, if necessary."

Eight Fascist reinforcements arrived here late to-night in a loud-speaker van.

OFFER REJECTED

Their arrival and camping arrangements were carried out with military precision, and soon after they lined up while their leader, Mr. B. Denny, instructed different members of the party to keep watch throughout the night.

They were told not to use violence.

"What we will do, if an attempt is made to cut the corn and barley, I cannot tell now," Mr. Denny told me.

He added that to-morrow the Fascists will move their camp to a "stategic position," close to the bailiffs' tent.

Arrangements have been made for a further party of Fascists, numbering between forty and fifty, to travel from London immediately an attempt is made to cut the crops.

King's College, Cambridge, to which tithes are owed, offered to allow the two fields to be cut by Mrs. Waspe, if she would make a token payment of £10. This offer was refused.

"Since that payment is not to be made, the authorities must gather the crops," I was told.

RESISTANCE THREAT

Bailiff Says "We Are Not Alarmed—We Will Stay Here"

I understand that none of the cutting tenders come from the immediate neighbourhood.

"Any attempt to interfere with the work of cutting will be resisted, but we are not alarmed by the opposition so far threatened," Mr. E. Robinson, the East Suffolk bailiff, told me to-night.

"We will remain here till the cutting is completed."

Mrs. Waspe's son Arthur, who farms the impounded property, told me to-day that in no circumstances would he make a tithe payment.

"Farm machinery value £50 has already been taken and sold for tithes which amounted to £47," he said.

"It is true the machinery realised only £5, of which £2 10s. went in costs, but I consider the debt should be looked upon as settled.

"The crops they now want to take are worth at least £200. It is a disgrace that my mother should lose that sum for a debt on a farm which cannot afford to pay tithes at all."

Mrs. Waspe, despite her years, is bearing up under the strain remarkably well.

"I still cannot believe that they will take my crops," she said.

Mr. Davis, the head cowman, who was left £1,000 in the will of Mrs. Gertrude Jane Austin, of Totteridge, Herts, with one of his charges, which is being sold. Mrs. Austin, who left £328,359, made bequests to all her servants and employees.

Members of the British Union of Fascists at their London headquarters yesterday.

Cutting from the *Daily Mirror*, 9 August 1933

Chapter 5

DANGEROUS TIMES

'Much of the incident connected with our distraint is already "news" so I need not touch on the march of our forty-five farm-workers to the rectory to ask the rector whether he thought he had a right to demand his tithe at the expense of their livelihood, nor on the spectacular round-up of eighteen Blackshirts by about 150 police – a musical-comedy act. But there are certain facts connected with the ultimate removal of the goods which have not obtained publicity. For some days and nights before this event, over thirty police had kept constant guard at our buildings – at whose expense? ... Further, I can assert without fear of contradiction, having abundant witnesses to prove it, that until appealed to by my husband, the police permitted a method of loading up the pigs which is prohibited in ordinary markets on account of its cruelty.'

Doreen Wallace, *The Tithe War* (1934)

ALONGSIDE THE COURT OFFICIALS and auctioneers at the almost daily scenes of distraint mayhem were the Police. They became concerned at how the policing of tithe sales and protest gatherings was perceived by the public. There was also the danger that an on-duty policeman would be injured and so damage the tithepayers' claim of passive resistance.

The cost of police presence at tithe raids increased, with sometimes over a hundred officers being needed to escort lorries off farms carrying terrified livestock. It was not unusual for a thousand or more angry farmers and supporters to turn up and jeer at the bailiffs as they went about the task of distraining stock and farm machinery. Parades would be held, the placard-carrying donkeys of the Kent distraints replaced by a man dressed as the Archbishop heading the procession, riding a horse and holding a shepherd's crook and banner reading 'Come Unto Me, Ye that are Heavily Laden – and I will Sell you Up!'.

In raids where tithepayers were supported by contingents of Mosley's 'Blackshirts' they created a potential breach of the peace. In *Constables of Suffolk* Leslie Jacobs records the 1934 distraint at Wortham, home of Doreen Wallace:

> *'Blackshirt activity in this normally peaceful quarter of East Anglia engendered expectations of confrontation, violence and a newsworthy episode. Consequently, large crowds were attracted ... including press and newsreel men. Spotter planes were also in use. Many thousands camped under canvas to witness the proceedings with 5,000 reported in the parish on one Sunday. Police presence at Wortham was not only required to maintain the peace, but also to deal with congestion on the narrow country roads caused by the indiscriminate parking of motor vehicles and bicycles. A contingent of up to 100 officers were stationed in the village at some stages, albeit great discretion was used with their actual deployment and many of their number were held in reserve. The Deputy Chief*

(This page) **Police at Wortham, 1934.**

(Opposite page) **Deputy Chief Constable and other police at Wortham.**

Constable, Superintendent Ernest Lancaster, was the overall commander, assisted by Superintendent Eade, and Inspector Bryant.'

Warrants were issued against the Blackshirts and around a hundred police officers arrived in two hired buses. The crowd shouted abuse at the police and on the front page of the *Sunday Pictorial* some of the one hundred and fifty police officers were shown escorting the arrested Blackshirts to the buses. Neither the tithepayers nor the British Union of Fascism could have bought such publicity. The entire episode became a flagship case for the anti-tithe movement and was recorded by Doreen Wallace in her book *The Tithe War* and fictionally in *So Long to Learn*.

In the aftermath of the Wortham raid many expressed disgust at the way the police had stood by and permitted a method of loading up stock that was prohibited in ordinary markets on account of its cruelty. Such accusations were made on more than one occasion, but it was not (then) an issue that carried with it a great deal of public outrage.

During August 1933 three officers were required to perform their duty in amazing circumstances, when they and a bailiff were sent to live in a tent beside a field of wheat at Ringshall in Suffolk. Both the wheat and the bailiff

(Above) The impounded bullocks at Wortham.
(Left) Crate used by the bailiffs to carry pigs
over ditches dug by the Blackshirts.
(Below) Pigs at Wortham.

were to be guarded on behalf of King's College, Cambridge. They stuck it out for nearly a month, but in the end the 'camping bailiff' ended his vigil without incident when it proved impossible to reach the Bursar of King's College. The *Daily Herald* reported that '*... by telephone and telegraph messages were sent to places up and down the country likely to be visited by [Mr Keynes] during his motoring holiday.*' Unconditional ownership of the wheat reverted to the farmer, Mrs Waspe.

The potential danger from firearms was another consideration for the police, and one commented on in retrospect by Doreen Wallace:

> '*... it followed that we had to behave ourselves. Had we used violence and injured a lorry driver or one of the hundreds of police brought in ... that would have made bad publicity. Some of our farmers were so desperate that they would have used guns – I had to hide some when my husband's big distraint was on in the winter of 1933-34.*'

In Kent, the police were in danger of public ridicule when officers attempted to disguise themselves as farm workers to enable Mr P Henderson, a London solicitor, to collect stock from farms in the Elham Valley on behalf of New College, Oxford. About two hundred officers were involved in a farcical cavalcade of vans, joined by hundreds of private cars, which moved slowly through the muddy lanes. The procession grew to be half a mile long and could only move forwards with little room for manoeuvre by the bailiff's lorries. At each stop Mr Henderson was escorted onto the farm, but he was unable to identify the stock he had come to collect so left empty-handed. When he got to Riverside Cottage Mr Henderson and the bailiff spent some time chasing about 250 Wyandotte hens round a field. Finally they managed to catch just two hens, one of which, when it was put in the lorry, promptly laid an egg. The press had a field day!

On more than one occasion questions were asked in the press about the role of police at tithe distraint sales, on which subject Captain Pitt Rivers wrote to Lord Cranborne, MP for South Dorset in 1933. Lord Cranborne was asked if he condoned the use of the police by titheowners at distraints that had, he said, been proved in the courts to be illegal. Pitt Rivers drew his attention to the Constabulary having been present in Shropshire on occasions of 'illegal' distraint which, he said, were not carried out according to the law and '*could be described as amounting to burglary*'. Lord Cranborne forwarded the letter to the Home Secretary who replied, somewhat predictably, that the function of the police was not to judge or question the County Court proceedings but to take such as action as was necessary to maintain order and prevent a breach of the peace.

Beyond farming, Britain was beginning to emerge from economic depression into what seemed a new light: J M Keynes published his General Theory of Employment, Interest and Money, Dali and Piccasso were pushing out the boundaries of accepted art, and people were reading Graham Greene, John Steinbeck, the detective novels of Dorothy L Sayers, while Doreen Wallace was cornering the market in popular fiction. Benny Goodman began developing Swing music from jazz and Gershwin's *Porgy and Bess* hit the American stage. Politically, Britain in the 1930s became a melting-pot for numerous factions that emerged to fill the vacuum of expectation created by an unsettled Europe. In 1933, David Lloyd George wrote to Roderick Kedward to commiserate on his failure to win the Ashford seat. He lamented the decline in Liberalism and warned about dictatorships:

> *'The result of the election must have been a great disappointment to you as it was to all of us, but I am convinced that no one else could have done nearly as well as you did. You put up a first-rate fight. You are the only man who would have polled 11,000 votes for Liberalism in a Kentish constituency. I am afraid that it means that for the time being Liberalism is down and out in the English constituencies. Its fortunes have been mishandled very badly during the last two years. We rallied 5,300,000 voters to our flag in 1929. I doubt now whether we could gather together one-third of that number. There is, of course, a reaction in the world against Liberal principles. That is what always happens in a panic. People everywhere are frightened and are calling for dictatorships.'*

It was just such a call that Oswald Mosley responded to with his British Union of Fascists (BUF) which came to prominence in the cities and – momentarily – infiltrated the highways and byways of rural Britain. Henry Williamson was one of those drawn to the ideas of Mosley and he wrote in a preface to *The Story of a Norfolk Farm*:

> *'An author writes a story; but he is not entirely free, in some circumstances, to persist in his personal wishes for its final (or original) form. The publishers have told me that certain passages, including an entire chapter, "are not essential to the story of the farming venture, and they are likely to excite a controversial interest at odds with the main theme of the book". I have therefore decided to remove them.'*

The item likely to excite controversial interest was his declared support for Oswald Mosley, whose political rise stemmed from the disillusionment felt by left-wingers at the failure of the 1929-1931 Government. During 1934 the MacDonald National Government was floundering. Sir Stafford Cripps organised the Socialist League, and in that year Mosley attracted the support of the press magnate, Lord Rothermere. The *Daily Mail* headlined 'Hurrah for the Blackshirts!' and Rothermere told his readers that Britain's survival as a Great Power would depend on the existence of a well-organised Party of the Right.

In the early 1930s, the two press barons Rothermere and Beaverbrook instigated the Agricultural Party. With some disdain, the *Land Worker* commented:

'... *a new Party has emerged – the Agricultural Party. It stands for Agriculture, first and last – full-blooded Protection for farmers. It takes its orders from Lords Beaverbrook and Rothermere. Farming is in the future to be conducted from Fleet Street. It is claimed that the labourers should in their own interest throw in their lot with the new Party. In this regard the Party has made a fatal mistake – it offers no concession to the labourers.*'

Lord Beaverbrook took his message to Norwich where it went down very well, and later caused ructions within the NFU whose Central Council came out against the new party. At a meeting of the Norfolk Executive of the Union in Norwich a representative of the Agricultural Party confirmed that tithe would be a 'plank' in its platform, which brought applause from the Norfolk audience. Mervyn Davies, then President of the NFU, cut short discussion on the Agricultural Party at the London AGM and a written protest was submitted by those members opposed to the Union's stance. The press, however, agreed with those urging debate, and given the appalling state of British agriculture, discussion of a new pro-farming voice could hardly make things worse.

A year or two later, when the full meaning of Fascism became clearer and rumblings of war a reality, many who had supported Mosley publicly were left in a difficult position. While most quietly forgot their initial interest and joined in the general condemnation of the BUF, there were many in the 1930s – not only tithepayers but also the wider agricultural community – who listened to what Mosley had to say (albeit many with an increasing degree of scepticism). He did, after all, offer a policy on agriculture, something sadly lacking in the mainstream parties.

**Blackshirts line up at Wortham beside their trench.
(Friends of Oswald Mosley)**

In 1934 Mosley was in Ipswich, a visit designed to coincide with the presence in the town of the (then) peripatetic Royal Show. He repeated his message about Great Britain being the dumping-ground for cheap foreign goods that undercut the British farmer and declared that *the Conservative Party has ceased to be the party of the country and has become the party of the City of London'*.

This was a sentiment guaranteed to find favour in rural England and the correspondence columns of the local press were aflame with opinion from all sides of the argument. The BUF had its share of local supporters, although in general the mood amongst farmers was guarded and, only a year after they had listened with open minds to the BUF message, farmers' leaders were warning of the dangers of alliance with Mosley.

In *The Blackshirt* one of Mosley's most loyal aids, Alexander Raven Thomson claimed that the Fascist approach to the question of tithes came solely from the religious angle:

'Obviously the average farmer and landowner receives little enough material service in return for the payment of tithe. Even in the matter of religious services we must take into account that many titheholders are laymen; and on the other hand, many tithepayers are not members of the Church of England. It is owing to this lack of justification in service that Fascism is opposed to the whole tithe system.'

By the time that was written, Mosley's Blackshirt followers had already involved themselves in the tithe war by way of a campaign led by the BUF's National Political Officer, Richard Plathen. Having attended tithe distraint sales in Worcestershire without intervening or exploiting the situation in any way, in 1934 the Blackshirts turned their attention to Suffolk and to Wortham in particular.

The Wortham distraint, immortalised in the writings of Doreen Wallace, was the culmination of the Blackshirts' involvement in the tithe war. After an eighteen-day siege, nineteen fascists were arrested. This made front-page news and gave the BUF an opportunity to be seen actively supporting British agriculture. In Worcestershire they had failed to make any impact on the situation, except in Evesham where William Joyce led 120 uniformed Blackshirts in an address to local farmers and market gardeners; but in East Anglia farmers were more militant and eager to put themselves on the line for the cause. The BUF policy that British agriculture should be protected at all costs gave them the excuse to take action. Nicholas Mosley writes in *Beyond the Pale*:

'... *local District officers thus saw the chance of a form of action which would be constructive and charitable. They were given legal advice that if members of the Fascist Defence Force went to farms at the invitation of farmers and just "by their passive presence" prevented bailiffs from doing their job, they would be within the law. Members went to farms and dug ditches and built barricades to make it difficult for bailiffs to carry away equipment and livestock; then they waited, in tents, while bailiffs and onlookers leaned on fences and watched. All this was photographed by the local press; small crowds turned out; there was genuine interest in what might be the outcome of such a challenge to authority.*'

This challenge to authority was important to the Blackshirts since, as a result of their non-intervention in Worcestershire '... *a self-proclaimed dynamic movement had been made to look somewhat ridiculous*'.

Wortham saw a coming together of all the factions involved in the tithe war: Rowland and Doreen Rash were allowing distraint as the only means they had of drawing public attention to what they saw as an injustice, in which endeavour they were supported by the tithepayers and their farm workers. The Blackshirts were hoping for some credibility as political rebels by thwarting the bailiffs in the course of their duties, and the men of the General Dealers were acting for the titheowner with the consent of QAB.

In *The Tithe War*, Doreen Wallace wrote:

'... *on the Wednesday there had been interesting developments. Some days before, a contingent of Blackshirts had arrived at the farm – uninvited, but not repulsed by us – to "protect the interests of the farmer", and this had occasioned certain police activity.*'

Afterwards, in an attempt to deflect criticism that the Blackshirts had, contrary to the 'rules of engagement', been invited to Wortham, AG Mobbs required Doreen Wallace to put in writing to him that she had not issued such an invitation. This she did, and in *The Tithe War* continued:

'... *the local superintendent and inspector came to our house, and without proffering any formal charge, warned my husband that what he said might be used in evidence against him, and asserted that the Director of Public Prosecutions had empowered them to investigate a "conspiracy". As we had conspired with no one – certainly not with the Blackshirts, who kept their plans, if any, very dark – we were not intimidated by this move. During the interview, the superintendent had occasion to remark that the presence of the police in tithe distraints was for the protection of the interests of the farmer as well as of the remover of the goods; we responded that evidently other farmers under distress had been less fortunate in their superintendent of police. After taking notes of my husband's answers with regard to certain alleged "obstructions" in the way of the removal of the goods, the officers withdrew.'*

She went on to endorse the point in *So Long to Learn* when a Blackshirt comes to the farmhouse door and offers help:

"'I don't know what your people stand for, but I'd take the help of the devil himself in this affair. The more the merrier," said Edward.'

In spite of the fact that *'half the newspapers lick their boots, and the other half damn them to hell'*, 'Edward' gives permission for them to camp on his land while making it clear that no invitation had been issued and they were to proceed with caution.

As a result of the Wortham arrests, nineteen of the thirty or forty Blackshirts who had attended over the few days were committed for trial at the Old Bailey. They first appeared before the Hartismere Bench at Eye, charged with causing a public mischief and conspiring to obstruct the course of justice. They were brought before Lord Henniker and nine other magistrates, dressed in their black shirts and wearing the badge of the Union. Among the defendants was Richard Plathen, who was said to have wielded a pick-axe and in the lengthy descriptions of proceedings in the *East Anglian Daily Times* was accused of being in charge:

'... the assistant bailiff, who looked after the eleven impounded beasts, spoke of a trench being dug at the farm, prisoner Plathen being apparently in charge of the work. He saw Plathen use a pick-axe. When Plathen commenced digging, witness asked him what he proposed to do. Plathen replied "To drain the water from the pond into the field".'

When they got to the Old Bailey, however, they pleaded guilty to the somewhat unusual charge that they had been in Suffolk *'... as an apparently organised force so as to cause alarm to His Majesty's subjects; to cause a public mischief by diverting the constables of the East Suffolk force from all ordinary duties; and by their action inciting to the commission of crime and a breach of the peace.'*

They received a conditional discharge from the judge, who told them:

'... I am told you are good fellows, and I hope you will remain good fellows, realising how badly advised you were in this matter.'

As an exercise in rebellious behaviour, the exploits of the Blackshirts in the tithe war were not entirely successful or fruitful, but their intervention succeeded in bringing the matter to the front pages of the nation's press. The National Union of Farm Workers was keeping a close eye on the situation and in *The Land Worker* condemned Fascism as 'this evil', deploring Mosley's remedy for British agriculture. In November 1933 the Union warned:

'At Aylesbury, Bucks, Sir Oswald Mosley outlined his agricultural policy – mainly one of encouraging home production, restricting imports, and State control of prices, to give a fair profit. How all this was to be brought about if not by the methods of the present Government or those proposed by the Labour Party (and Sir Oswald condemned both) is by no means clear. Sir Oswald, according to the Press report, declared he was out to "break down the barriers of class and snobbery which were the curse of the country". Fascism was out to destroy Communism. They made no promises, but told the people what they were going to do and asked them to help. Apparently voters are to sign "a blank cheque" which Sir Oswald Mosley will fill as he pleases.'

NUAW member Arthur Barker of Kenton near Stowmarket, a supporter of Mosley's proposals for a Credit Bank solely for agriculture, was asked what the locals made of the Blackshirts and replied that the farm workers *'watched the Fascists with bemused curiosity, neither for nor against them'*, adding:

'The 'Fascist Week' claimed that the police were booed as they arrested the Blackshirts, no doubt they were, but this was probably more in anger against the tithe than in support of fascism.'

Another East Anglian Mosley supporter, George Hoggarth saw things slightly differently. Writing in *Mosley's Blackshirts* he remembered:

'In 1934, as a Committee Member of the Suffolk Tithepayers' Association, I worked with Albert Mobbs and other Suffolk Farmers' Union supporters in the battle against the extortion of tithes and the enforced sale of farmers' goods ...When Wortham Manor ... was under threat of distraint I went along to lend support ... There I came across a group of Blackshirts, who under the command of Dick Plathen had come down from London to give us a hand. I got into conversation with these men, found their policy for overcoming the agricultural depression sensible, and bought their literature.'

Hoggarth was ever afterwards indignant at the way the BUF members were portrayed by history, and *'all the lies told about us in the press and on the radio'.* He wrote:

'Dick Plathen and his colleagues had taken legal advice before coming down to Suffolk and had been told that if they were present at an enforced sale with the farmer's permission and hindered the bailiffs without using force, they would be within the law. So they felled trees across the private road leading to the farm buildings, dug trenches and put up barbed wire ... Then police reinforcements were brought in and the Blackshirts were arrested under a long-forgotten statute ... I was extremely indignant about these arrests and with others, including my brother, decided to join the local branch of the BUF. A year or two later I became branch treasurer.'

It seemed that everyone was trying to keep on the right side of the law, while at the same time milking the publicity opportunity. In *The Fascists in Britain* Colin Cross refers to the BUF's 'energetic campaign in the countryside':

'... the Fascists cherished the hope, common in new political movements, that if only they could pierce the farmworkers' stubborn regard for tradition they could, without difficulty, win the countryside from the Conservatives. Accordingly the BUF muscled into the 'tithe war' ... Mosley, declaring that he opposed not the principle of State support for the Church of England but only the method of providing support through tithes, sent his men to the countryside with instructions to obstruct the county-court bailiffs.'

Farm workers, however, were not that easily impressed, although one thing that did have an impact was a special brand of cigarettes which bore the Fascist 'flash in the pan'. Lord Rothermere had thought up the scheme as an advertising gimmick for the BUF. He would produce them if the Blackshirts would distribute them, thus profiting both parties. Whether or not the enterprise made a profit is unclear, but the stunt had the power to impress the locals in rural Suffolk, if nothing else.

Lady Eve Balfour, while acknowledging a deficiency in 'the old monetary system' which she thought inadequate to deal with the country's present difficulties, did not think Mosley's proposed Credit Bank for agriculture a likely solution. She expressed her fear that if nothing new was found '... there is a very grave danger that if [Mosley's] remains the only party with such a policy the whole of rural England will go black-shirt'.

F R Allen had also been aware of the potential dangers of alliance with the BUF and in 1933 wrote to AG:

'I have at last found time to congratulate you on the result at Mr Waspe's farm. I am glad that it ended without a disturbance, and without *anything very active on the part of the Fascists. You were right in disclaiming their intervention.'*

Shortly afterwards, at a meeting of the TPA in Ipswich, AG warned:

'There is a rumour abroad that the Tithepayers' Association are linking up with the Fascist movement, and I feel therefore that we should make our position quite clear. We started this association as a non-political and a non-sectarian organisation, and will remain so. What individual tithepayers do, however, is another matter. I suppose a tithepayer has as much right to become a Fascist as to become a Conservative or a Socialist. After all, there is an old saying that a drowning man will clutch at a straw. Personally, I have not joined the Fascist movement, but I know of nothing in this country more calculated to encourage the growth of Fascism than the apparent indifference of Parliament to the grievances of the tithepayers.'

Association between the BUF and tithepayers had no lasting effect on either group and in *Mosley's Men* J D Brewer writes:

'[An] Agricultural Party was formed specifically to agitate on farming matters but it was dominated by those dynasts of the political centre, Lords Rothermere and Beaverbrook. The NFU, Tithepayers' Association, the various Chambers of Agriculture and Farmers Clubs remained strictly non-political. And unlike the Nazis, the BUF did not form specifically farming organisations, nor did it attempt to infiltrate existing farming bodies. This reflected three things: the lack of success for the BUF that was likely to result; the lack of both farming and non-farming membership in the BUF to allow them to do all this; and the lack of a serious interest in agriculture by the BUF. Its link with British farmers came only from opportunistically exploiting a number of localised disturbances in the circumscribed area of East Anglia.'

~ o ~

JUNE 11, 1934. *THE FARMER AND STOCK-BREEDER.* 1353

A Royal Commission on Tithe

Bill Withdrawn in Face of Opposition

Government Not Justified in Forcing Proposals in View of Dissatisfaction

By Our Parliamentary Correspondent

In face of the strong opposition which had developed since the Tithe Bill was given a second reading in the House of Lords on April 17 by 45 votes against 18, the Government announced the withdrawal of the measure in the Upper House on Thursday and the appointment of a Royal Commission to enquire into the whole question of tithe rent charge in England and Wales, and its incidence, with special reference to stabilised value, statutory remission powers for recovery, and the method and terms of redemption.

SUBSEQUENT to the second reading the Central and Associated Chambers of Agriculture passed a resolution asking the Government not to proceed with the Bill, but to set up an enquiry, while the Council of the National Farmers' Union referred back a resolution of its Tithe Committee welcoming the introduction of the measure.

In a leading article on April 16 the FARMER AND STOCK-BREEDER said: "A great outcry has arisen all over the country against the Government's Tithe Bill. It was suggested that there was a certain amount of agreement, on the basis of a compromise, but we have been unable to discern any of it . . . . there is no cessation in demands for a full enquiry. It is difficult to see on what grounds it can be maintained that such an enquiry is not called for. To obtain a settlement agreeable to moderate men the whole question must be brought under review immediately."

A Belief Not Justified

In conveying the Government's decision Lord Hailsham explained that before bringing the Tithe Bill before Parliament the Government had ground for believing that its proposals would

DEALER HAILSHAM: "TAKE 'IM AWAY, BILL, NOBODY SEEMS TO WANT 'IM."

recommend themselves to the great body of moderate opinion among both tithe-owners and tithe-payers. In the event, however, this belief had not been justified.

Possibly the fact that neither party was satisfied was an argument in favour of the view that the proposed compromise was essentially fair. The Government had come to the conclusion that they would not be justified in attempting to force their proposals upon the contending parties when neither professed to be satisfied.

The dropping of the Bill involved that existing conditions would continue, but it would not be right to leave matters in such a position indefinitely, and the Government considered it proper to give all parties concerned a full opportunity of having the facts investigated by a body with the widest terms of reference.

Lord Cranworth congratulated the Government on the step taken, and the Bishop of Norwich expressed the hope that the work of the Royal Commission would be expedited.

Farmer & Stock-Breeder cutting, 11 June 1934.

Chapter 6

A ROYAL COMMISSION IS ANNOUNCED

'It was announced last night that the King has appointed a Royal Commission "to inquire into, and report upon, the whole question of tithe rentcharge in England and Wales, and its incidence, with special reference to stabilised value, statutory remission, power of recovery, and methods of terms of redemption".'

East Anglian Daily Times, 28 August 1934

IN 1934 Sir John Fischer Williams, KC, who had recently been the British legal representative on the Reparation Commission under the Treaty of Versailles, was appointed Chairman of the Royal Commission on Tithe Rentcharge in England and Wales. Other members were Sir Leonard James Coates (a partner in a firm of Chartered Accountants): Lord Cornwallis (a former President of the Royal Agricultural Society of England and former Chairman of Kent County Council); Sir John Edward Lloyd (Professor of History at the University College of North Wales, Chairman of the Board of Celtic Studies and President of the Welsh Language Society); and Sir Edward Robert Peacock (a director of Baring Brothers & Co and the Bank of England). This five-man team, together with two secretaries, Mr E Lawrence

Mitchell (assistant secretary at the Ministry of Agriculture) and Mr A S Allen (also of the Ministry), was charged with enquiring into and reporting on the whole question of tithe rentcharge.

Sir John Fischer Williams was a Governor of QAB, as Roderick Kedward pointed out, but this objection was quickly sat on by George Middleton, who said that all KCs and some of the principal officers of State automatically became Governors on their appointment. *'I daresay,'* he told the press, *'that many of the Governors are unaware of this fact'*, by which he presumably meant that there were QAB Governors who did not know they were Governors.

At the start of 1934 it looked as though the tithepayers' message was starting to be taken seriously within both the Government and the country and their leaders took the announcement of a Royal Commission as a sign that protest had been raised to a new level. Indeed, it was impossible to ignore. The County Courts were dealing with hundreds, and in some counties thousands, of non-payment cases. Every few days another picture of yet another distraint sale would reach the front pages of the national dailies. The Ashford, Kent & Sussex TPA told their members that:

> *'...thousands of court orders are issued. Four hundred and twenty-two Orders were issued in one day at one Court, and many Court Bailiffs were assaulted. One Bailiff called at a farm to seize cows for tithe, but the cowmen seized the Bailiff and dropped him in the cesspool! Here and there, all over Christian England, Church Authorities are threatening and chasing farmers for tithe.'*

It was estimated that in 1932 alone some sixteen thousand applications had been made to the courts in respect of tithe non-payment. Not only were the Courts dealing with tithepayers refusing to pay, but also with tithepayers incurring heavy legal bills. Some who bought their farms under onerous mortgage conditions had overdue repayments outstanding and choices had to be made as to whether to pay tithe or mortgage demands.

Resistance to distraint attempts was acute as QAB scrambled to obtain farmers' goods and chattels for tithe payment. Farmers' wives lost their furniture, ducks and chickens, farmers their cows, sheep, corn and farm implements. Auctioneers were chased off farms after the sales, some taking shelter in public houses with a police guard on the door, and their cars were tarred and feathered inside. Whenever possible, a member of the NTA 'flying squad' would be standing by to assist with the proceedings and give press interviews where necessary.

Collection was a huge problem for QAB and, with agriculture's problems deepening almost daily, even those tithepayers willing to pay were finding it impossible to do so out of profits and most had no capital reserves to draw on. In their sixth report QAB's Tithe Committee admitted that the cost of collection, including convener's salary, audit fees and office expenses, was £3 6s 6d per £100 tithe money and was an increase over the average cost in the previous year. However, '...*taking the country as a whole, of the two half-years' tithe becoming due during the year 1932, over 37 percent was collected by November 30th 1933, and nearly three-quarters of the half-years' tithe due in April 1933 was collected within eight months.*'

Although claiming success, the Committee made no mention of the real costs, particularly those relating to the erosion of the Church's reputation. It did, however, admit that due to the 'low produce prices and high costs of production' within agriculture, concessions were being made to tithepayers amounting to over £48,000 in settlement of nearly 3,800 hardship cases. The amount collected, therefore, was well below that which was due.

The Committee reaffirmed its belief that there was no need for an official inquiry and that Government already 'had all relevant facts concerning both tithe and agriculture at their disposal'. This was a point emphasised in the *East Anglian Daily Times*, which agreed that there was no need for a protracted consultation period since '... all the essential facts concerning the effect of the tithe problem must be known'.

The final point in the Committee's report was predictable:
'*Tithe rent-charge is payable by the farmer only in cases in which he is the owner of the land which he farms.*'

It went on to say that tithe bore no relation whatsoever to the profit which might be made from the land:
'... *even tithes in kind bore no relation to profits, the titheowner was entitled to take every tenth sheaf of corn or every tenth lamb and so on, whether or not produced at a profit.*'

The 'tenth' portion of produce, in the form of a sheaf of corn or a lamb, had not existed since 1836 but it was plainly inaccurate to say that tithes in kind had had no relation to profits. That, argued the tithepayers, was the point: tithe in kind had been a portion of each season's produce and therefore varied annually.

The Committee estimated that tithe accounted for only £3 million of nearly £140 million worth of produce, about two percent, sold annually off farms in England and Wales. By itself it sounded an insignificant figure, but in terms of the nation's agricultural profitability the figure of £140 million was very low relative to those enjoyed during 1919 and 1920.

Newspaper headlines resulting from the effigy-burning distraint sales showed, at the very least, undignified behaviour from the Church which appeared to be losing the battle on the publicity front. In a pre-television age, publicity consisted of newspapers and journals, radio and cinema newsreels. Numerous articles and letters from the correspondence columns were reproduced in leaflet form for the TPAs to use as propaganda. This entailed a huge amount of work for the Secretary, F R Allen, who wrote to AG in 1935:

'I enclose a revised copy of "Notes on Policy" ... The cost of setting this leaflet up and 200 copies is £2 14s 6d. Extra copies will be at the rate of about 5 shillings per 100. I am told that the movement will only be kept together by the continuous issue of leaflets. But I am troubled about the question of finance. There is (1) the cost of printing (2) the cost of postage and carriage (sometimes heavy) and (3) there is the question of my time preparing and distributing the leaflets. I would gladly give all this, but I have to put some limit to the amount I can give as my living depends on my employment in some sort of remunerative occupation. The preparation of these leaflets takes a great deal more time than may appear to some as I feel bound to do my best to make them "water-tight" and this means casting and re-casting them again and again.'

In one of her many later articles in the *East Anglian Daily Times*, Doreen Wallace wrote:

'... newspapers, radio, cinema newsreels (there was no telly then) featured the Tithe War, which kept breaking out in new places, conspicuously month by month, year by year. The correspondence-columns raged. We could not have asked for more.'

Unfortunately, a casualty of the newsreel was the friendship of Doreen Wallace and her Oxford contemporary, Dorothy L Sayers. Both Doreen and Dorothy used tithe in their novels but from different viewpoints. Janet Hitchman recounts in her biography of Sayers, *Such a Strange Lady*:

'Doreen, who had, in 1922, married a well-known Suffolk farmer, Rowland Rash, became involved in agitation for the abolition of tithes. In the days of the great agricultural depression many farmers were being made bankrupt and their farms and stock sold ... The ecclesiastical authorities behaved, to say the least, with consummate stupidity. Dorothy,

*a clergyman's daughter, was naturally in favour of the continued payment
of these charges. She had, as she said, been educated by the tithes.'*
Eventually, after a heated correspondence, Janet Hitchman recounts:
*'Did Dorothy pay the church one tenth of her income from her books?
Back and forth flew the letters, until, horror of horrors, from her seat in
the cinema Dorothy saw on the news-reel her old Somerville crony
bawling from a farm wagon in Hyde Park!'*

All communication between Doreen and Dorothy ceased and the rift was
never healed. Janet Hitchman dedicated *Such a Strange Lady* to Doreen,
having moved down to Suffolk to live at Wortham with the Rashes for about
eighteen months. Later she was to write the script for a film about the tithe
wars for the BBC that used archive film from the 1936 Hyde Park
demonstration that had so horrified Dorothy L Sayers.

Publicity continued as the life-blood of the anti-tithe movement, and
addressing a public meeting in November 1933 AG echoed sentiments akin
to those made by Doreen Wallace:

*'The tithepayer has no option therefore but to allow the law to take its
course and to rely on the support of public opinion. He knows that he is
fighting a just cause and his only hope is publicity. The public, and may
I add the Press, have supported us in no uncertain way. But the Bounty
with its six hundred-odd Governors goes blindly on while the tithe law
breaks down under its own weight.'*

As a variation on a theme, tithepayers burnt a paraffin-soaked effigy of
titheowner Lord St Audries at a farm auction in Sussex watched by three
hundred farmers. The auctioneer found no bids for a haystack and only £1
for six heifers, but this was one of the last such auctions. QAB and some of
the lay impropriators changed their collection tactics. Instead of auctions they
requested the Courts to issue orders for sale by tender, a device more difficult
for the tithepayers to disrupt. In one way, therefore, the publicity that the
auctions attracted was a doubled-edged sword, as M C McCreagh had already
pointed out in a letter to AG in March 1932:

*'The tithepayers should discuss their business and make their plans in
private. I know the tithepayers are scared by tender sales, but that also
is due to the same mistake. In October 1931 on a public platform you
said that farmers have the power to make distress sales ridiculous. The
telephone and mechanical transport have given them the power to
break an agricultural injustice. Some others boasted in public of their*

*ability to make tithe sales a farce. In consequence of the publication
of such statements, the tithe claimants had a meeting with their
advisors in London and devised the tender sale. If the tithepayers had
kept their mouths shut and issued their instructions privately instead
of through the press, there would probably have been no tender sales.
The tithepayers by boasting in public over every success and squealing
over every success are helping their opponents. It is important to
distinguish between what should be said to the tithepayers in private,
and what should be said in public.'*

On balance, however, it was decided that they were not in the business of
keeping their mouths shut and public defiance seemed the best strategy.

In spite of all this, Prime Minister Stanley Baldwin stood by his
declaration made to the House of Commons in June 1932 that the
Government could hold out no prospect of an inquiry. He acknowledged that
farmers had problems paying their tithe, but he had been assured that QAB
was giving sympathetic consideration to individual cases. A new Tithe Bill
would, he said, be introduced into Parliament that would 'solve' the matter.
Earl de la Warr, Parliamentary Secretary to the Ministry of Agriculture,
opened a House of Lords debate on the new Bill in April 1934:

*'My Lords, I beg to move that this Bill be now read a second time. When
my right honourable friend, the Minister, first brought up this question
within the Department, I can assure your Lordships that he realised to the
full how very difficult and indeed dangerous a subject he was raising. He
realised, also, that he was raising a question which concerns itself with the
very deepest prejudices that can be felt on the countryside – prejudices that
go right back into history for very many centuries.'*

Hardly were the noble Lords on their feet than the old argument about
tithe being property was raised. The Archbishop of Canterbury said:

*'... widespread fallacies ... fallacies, for example, such as that tithe is a tax
imposed on agriculture for the support of the church ... it has been
abundantly pointed out already that tithe rentcharge is a form of property
like any other.'*

As a form of property, he said, the Church and lay owners were legally
entitled to a rentcharge and the fact of its being levied indiscriminately on
some landowners and not others was irrelevant. He again cited the worn-out
argument that purchasers of land had paid less for it because of the tithe
rentcharge but said nothing about those who had taken on family farms or

who had been forced to buy tenanted land at inflated post-war prices. He made no reference, either, to the suggestion put forward by the NFU that it should be made compulsory on the vendor of agricultural land to disclose the existence of tithe rentcharge in the deeds. Archbishop Lang, however, thought it unfair that tithe should be considered a burden:

'... I think it is not unnatural that in their stress [farmers] should turn to tithe as affording a possible means of relief, but I submit that it is not fair to select tithe and treat it differently from any other legal charge or interest. Indeed I will venture, perhaps rather daringly, to say that the degree and expense of the hardship have been considerably exaggerated.'

Possibly such landowners as his Lordship consorted with were not subject to the same hand-to-mouth existence as most of the nation's family farmers, and they were certainly not dependent on farming for their livelihood. The Archbishop went on:

'There is the fact, though it is often forgotten, to which the noble Lord alluded, that at the present time over four-fifths of the country tithe is collected without any difficulty whatsoever. The difficult counties are mainly in the East. Suffolk is the worst, and after it come Essex, Norfolk, Berks and East Kent. Elsewhere there is very little difficulty. Let us keep a sense of proportion in this matter.'

The Archbishop had not been reading the newspapers or he would have known that tithe countrywide was rarely collected 'without any difficulty whatsoever'. He cannot have been unaware that his effigy was burned amid jeers and

Reprinted from the "Andover Advertiser"
October 30, 1931.

☞ Your assistance in making this Meeting known to other Tithepayers will be much appreciated.

South Wilts TITHEPAYERS' Association

A Mass Meeting

Will be held in the

GUILDHALL, ANDOVER,

On FRIDAY, 6th NOVEMBER, 1931,

At SEVEN p.m.

Chairman : The Mayor of Andover
(Councillor E. C. Lovell).

VISCOUNT LYMINGTON, M P.,

AND

F. R. ALLEN, Esq.,

President and Hon. Sec. respectively of the National Tithepayers' Association, have been invited to speak.

All Tithepayers interested are cordially invited to attend.

Wiltshire Agricultural Association

NO SHOW IN 1932.

In view of the fact that Andover were arranging to welcome the Wiltshire Agricultural Association to the Town next May, the news received this week that no show at all will be held in 1932 will come as a great disappointment to many people.

The information was conveyed to the Mayor, who was the chairman of the local Committee, and Mr. H. R. Miller, the hon. secretary, also received the intimation, in a letter sent by the Secretary of the Association, which was in the following terms :—

WILTSHIRE AGRICULTURAL ASSOCIATION.
Secretary's Office,
4, Market Place, Devizes,
23rd October, 1931.

DEAR MR. MAYOR,—At a meeting of our Council held yesterday, after a very long discussion, it was finally decided that in view of the present economic situation and the financial state of the country, that it would be impolitic to hold a Show in 1932.

The fact of the Royal Show being at Southampton in the same year was also taken into consideration, and although the Council very much regret to have to take this step after all the trouble that you and your Council have taken, they were of opinion that it would be most unwise to risk the Show, as any failure would mean a very serious financial position for the Association.

They wish me, however, to express their great gratitude to yourself and your Council for your kind invitation and they feel sure that you will under⸴   ⸴ces
that ⸴   ⸴.—
Yours   ⸴.
His   **Example of a newspaper**
    T
The   **article made into a**   nen
who s⸴   eral
and L⸴   **pamphlet for propaganda.**   all
look forward with hope to the future," states the Mayor in his communication to this office.

The preliminary arrangements for holding the Show in Andover were well in hand, and all were anticipating as great a success for the Show as was the case on two previous occasions when the Association came to the Town.

[P.T.O.

insults on farms up and down the country, often within short distances from the parish church and to the distress of his rural clergy.

Both the Lord Chancellor, Viscount Sankey and Lord Cranworth (who spoke as a tithepayer) went on to outline clearly that collection was most certainly a problem. Viscount Sankey said:

'... the remedy worked tolerably well when tithepayers behaved in a normal law-abiding fashion, but in the face of organised opposition it has not worked well. Experience has shown that during such violent agitations as we have recently witnessed – and this is a point which, standing here, I do desire to press home to your Lordships – the County Court cannot perform the tasks imposed upon it by the Act of 1891.'

Lord Cranworth called for an inquiry:

'... there should be an inquiry by an impartial Government Committee into the whole matter. As that committee would naturally take time ... some alteration of Clause 8 of the Act of 1891 should take place to give relief while that committee was forming an opinion.'

Lord Hastings agreed:

'We all know of the unfortunate incidents that have occurred arising out of distraints which have had to be levied on certain reluctant tithepayers in certain parts of England. It has brought the Bounty into some disrepute just as it has brought the parties who have taken an active part in resisting distraint into disrepute.'

One of the main concerns of those who opposed the Bill was Clause 2, which allowed for power of distraint. Earl de la Warr explained to the House:

'The change proposed in Clause 2 of the Bill does raise very important and very serious principles. It means that from henceforth, if this Bill is passed into law, tithe will be collected as an ordinary debt at the County Court; in effect, that tithe becomes a personal debt, which hitherto it has never been.'

The Earl consoled himself with the thought that this important change in the law would only affect those who did not pay up. He thought it would put an end to evasion, obstruction and defiance of the legal system but would make 'not the slightest difference' to the man or woman who signed the cheque for tithe.

There were strong words on both sides and Viscount Astor joined the ranks of those seeking a full inquiry, but in the end the 'Contents' carried the day and the Bill was commended to a Committee of the Whole House.

By June, though, it was obvious that the tithe question was by no means settled and the current Bill unlikely to satisfy anyone. No progress was made with the legislation after the April debate in the House of Lords. Finally, over the summer, those trying to push the Bill through gave way: the Bill was withdrawn and Viscount Hailsham announced the setting up of a Royal Commission. At last it seemed that after five years of organised protest all sides would have a chance to have their say. Under the headline 'Tithe Bill Dead' the *Eastern Daily Press* told its readers that the fact was that neither party in the debate was satisfied with the Bill and that a Royal Commission was 'essentially fair'.

The Commission started sitting late in 1934 and continued for well over a year. AG, who had led a farmers' deputation at the House of Commons in early February, attended most of the sittings and gave evidence before the Commission, as did many within the TPAs. AG complained that, due to a lack of space for the public to sit in at meetings, people were often not able to get a seat. However, he got in often enough to hear yet more tales of injustice, much of it convoluted and unintelligible to the average tithepayer. It seemed that although £600,000 a year was paid out of the Treasury towards the rates charged on ecclesiastical tithe, the ecclesiastical titheowners were deducting that amount from income tax returns. The Commission declared itself amazed at this and countless other anomalies to do with tax and rates. Various rating authorities were challenged to explain when tithe first became liable for rates but they were unable to do so, and indeed the complicated relationship between rates and tithe was incomprehensible to anyone but dedicated accountants.

There were also questions that never reached the Commission but which show a sense of fear bordering on paranoia that was creeping into some parishes. An anonymous letter writer challenged AG:

'Are you aware that the financial statement of the farmers, forced from them in the stress of circumstances by QAB, are returned by them to the incumbent and kept at the Rectory? Mortgages, overdrafts, land credits, etc. are all known to the parson on our doorstep. If it has not already been done, it ought to be brought before the Royal Commission and Mr George Middleton questioned on the fact. In our case the parson's wife got the papers, and how we all have suffered. Is such a low-down, unprincipled thing going on all over the country against the farmer? I dare not sign my name for if QAB knew where the information

came from they could ruin us (they probably would) and others are involved. Others who are also afraid.'

The *Farmers Weekly* reported:

'The Royal Commission ... were told of a number of small freeholds in the New Forest where the tithes represented 1d, 2d and 3d. There were 573 people liable each year to pay sums below 20s; there were 27 people who had to pay between 20s and 60s; and 58 who paid sums over 40s. The collection of these small sums, the Commission were informed, caused great irritation to the payers and the incumbent.'

Reports of anomalies dating back to 1838 were cited, when some fields that had been under corn were levied at the higher rate and had remained at the Great Tithe levels thereafter, whether or not the land had been used for cereals. Very high rentcharge was demanded on land that produced crops of much less value than previously (or no crops at all in some places) especially where hop tithe still applied.

A witness for the Inland Revenue revealed that, for estate duty purposes, tithe was calculated at between ten and fourteen years' purchase, but these values were not always endorsed by MAFF figures, thus causing prolonged arguments over probate settlements. The Commission also heard of problems where the transference of tithe obligations became especially acute when tithed land was sold for building and redemption values had to be assessed and shared between the new owners.

Tithepayers' witnesses pointed to the huge administrative cost of QAB, not just for collection but in reference to the convener's salary, audit fees, office expenses, not to mention all the expenses of the central administration. The Essex TPA witness urged the Commission to have a regard to the moral issues and *The Times* reported Mr W H Harvey as saying that the principle of tithe was an obsolete and unnecessary survival of medieval times, and:

'In the parish of Great Holland, Essex, the total value of the tithe in 1770 was £319. After the Commutation Act it rose in 1837 to £770 16s. The 1925 Act established tithe unfairly on War prices at some 35 percent above its value in the years immediately after the War. The present value was something like 50 percent above its true value compared with the 1836 standard. Seven farms in Essex were instanced where the tithe was 60 percent above what it was in 1901; costs had increased and prices dropped.'

Roderick Kedward was quoted in the *News Chronicle* on the theme of morality when, supported by AG, F R Allen and E F Iwi (legal adviser), he gave evidence to the Commission in December 1934:

> *'We recognise no moral obligation to pay tithe or redeem it, declared Mr R M Kedward, chairman of the National Tithepayers' Association, giving evidence yesterday before the Royal Commission on Tithes. But, he added, tithepayers were prepared to contribute towards abolishing the system in the same way and for similar reasons that those who abolished slavery recompensed the slave owners. It was a question of expediency. The association proposed that all tithe rentcharge should be bought out at ten years' purchase – the average market value of lay tithe – instead of the 31 years' purchase now demanded for ecclesiastical tithe.'*

Witness for the rural clergy came from the Reverend Arthur Ogle, rector of East Ilsley, Berkshire, who said that the clergy had been 'on the dole' since 1899 and the confusion over what was to happen during the Commission's sitting made things worse. The Bishop of Norwich, speaking as a Governor of QAB, was on record as saying that he looked with some anxiety at what the position of the clergy dependent on tithe might be during the course of the inquiry. He thought that the Bill should be forced through and the inquiry take place afterwards.

That was exactly what the opponents of the Bill feared, not least because there was a danger that farming prices might recover slightly, adding fuel to the QAB argument that it was only when agriculture was in the doldrums that farmers made a fuss about paying. Tithepayers consistently tried to make the point that the degree of agricultural profitability had nothing to do with the injustice, as they saw it, of tithe. QAB made it clear that it considered the worst of the agricultural depression to be over and, as a consequence, could see no reason for changing the legislation or for setting up an inquiry. In response to a statement by Roderick Kedward, George Middleton added to the pile of letters on editorial desks across England and Wales to the effect that the tithepayers exaggerated the burden of tithe on agriculture. He reiterated that it was only when a farmer owned the land that he paid the tithe and that it should be looked on as no more than a mortgage payment on the farm. He hotly disputed the fact that invariably the amount of rentcharge was equivalent to a farm rental and repeated endlessly that where the Bounty thought it necessary they were prepared to consider temporary abatement. He gave optimistic assurance that even the very worst trough of the farming depression would be 'mitigated before long'. George Middleton might have known something about the Post Office, but he appeared to know very little about the fortunes of peacetime agriculture and ignored the root objections to the unfairness of arbitrary tithe and its redemption cost.

Indeed, many were worried that although the number of tithe redemption cases completed during 1932 was announced to have been 1,436, the redemption cost was considered by many to be nothing less than 'daylight robbery'. If a tithepayer could not afford to pay the annual rentcharge, how was he expected to redeem the liability for a capital sum several times the amount?

A number of other clergymen expressed views to the Commission, including those on behalf of the Chapter of the Rural Deanery of Wickford, followed by the Reverend J Bazille Corbin (Rector of Runwell) who was accompanied by the Reverend Henry Iselin (Rector of Rawreth). They all agreed that something had to be done, although opinions varied as to what. One parson said that people came to him to say that they do not approve of tithe, but he told them that '... *as a matter of fact, neither do I, but we are both cogs in the same machinery*'.

Shortly after the announcement that the Government had abandoned the Bill, Cosmo Lang told the House of Lords that he thought there was a misunderstanding among tithepayers that the setting up of a Royal Commission put the matter on hold. It did not, he said. The Church would not countenance the request of tithepayers who were urging that they should be relieved of their responsibilities in the meantime and he urged them to stop their protest for the duration. A clergyman wrote to Doreen Wallace saying the same thing, to which she replied:

'Why should we, when the other side are still acting harshly, and are even more vindictive. We don't mind a reasonable truce, but the tithe demands must be consistent with the state of farming. The continuing of the tithe agitation rests not with the tithepayers but with the titheowners.'

In Devon Mr A Turner, Chairman of the North Devon TPA was caught off guard when eight bailiffs and several members of the Devon Constabulary arrived at his farm to seize, mark and impound his cattle. Mr Turner was in London for the day on the understanding that QAB were 'on hold' pending the result of the Commission. It turned out that they were not.

The *Farmers Weekly* reported that the NTA had sent a resolution to the Minister of Agriculture and the Commission expressing regret '*that the Archbishop of Canterbury and the Bishop of Norwich speaking in the House of*

(Above)
Doreen Wallace.

(Below) Letter to
Doreen Wallace
from the Royal
Commission on
Tithe Rentcharge,
1935.

Lords on behalf of the ecclesiastical titheowner, repudiated the suggestion made by tithepayers for a truce during the sitting of the Royal Commission'.

Following adverse publicity about the role of the NFU, the Reverend S H Osborne, Rector of Eardisley asked the Commission to define the role of the farmers' union. He said he had heard of an inquiry that had taken place prior to the 1925 Tithe Act, which had been a compromise between titheowners and tithepayers in collaboration with the NFU. AG was called upon to answer, but said that while the Union had been in discussion with ministers it had made a statement to all MPs to the effect that if the Act was passed, tithepayers country-wide would commence agitation against it and there had been no collaboration. Mr Osborne still expressed concern that there had been collusion to the detriment of the clergy in 1925 and he did not want it repeated in 1935. He urged George Middleton to accept an invitation to attend a public meeting in Hereford to put the case for the clergy. Middleton did not attend the meeting and much was made of it, although in his own defence he wrote in the *Hereford Times* that he had been elsewhere and not able, as requested, to send anyone to represent QAB.

Landowners also provided witness to the Commission: Lord Hastings and Brigadier-General H Clifton Brown MP supported a memorandum submitted by the CLA whose membership of 11,500 included most of the large estate owners, many of whom were tithepayers. Chairman of the CLA's Somerset branch was R S Strachey (a cousin of Lord Strachie) whose name featured regularly in the correspondence columns and who wrote *Freedom from the Tithe Act 1925*.

---

hone:—VICTORIA 8740.

ROYAL COMMISSION ON TITHE RENTCHARGE.

id delay, address all
munications to :—
THE SECRETARY.

3, SANCTUARY BUILDINGS,
GREAT SMITH STREET,
WESTMINSTER,
LONDON, S.W.I.

14th January, 1935.

Dear Mrs. Rash,

    With reference to the evidence which you submitted to the Commission, I am desired by the Chairman to inform you that he has received a communication calling attention, in the interests of historical accuracy, to the fact that you appear to have been under a misapprehension as to the figures which you found in Ecton's Liber Valorum. It is stated that the figures do not represent the value of livings in 1711, but their value in King Henry VIII's books for the purpose of the payment of first fruits and tenths taken over by the crown from the papacy. The writer states that he does not know how Henry VIII's valuation was made, but he has always suspected that it was a mere continuation of an earlier mediaeval valuation, and even at Henry VIII's time did not represent the true value of the livings.

    Although the writer has not seen Ecton's Liber Valorum, he has a copy of the 1742 edition of the name author's Thesaurus, and he finds that your figures for 1711 are, in each case that he has looked up, the figures given by the Thesaurus under the heading of "King's Books". It is suggested that your mistake, if it is a mistake, is intelligible, as Ecton in the Thesaurus nowhere gives any indication of what the figures are beyond the head "King's Books". In the Thesaurus, however, in some cases, he puts under the figure from "King's Books", but in small type, a second and much larger value, which he sometimes calls "certified value". The writer has not been able to discover what those values are, but believes they represent the true value at the time Ecton was writing. For instance, the living of Saham Tonye, which was valued in the"King's Books" at £21.14s.9¾d. (your figure £24 is perhaps a misprint) has inserted under it a value of £120 in small type.

The

D.A.E. Rash.

*Telephone :—*CITY 2261.　　　　　　　*Telegrams :—*AGRITITRE—CENT—LONDON.

MINISTRY OF AGRICULTURE AND FISHERIES.

To avoid delay address all
communications to:
　　THE SECRETARY.

7, OLD BAILEY,

LONDON, E.C.4.

REDEMPTION OF TITHE RENTCHARGE
2 7 JUL 1935

No. L.T. 43412

Parish ✗✗✗✗✗✗✗✗✗✗✗ CARLTON COLVILE

County **SUFFOLK**

SIR,

I am directed to inform you that, in pursuance of an application under the Tithe Acts, an Order has been made directing the redemption of the annual Tithe Rentcharge on certain tithe areas situate in the above-mentioned parish, in a portion of which areas, as the Ministry is informed, you are interested as owner.

A Schedule, with plan attached, showing the total amount of the redemption money and the incidental expenses, and the share thereof to be borne by each owner, has been deposited in the Parish in the custody of Mr. W. B. Hoseasen, of The Oulton Broad Harbour Master's Office, Nicholas Everitt Park, Oulton Broad for inspection by persons affected. Objections, if any, to such proposed apportionment of the redemption money and expenses must be signified in writing to the Ministry at the above address on or before the 1 9 AUG 1935

The share proposed to be apportioned in respect of the property stated to be owned by you is £ 39 : 17 : 3d , and in due course you will receive notice of the time and manner in which payment of your share should be made. The property is numbered as below on the deposited plan.

Your attention is directed to the explanation which is printed on the back of this letter.

I am, SIR,

Your obedient Servant,

Charles J. W. Thomas.

		Tithe Field.	No. on Plan.
J. Long, Esq.,		216 .	3c .
"Rosedale Cottage,		217 .	42 .
Elmtree Road,			
Carlton Colville			
Lowestoft,			
Suffolk			

Letter No. 129/L.T.　　　　　(X2750)　Wt 29791/2010　10,000(2)　2/35　H & Sp　Gp 642

Compulsory notice from MAFF, July 1935.

The CLA advocated immediate redemption and would, said Lord Hastings, remove forever *'the disabilities which the Church suffered and would remove the whole question from future politics'.* The CLA had been active on the side of the tithepayers and in November 1933 had sent a Deputation to the House of Commons urging the Minister of Agriculture, Walter Elliott to take the issue more seriously. The Minister declined to make any statement in reply as he was receiving a deputation from titheowners at a later date, plus an NFU Tithe Committee Deputation, and was therefore not in full possession of the facts.

As usual, life in the NFU's Bedford Square headquarters was not running smoothly. The Union faced a crisis: membership was falling in several counties because of dissatisfaction among the rank and file over the leadership's handling of negotiations concerning the new Bill. The *Gloucester Journal* reported a 'clash' between tithepayers and the NFU which claimed that it weakened its stance if the county had a Union branch and a TPA. But tithepayers thought the NFU was not sufficiently alert to the situation and Headquarters 'had done nothing about the matter except talk'. It was only in 1933 that AG and Makens Turner persuaded the NFU Annual Meeting to form a Tithe Committee.

Although the newly formed NFU Tithe Committee sent a deputation to the Minister of Agriculture, members argued that it had achieved little, and over a month afterwards there was still no word of reply from the Minister. The argument was put forward forcibly by deputation members J W Rickeard, Makens Turner and AG from Suffolk and D Gemmill from Essex but several weeks later they were still waiting for an intelligible reply from Walter Elliot, in spite of a resolution put forward by one-third of the Members of the House of Commons urging for a permanent, long-term tithe policy.

In view of what was happening in the fields and farmyards of rural England and Wales, the machinery of government and interminable NFU meetings seemed irrelevant and frustrating to those on the ground. Although the findings of the Tithe Committee were gradually making their way up the Council's agenda, it had nowhere near the momentum that those interested members thought it should. When they did, finally, hear from the Minister it was to the effect that he thought that if there was a grievance it was primarily one for the titheowners and the tithepayers to settle amongst themselves. In the Union debate on the Minister's reply Mr A H Brown from the Hampshire branch moved a resolution to the effect that unless the 1925 Act was repealed or revised the Union should instruct its tithepaying membership to make a token payment of one shilling in the pound until such time as the Act was repealed. The General Secretary, Cleveland Fyfe said that he had met George Middleton and Mr Hannah, the Principal Assistant Secretary to QAB, to discuss the Ministerial answers though none of them had come to any conclusions on the matter. QAB had said categorically that it would not enter into any conference that had as its objective the repeal of the 1925 Tithe Act and would not enter any joint negotiations to lobby in favour of an inquiry.

Even by April 1934, as the Bill reached the House of Lords, Union committees were still discussing whether or not to consult with other organisations and constantly putting off any decision while waiting to hear from the Minister. County delegates representing angry tithepaying members were rendered impotent by the Union's bureaucracy and constant referrals. At one meeting those anxious to discuss a report of the Tithe Committee had to sit through a discussion on the theft of mushrooms from fields, and whether steps should be taken to make stealing mushrooms an offence.

The Union was constantly in the position of having to defend itself to its members and justify the proceedings of its Tithe Committee, whose members were valiantly attempting to inject a sense of urgency into the proceedings. Many were already panicking with regard to Clause 2, which would make tithe a personal debt. After canvassing opinion from the counties – a lengthy, bureaucratic process – there was a 21 to 1 vote in favour of recommending either amendment or deletion of Clause 2 from the Bill. The President was pressed to inform Earl de la Warr of the Union's total opposition to the entire Bill, and convey in the strongest terms the membership's opposition to the Minister of Agriculture.

When the Royal Commission was announced the Union took much of the credit for it, but rumours that it had recommended approval of the Bill with no inquiry reached the press. The *East Anglian Daily Times* demanded to know what was behind the Union's recommendation:

> 'It is a pity that publicity should have been obtained for the recent decision of the Tithe Committee of the Farmers' Union to the effect that it recommended the Council not only to approve of the Tithe Bill now before Parliament for the settlement of the tithe question, but that the Union should agree there was no necessity for a prolonged inquiry into tithe. It is inconceivable that proposals of such a character should have even been put forward, let alone recommended by a Committee of the Union. That

*appears to be the general view of tithepayers. It is only fair to say that on
the Union's Tithe Committee there was a considerable minority against
the recommendation.'*

The Union, though, had taken the President's lead and submitted the
recommendations that included acceptance.

Messrs Rickeard and Gemmill, the minority who had done much to
convey the urgency of the situation, were elected to help form the Union's
evidence. Representatives from Berkshire, Cornwall, Hampshire, Hereford,
Kent, Norfolk, Oxford and Worcestershire, together with a delegate from the
Welsh Committee, were voted onto the Tithe Committee in July 1934. Only
a few months later the *News Chronicle* reported that at least three counties had
launched a further attack on NFU policy:

*'The counties are Norfolk, Suffolk, and Essex. With the exception of Kent,
they are the most heavily burdened by the tithe law. Rumblings of revolt
by the rank and file of the NFU against the officials of the National
Executive have been growing. If the NFU Executive persists in the
proposals they intend to make to the Royal Commission on tithe – that a
return be made to the 1836 corn crisis as a basis of payment – I learn that
the East Anglian branches, with the support of many others, will formally
disclaim the official representation and apply to the Commission for
permission to give evidence on their own account.'*

Another report said:

*'Executives of five county branches of the National Farmers' Union –
Cambridgeshire, Norfolk, Suffolk, Essex, and Kent – are to meet in
London today to discuss the "secrecy" which they feel covers the union's
official attitude on tithes ... Though the Royal Commission on Tithe has
repeatedly invited all who wish to give evidence to submit written
statements ... the tithe committee of the NFU which is preparing the
evidence to be given on behalf of the union has not reported progress to the
executive for at least two months.'*

Probably in an attempt to dampen down the fires, AG was originally left
off the NFU Tithe Committee but was quickly voted on after complaint from
the other members. But he, together with Doreen and Rowland Rash and
Lady Eve Balfour (whose fight with the NFU eventually ended in her
resignation from the Union), decided to request that they and Roderick
Kedward be allowed to give individual witness to the Commission and not
rely on the Union for representation. Lady Eve, well known in so many circles

FRIDAY, THE DAILY EXPRESS. AUGUST 4, 1

Harvest Interrupts A Tithe W
Charge Against 36 Farmers

S. MARGARET GARDNER, one
he two women defendants, carrying
r "lucky horseshoe" yesterday.

day's Human Story

'hen The
Law Is Blind

LADY EVE
BALFOUR IN
THE DOCK

SOLICITOR TELLS OF
'IMPRISONMENT'
IN A BARN

PELTED WITH EGGS

"Daily Express" Special
Correspondent.
CASTLE HEDINGHAM
(Essex), Thursday.
THIS little town, set deep in the
heart of a farming district,
became to-day the focus of the
country when Lady Eve Balfour
and thirty-five other farmers were

LADY EVE BALFOUR and Mr. Holes, a seventy-four-year-old farmer, two of
the defendants charged with "unlawful assembly."

Cutting from the *Daily Express*, 4 August 1933.

not least as the niece of the Conservative Prime Minister, Arthur Balfour,
added her not inconsiderable support. She was taken to court both for tithe
arrears and for her part in the famous tithe distraint raid of the Gardiner farm
at Gestingthorpe, Essex. In a speech to the Women's Branch of the National
TPA in July 1934 she said:

> 'On the tithe issue the policy of the NFU has done as much harm as
> anybody or anything else. It is my opinion that if they don't alter their
> tactics soon every occupying owner-farmer should leave the Union as a
> protest. The NFU has split itself right down the back, and I intend to send
> in my resignation when my subscription expires.'

Lady Eve's application to give evidence in person was accepted, as was that
from the NTA, AG and the Rashes. Like many farmers, Lady Eve bought her
farm in 1919 when land prices were between £20 to £25 per acre. By 1933
the same land was worth £10 an acre. In 1928 she was paying the titheowner,
Dr Triplet's Charity, out of capital and by 1930 she was borrowing money to keep

the farm running and to pay tithe. In her evidence Lady Eve outlined in detail the Court's seizure at her Suffolk farm. Having offered a fifty percent settlement to the charity, which was refused, she allowed the law to take its course:

> '... at 5 o'clock in the morning the lock on my gate was broken and two lorries arrived in my yard. General Dealers, Ltd., sent a man ahead to break all my locks on every gate ... the Bailiff, a Superintendent of Police, and about forty Constables were present. The police removed any walking sticks that my friends happened to have, but left the employees of General Dealers armed with sticks and cudgels.'

Photographs of Lady Eve leaving an Essex Police Court in the company of thirty-five other farmers brought there on a charge of unlawful assembly had been invaluable publicity for the tithepayers' cause. The *Daily Express* carried a picture of Lady Eve and seventy-four-year-old Mr Holes with a report of the court proceedings that related to the high-profile distraint on Delvyn's Farm, Gestingthorpe. It was a particularly hot day and *the farmers, nearly all in heavy tweeds, with tanned faces which glistened as the sun beat down on the little red-brick court, listened intently to the battle of wits between counsel for the defence and the prosecution*'. Lady Eve was reported as removing her coat *'under which she was wearing an open-necked white shirt'* and also removed her hat, although the other woman defendant, Mrs Margaret Gardiner (whose farm had been at the centre of the distraint raid), kept hers on to the end. Eventually the sitting had to be abandoned so that the farmers could get on with the harvest, and '... *by the end of the day the whole court had wilted under the heat: the strong feelings which had caused the scene which, in turn, had given rise to the court case, had been defeated by the weather. It was much too hot*'.

Lady Eve and the other defendants were charged with pelting the solicitor and bailiff with rotten eggs and chaff, threatening them with a hive of bees and with personal assault. It was also alleged that they had used foul and abusive language, most of which was directed at a contingent of unemployed Welsh miners who acted as carriers. Later, in the Essex Assizes Court, a local farmer named Norman Stebbings claimed that the only egg he saw thrown hit another of the defendants. Another said that the only reason he had thrown chaff at the man was to stop the egg running down his face and into his eyes.

The Reverend H M Greening, Rector of Gestingthorpe, refused point-blank to receive anything but the full amount of tithe and, reported the *Daily Mail*, in a spirit of bravado he faced the loud and spirited protests from the farmers 'smoking a cigarette'.

The *Daily Express* (who tagged Lady Eve 'Trousered Daughter of Peer') ran a fund-raising campaign for the £200 court costs required by Lady Eve and her co-defendants in protest at the nature of the charge. The paper's Agricultural Correspondent, Kenneth P Pipe involved himself personally when he discovered that the 'unlawful assembly' charge had been described as *'an occasion on which three or more persons meet together to support each other in carrying out a purpose which is likely to involve violence'.* Contributions were invited up to, but not to exceed £1.

Lady Eve's condemnation to the Commission of a company called General Dealers Limited highlighted how tithepayers dealt with another weapon in the armoury of QAB. This time, though, there was a more sinister aspect to proceedings. During 1933 tithepayers made the acquaintance of the 'Black and Tans', a semi-military police force raised in 1920 for the suppression of the IRA in Ireland, operating now in a new guise which gave the potential for violence that could damage the cause and needed careful handling.

QAB's announcement of higher collection rates in 1933 coincided with the appearance of the newly formed company called General Dealers Limited. Its offices were at High Holborn in London and it had two shareholders – solicitors' clerks – who had each subscribed £1. The chairman of directors was Major Thornton Miller, a retired Army officer, and his right hand man was Percy Knight Rennie. There was no direct proof that General Dealers (renamed 'General Stealers' by the tithepayers) was set up by QAB, but Reginald Primrose of Deacon & Company, solicitors to General Dealers was quoted in the press as saying that obviously '... *the actions of the company are such as to benefit the titheowners, and one can scarcely believe that it should have been formed quite fortuitously'.*

No one believed for a moment that it had been formed fortuitously, especially as it was estimated there were over 5,000 tithe orders outstanding throughout the country; in Kent over 200 orders

N ANNE

AND HER

Y FRIEND

(Left) Effigies of Queen Anne and her boyfriend from General Dealers were ritually burned at distraint sales throughout the 1930s.

were outstanding in the Ashford District alone, with over 1,000 in the rest of the county. Mr Primrose went on to say that the company was carrying on a legal trade and hoped to make a profit. It would, he said somewhat threateningly, be unfortunate if *'in taking possession of goods which the company had bought opposition were encountered'*.

Major Thornton Miller went further and said that on at least two occasions the company had met with such opposition that it was necessary to augment the normal staff by 'hiring' police to accompany them. If they were hired it was strange

General Dealers man at Wortham.

behaviour, since the police would have been bound to protect a company in pursuit of lawful and legitimate business.

The tithepayers' tactic of disrupting distraint sales was clogging the County Courts and even where goods were successfully seized it was difficult to dispose of them. Since the only people interested in buying farm stock and implements were other farmers and no farmer would touch distrained goods, it was necessary to change from auction sales to tendering. If QAB had its own version of the TPA 'flying squad', which could buy up and market the distrained goods anonymously, it would not only speed up collection but also increase money realised. Titheowners themselves were not allowed by law to buy distrained goods, but as a third party General Dealers could lawfully tender for goods and remove them to their own farms in the North of England (where tithe was not so contentious). It is to be presumed that like other such debt-collectors, their profit was whatever they made over and above the value of the debt.

One of the first indications that General Dealers was at work came at Haughley in Suffolk, where several lorries arrived at New Bells Farm to seize a number of cattle in lieu of Lady Eve's tithe. It became clear that the same outfit was operating in Cornwall (where lorries and men swooped on a farm at four o'clock in the morning to seize cattle), Gloucester, Denbighshire, Kent and East Anglia. It was discovered that a Captain William Parlour was also a director of General Dealers, and land belonging to him in Oxfordshire was used as a 'dumping ground' for stock brought up from the southern counties of England. The stock could be sold anonymously at Banbury and other markets. Another of these clearing farms was in Yorkshire, another in South Wales, and there was a lorry depot in Durham.

In her evidence to the Commission, Lady Eve said:

'... I took some trouble to ensure that I did not [break the law] by asking the Registrar what the correct methods of seizure should be. I went to the Superintendent of Police and asked for the warrant. He referred me to the representative of General Dealers, who in turn referred me to the bailiff, who walked away without answering. None of the three would give me any explanation as to why no warrant was produced, or why my property had been deliberately and wantonly broken.'

Lady Eve emphasised that she was prepared to allow the law to take its course and not impede it in any way, but she thought the County Court had ignored the legal proceedings of the warrant procedure:

'[The Registrar] informed me that whoever bought the cows would bring a warrant, signed by the Registrar himself, to say that the bearer was now the legal owner of the goods impounded, and that the law did not require me to hand them over until such warrant was produced ... While I was asking for the warrant my men and friends attempted to hold up the loading of the cows. Several men were deliberately knocked down, but kept their promise to me and did not retaliate.'

Percy Rennie, ably assisted by a 'big and heavy man' named Burgess, took command and

IN THE DARK

a neighbouring farmer was struck. The farmer, Mr Stribling, although in a semi-conscious state and with blood streaming down his face, was arrested by police and the cows were rounded up and loaded with what Lady Eve and the other farmers considered was unnecessary cruelty:

> *'The loading of the last cows has left a lasting impression on the memories of all who saw it. The lorry was overfull with three cows in it. The fourth was dragged in by a rope on her horns till her head was between the legs of the other cows, and then five or six employees of General Dealers slammed the tail-board up. I still do not understand why that cow's back was not broken. Had any farmer attempted to do such a thing on any market in England he would have been arrested, but this wanton cruelty was carried out under police supervision, and when my sister attempted to take a photograph of the loading the superintendent of police ordered a constable to prevent her.'*

Tithepayers, however, were in a position to monitor what was happening at the London headquarters, about which AG wrote:

> *'General Dealers came into being. Their origin was very obscure but pretty obvious. Two ex-army officers were in charge. They ran new lorries which they kept in a hotel yard in London, and staffed them mostly with unemployed men. The lorries were equipped with axes and saws to remove obstacles such as trees felled across farm roads. They were, however, unaware that within view of the hotel yard resided relatives of Lady Eve Balfour. This meant that any lorry activities were telephoned to Suffolk and members immediately alerted. This happened when a portion of Her Ladyship's herd had been tendered for by the Company. An evening's preparation in the hotel yard meant that an early morning visit might be expected and as many members as possible were contacted. It was late when I got the message on this occasion and my family were retiring for the night, but I proceeded on a sixty-mile drive to Haughley, near Stowmarket. At the farm entrance, some distance from the house and buildings, sat our two ex-army officers in a car, which left me in no doubt as to what was happening.'*

Just as there is little safe evidence that General Dealers had been set up on the direct orders of QAB, so it was difficult to prove the allegation that the men were, in fact, members of the 'Black and Tans'. These unemployed ex-Army men wore a mixture of police (black) and army (tan) uniforms and had acquired a reputation for murder and mayhem in Ireland. Certainly the men

Addressing the crowds after a distraint sale on one of his Kentish farms are (left to right) Doreen Wallace, Roderick Kedward (speaking), AG Mobbs and Rowland Rash. The journalists take down his speech verbatim, while effigies representing Queen Anne and General Dealers are on show for the press cameras.

who drove the lorries and loaded the stock worked as a team and were adept at using axes and saws. Contemporary opinion was that the men were ex-military, although one newspaper report said:

> 'General Dealers, Ltd., the London company formed with a paid-up capital of £2 for the avowed purpose of dealing in goods distrained for tithe, has assembled its staff from the hotel in Holborn where they work between tithe raids.'

Some years later, the Kent & Sussex TPA published a first-hand account by a General Dealers man:

> 'I was a member of a gang of six desperate men, glad to have any sort of work after long periods of unemployment, who formed the tithe raiding gang of General Dealers Limited – we had to be ready to leave on a tithe raid at any time of the day or night. The two cattle lorries used for the work were always standing by in the yard. They were fully equipped to deal with any obstructions and carried picks, shovels, wire cutters, crowbars, planks and ropes.'

The destination of the raids was always kept secret so that only the driver of the leading lorry knew where they were going. But the raids were never carried out haphazardly, the farm always being reconnoitred beforehand:

> '... a campaign of action was only known to our foreman. Often I have travelled hundreds of miles in the pouring rain crouching with five other raiders in the back of one of these open lorries with only two blankets between us, to arrive before dawn at the farm where the cattle were to be claimed. Sometimes we have managed to take the cattle without awakening the farmer, but usually he was waiting to defend his stock. Obstructions meant nothing to us because we had the law on our side, and in any case we were prepared for violence.'

The man told of farmers and workers who were 'roughly handled without the slightest provocation' and if a summons for assault was brought the men were instructed as to what they had to say in evidence, should any of them be called.

> 'I have seen gates torn off their hinges, hedges broken down, and at one farm I saw a motor car rolled into a ditch, a cart pushed into a pond and cattle we had no right to touch brutally ill-treated. None of the men were experienced at handling animals, and I remember one raid when we had to take away three heifers and some pigs, which were all bleeding by the time we had finished. The heifers were herded into the front of the lorry

and a barrier erected, then the tailboard was closed and the pigs were thrown into the remaining space like sacks of coal. When we left the farm all the pigs were bleeding from nose and ears.'

In one such incident at Kersey in Suffolk two General Dealers lorries turned up at a farm early in the morning. There were about fifteen men with more than a dozen police guarding them and it was noted, somewhat wryly by onlookers, that twelve of the cattle had been those which had escaped from the pound the previous night. It took over forty minutes to load the exhausted and frightened cattle. The fact that the animals had been retrieved and driven back to the pound by Blackshirts, who were supposed to be there to hinder the bailiffs, not help them, added to the rumours that some of them were not very bright. The confused Blackshirts left as the bailiff and lorries disappeared at speed in the direction of Colchester.

Other activities of General Dealers included the supplying of bailiffs in cases considered too difficult or dangerous for the County Court Bailiff. For this 'service' a charge of ten shillings a man per day was made, of which QAB paid three shillings and the County Court seven shillings. By such gangster methods many farmers were forced into submission. The former General Dealers man alleged that two men were killed in Wales.

In the face of such uncompromising tactics, not just individual cases of violence but actual mass violent confrontation seemed a possibility and the NTA decided that enough was enough. The sacrifice made by tithepayers was too great and it would certainly damage their cause if anyone got badly hurt or killed. The Association decided to ask the courts for a reversion to auction sales with an undertaking that a successful sale would ensue and the arrears recovered in full. It took only one court – under the jurisdiction of Judge H J Rowlands at Lowestoft – to agree to this and the courts generally concurred that an orderly, successful sale was preferable to the questionable antics of General Dealers Limited. AG and his associates were soon back in the courts, where they would advise the tithepayer to oppose the application for tendering and then give the judge the required undertaking. Thus they would arrange orderly sales from which all parties drew honourable satisfaction.

Major Thornton Miller, Captain William Parlour, Percy Rennie and Mr Primrose dissolved General Dealers Limited and disappeared from the scene. In a newspaper report dated July 1935 General Dealers were named as the purchasers of goods distrained from the Westwell farm belonging to Roderick Kedward, but little was heard of them after that. It is doubtful if they made the expected financial 'killing' and probably lost the capital expended on men and lorries. It is difficult to know the precise date of its demise, but the memory of 'General Stealers' lived on in placard and poster form well into 1936, although by then it had ceased to exist.

During its sitting the Commission found that time and time again the notion of tithe as property and its attendant arguments would be raised. During 1935 Doreen Wallace was writing her novel *So Long to Learn*, in which a character is putting his land on the market to test the theory that tithe-free land is dearer than land subject to tithe:

> *'You bought your land cheaper because the tithe was on it ... That's what Baldwin and the titheowners say. Let 'em try it. We'll put the place up for auction at Michaelmas, with a reserve on it to cover the tithe redemption; and I bet you anything it won't sell; and it'll provide us with one more set of facts and figures to put before the Royal Commission. I'm not sure, by the way, if this Commission is a feather in our caps or not. We are glad to have the whole situation made public: that's all to the good. But as a rule Royal Commissions are a government's way of shelving questions they don't want to tackle. This one'll sit for a year and refuse to hatch till the government's just going out; and its report will be overlaid in the general upset, you'll see.'*

All eyes were turned on Sir John Fischer Williams as the Royal Commission took evidence in what seemed slow motion throughout 1935. In the conclusion of the Commission's findings a paragraph reads:

> *'The surprising thing about the tithe system in this country of which Tithe Rentcharge is the present form, is not that it has provoked recurrent discontent, but that it has endured so long.'*

It remained to be seen how the legislators would interpret the findings and what it would mean to the 100,000 tithepayers across England and Wales and to agriculture.

~ o ~

Chapter 7

THE GREAT
LONDON MARCH
Midsummer Day, 1936

'A conference of tithepayers organised a March and demonstration against the Government's Tithe Bill, to take place on Midsummer Day, 1936, in London. About 5,000 tithepayers assembled on the Victoria Embankment from all parts of England, and even some from Wales, and marched through interested crowds to Hyde Park, where four platforms had been provided for the speakers. The March itself was designed to bring to the notice of townspeople the fact of the very existence of this archaic tax.'

George J Gill, *A Fight against Tithes*

THE FOUR PLATFORMS were large wagons, each having a Chairman, a proposer for the Resolution, and three supporters. Speeches were timed and stopped by a bugle call, when the Resolution would be put simultaneously from the four platforms. The Resolution was:

'That this mass meeting of the yeoman tithepayers of England and their sympathisers absolutely refuse to accept the Government Tithe Bill.

'First, because it prolongs for another sixty years the monstrous injustice of compelling the single industry of agriculture to bear practically the whole tax-cost of maintaining the State Church in town and country.

'Secondly, because it makes no effective reduction in the financial burden on the farmer.

'Thirdly, because it confers for the first time in the history of the tithe rentcharge the power to send tithepayers to gaol, or to make them bankrupt, or to sell their homesteads to enforce payment of this wicked tax.

'Fourthly, because, having drafted the Bill as a grossly partisan measure, the Government have, by their financial resolution, prevented it from being amended in the interests of the tithepayers.

'We therefore demand the immediate withdrawal of the Bill, and pledge ourselves to continue the fight until we obtain justice at the hands of the King, Parliament, and the people.

'That this Resolution be handed to the Prime Minister and to the leaders of the Labour and Liberal opposition, by a deputation of five.'

In February the findings of the Royal Commission were made public and in May the text of the new Tithe Bill was issued. The Bill had forty-three clauses, with nine schedules, which changed the whole character of tithe payments. For the first time in history tithe on the land was to be made a personal debt, thereby making any tithe-resisting landowner subject to bankruptcy and imprisonment. In October 1936 tithepayers would receive their usual demand for tithe on the full £109 10s scale, but from the following April titheable land in agricultural production would be allowed to pay at a new lower £91 11s 2d rate.

Maps were to be displayed in the parishes showing details of the annuities which the Commission proposed to fix on the land and it was up to the individual tithepayers to make sure that the information was correct. Any apparent discrepancies must be made in writing to the Tithe Commission. After that the tithepayer would receive an official notice registering him or her as the owner of the land and thereafter the Commission had to be informed within one month of all sales affecting the tithed land, failure to do so incurring a fine of £5.

Small tithepayers of twenty shillings and below were to be compelled to redeem their tithe, so reducing both the number of tithepayers and the cost of collection. There was to be a special vommittee with full powers to deal with existing arrears, although any plea of inability to pay must also be sent in writing to the Commission, who would refer the matter to the Arrears Investigation Committee. Tithepayers were advised not to do this 'for fun' since, if they threw the case out, the Commissioners would charge the costs of the investigation to the applicant.

Government was effectively buying off tithe by a form of compensation equivalent to a capital sum of £70 million. QAB were to be issued with gilt-edged stock carrying a three percent interest, which over the next sixty years tithepayers were to reimburse by means of annual payments similar to the old rentcharge. By 1996, therefore, tithe would be redeemed for all time. In theory, agricultural tithe was dead, but for tithepayers it meant another sixty years of payments, albeit in reduced amounts. Furthermore, it was to be administered by a Government that had been granted collection powers far beyond anything with which QAB had been endowed. Tithe had become a compulsory state tax.

On the plus side, Eric Evans writes in *The Contentious Tithe*:

'The Royal Commission of 1934 had recommended a maximum redemption period of forty years. The Government, however, argued that this would prove too great a burden for the agricultural interest and extended it to sixty. The low level of annuities was also deliberately set to placate the farmers. Annuities were payable at £91.56 for every £100 of rent charge to be extinguished. Many farmers ... argued that even this level gave too much to the church, and pressed for a redemption annuity rate somewhere in the low 80s. The Government were not to be pushed this far, however, despite demonstrations in Hyde Park and other vociferous expressions of feeling.'

It was in the hope of influencing the passage of the Bill through Parliament that the London March was organised. AG wrote:

'As soon as the contents of the Bill were published, every possible effort was made to organise opposition to it. We arranged a mass demonstration in London in which several thousand people took part. On a very hot day we tramped the streets and finished with meetings from four platforms in Hyde Park. Sir Stafford Cripps, a former Chancellor of the Exchequer, and other MPs were some of the speakers, which included Lady Eve Balfour, Mr Kedward and myself.'

Tithepayers from all over the country left their farms – at no small cost, since it was haymaking – to assemble on the Victoria Embankment, from where they began the three-and-a-half mile march to Hyde Park. They arrived

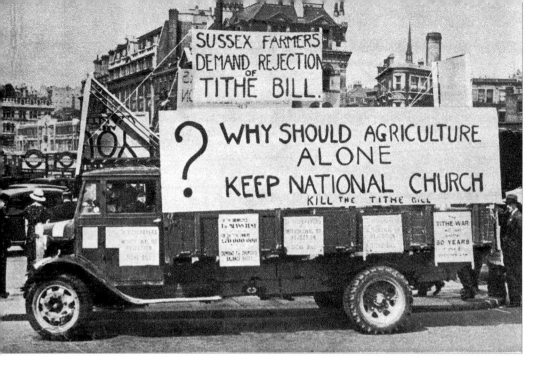

Part of the Great London March, 1936.

in private cars and carts, sixteen special trains and hundreds of coaches. The *Eastern Daily Press* read:

> 'Considerable excitement prevailed at Diss yesterday when an excursion train left the town station conveying tithepayers to London ... nearly 150 boarded the train at Diss in the highest of spirits. They included farmers and farm workers and their wives.'

Nearly a hundred farmers were reported to have left Dereham, and some 400 boarded trains leaving Ipswich station. Over a hundred came from Cornwall, and many hundreds more from Kent and the Home Counties.

Police were on hand to warn protestors about possible incitement charges and were told they must fold their banners except on the Embankment. Under the picture of a policeman raising a baton at Rowland Rash (which appeared in almost every newspaper report the following day) the caption in the *Weekly Illustrated* ran:

> 'No Banners on the March. They have to pay tithes and they can't even carry banners saying so. Police tell demonstrators to take banners down before leaving Embankment.'

The procession left by way of Surrey Street and eventually turned down Aldwych into Kingsway, led by men dressed as Cromwellian soldiers and mock-clergymen. The *Daily Herald* reported:

> 'Tithe rebels, armed with hoes, hay-rakes and scythes, marched against the Government yesterday and dislocated the rush-hour traffic of London.

Londoners, in the traffic jams, stood helpless and agape at the sun-tanned marchers behind banners which, to the city bred, bore a strange device.'

The banners which brought the unfamiliar word 'tithe' to the Metropolis came from Cornwall, Devon, Wales, the Midlands, Norfolk, Suffolk, Essex, Kent, Sussex, Hampshire, Dorset, Somerset, Oxford, Berkshire, Buckingham-shire, and nearly every county in England was represented.

"What's a tithe?" asked a city typist at the corner of Oxford-street as the resolute farmers, several of them nearly eighty years of age, plodded over the blistering asphalt, which thousands of them were treading for the first time. By the time, willy-nilly, she had watched that army passing for half an hour, she had no excuse for not knowing.'

Behind the Cromwellians came a 'yeoman' farmer and a dairymaid in Tudor costume carrying a banner to which was chained an old farmer in a smock and another old grey-bearded, beaver-hatted farmer carrying a scythe. Further down the procession came a company in the helmets and costumes of 'Roundheads', carrying pikes. They were there to represent descendants of the men who had joined the Buckinghamshire Puritan John Hampden in his fight for freedom against tyranny. In 1637, Hampden had been condemned for refusing to pay Ship Money, disputing its legality as a legitimate and honest tax. Hampden was related to Oliver Cromwell and Doreen Wallace used both characters in her novel *Land from the Waters*, published in 1944.

Other rebellions were recalled, the *News Chronicle* saying that rural England had not invaded the capital in such organised force since Jack Cade, the Kentish rebel, brought his 'army' to London in 1450 to protest against waste, corruption and oppression in high places.

Lorries carried sheaves of corn, bales of hay and farm stock, and, said the *Daily Herald*:

'... one carried the furniture of a family dispossessed and sold-up for non-payment of tithes. An old, white-bearded farmer, the victim, lay on the chair which had been bought back at the auction by his sympathetic neighbours. Two old farmers, crippled with rheumatism, were pushed along in bathchairs. With the farmers marched their wives.'

The *Eastern Daily Press* gave the exact route:

'The long procession left the Embankment by way of Surrey Street, and made its way to the offices of the National Farmers' Union in Bedford Square, where the deputation remained to discuss the position, and from there the main procession went along Shaftesbury Avenue, across New

Oxford Street, and Tottenham Court Road by Cavendish Square, Wigmore Street and Tyburn Gate. Crowds of shoppers and business people cheered them on their trek to Hyde Park, and the farmers' march had all the enthusiasm of a march of triumph. Despite the heat the men, and women too, marched buoyantly into the park.'

The newspapers marvelled at the speed with which the marchers assembled and the orderly character of what was, in effect, an informal procession. The Metropolitan Police had been prepared for only two thousand at the most, but more than twice that number arrived. The protesters, though, were not there to make trouble, and the *East Anglian Daily Times* reported:

'They marched on a sweltering June day through miles of London's streets for the one purpose of demonstrating their unalterable objection to a Bill which, they claim, enforces heavy tithe payments without any prospect of redress. Their mien depicted their determination. It was far removed from being a pleasant trip to Town. The silent passing of the procession through the thronged streets of men and women of all ages, gravely concerned and preoccupied with the object of their presence in London, produced not banter or ridicule from bystanders in the

Kent farmers arrive at Charing Cross Station.

(Above) Protesters
carried posters featuring
a cartoon from the
Daily Herald (below).

The Sky-pilot—a farmer's nightmare.

crowded streets, or from those gathered at the
windows and doors offices, and shops, but
sympathy. The friendly attitude exhibited
towards the processionists was evidently
appreciated and occasional remarks indicate
that the difficulties of the farming community
have at last dawned on town folk.'

The *Daily Sketch* headlined 'London sees Men
in Chains' and said: '

*...London opened its eyes at the angry note
which characterised the banner inscriptions
accompanying the emblems of resposeful rural
England.'*

Two full pages were given over to the march
in the *Weekly Illustrated* with the comment
*'... they marched in column through the West
End, giving Londoners a reminder that there
are some other parts of Britain besides the one
they live in'.*

The *News Chronicle's* front page carried
representative portraits of the marchers and the
Daily Express headlined 'Country came to
London, with Tithe Grievance'. Indeed, the
procession would have been even more
spectacular had the police not intervened. *'Two
hundred horsemen were to have ridden in the
procession,'* reported the *News Chronicle*, *'but
permission was refused by the police.'*

There is no doubt that twentieth-century
London had seen nothing like it. Not for a very
long time had rural protest been seen in the
capital on such a scale and the organisation that
went into it had been both phenomenal and
spontaneous. The success of the day was entirely
due to the genuine depth of feeling of protest
and indignant outrage at the blatant unfairness
of the proposed Bill that gave new impetus to an

extraordinary display of unity. The title of the organising committee, the United Committee of Protest, said it all. Chairman George Gill made it quite clear that the initiative had come from the countryside and the marchers had paid their own expenses. There was no central fund; each man and woman paid his or her own way and was prepared to lose a day's work on the farm. This was a people's protest in every sense.

However, in reality, the plight of thousands of tithepaying farmers, tucked away in rural backwaters, was minimal and of very little consequence to most Londoners and town dwellers generally. Few concerned themselves, either, with how the rural clergy should be paid, and gave no thought at all to the problems facing the Archbishop of Canterbury and church finance (which was anyway a closely guarded secret), or to the relationship between church and agriculture. Nothing of the long fight between tithepayers and titheowners had impinged on their lives, except as items in their newspaper. While some of the general public had a vague grasp of what the countryside was all about (chiefly because of the importance of First World War agriculture), by and large it really cared very little.

After 1918 food imports had resumed and few looked with any real foreboding at what was happening in Hitler's Germany. Already the countryside was seen as somewhere for the new car owners to drive their vehicles, and by encouraging the establishment of smallholdings the Government had given the wrong signals in terms of the economic future for agriculture. Even by 1928 Stanley Baldwin warned of the threat to the countryside of 'advertisement hoardings, tasteless petrol stations, and ill-planned housing estates'. Osbert Lancaster referred to the ribbon development as 'Bypass Tudor' and writers such as G M Trevelyan and C E M Joad warned of the dichotomy between urban and rural growth. The former was expected to modernise, which was to be considered a Good Thing, while the countryside must be preserved in such a way as to freeze progress but provide a playground for town dwellers. Trevelyan's *English Social History* attacked the unplanned and unhealthy state of the cities, and pointed out that *'British agriculture as an economic proposition had collapsed'.*

The wider debate about British agriculture was only just beginning in 1936 and was destined to be put on hold for another sixty years by the Second World War. It was only after 1945 that anyone in any kind of authority came to understand that what happens in the countryside cannot be weighed on the same scales as that of the towns and cities.

DAILY SKETCH, THURSDAY, JUNE 25, 1936

WIFE THRASHES OTHER WOMAN: Page 4

WIRELESS: Page 16

DAILY SKETCH

THE QUEEN AT JUBILEE HOUSE —Page 14

No. 8,473   THURSDAY, JUNE 25, 1936   ONE PENNY

THE FARMERS MOBILISE

TO FIGHT TITHE BILL

Great March To Hyde Park Meeting

Thousands of farmers and farm workers took part in the great march to Hyde Park to demonstrate against the Tithe Bill, and many tableaux were in the procession.

On the right is a sheep cart laden with women and live sheep and farm produce on its way along the Embankment.

Left: Mr. E. J. Haffenden, of Pluckley, Kent, the first farmer in England to suffer distraint for tithe. He declares that "the Bill is absolute rot."

Many picturesque characters in medieval garb gave an effect of pageantry to the demonstration.

Among those who took part were this old-time farmer in beaver hat and his dairymaids, complete with scythe and sickle.

Right: A group of halberdiers and civilians of Roundhead days. Full story on page 7.

PAGE 20   **Daily Express**   THURSDAY, JUNE 25, 1936

PHOTONEWS

COUNTRY CAME TO LONDON—WITH TITHE GRIEVANC

Three thousand farmers marched from the Embankment to Hyde Park to protest against the Tithe Bill yesterday. Pictures show: Farmerette, holding up emblem of "tithe pig" in one hand horn in other; men in Cromwellian armour bearing banners; policeman telling demonstrators "banners not allowed except on Embankment"; (in circle below) farmwoman from Rye.

NEWS CHRONICLE, Thursday, June 25, 1936.

Burnt Ochre, Burnt Copper
new "Contrast" shades in

Bear Brand

Chiffon Stockings

No. 28,131   ONE PENNY   THURSDAY, JUNE 25, 1936

News C

5,000 FARMERS' PROTEST MA
THROUGH WEST

"Drop
The
Tithe
Bill"
Call

The pig—the scavenger of the farm —was used by a demonstrator in yesterday's London march to represent her opinion of tithes

Mr. J. Buss, of Kent, decorated his hat with cards epitomising the history of tithes from "every tenth shock" of corn to a "shocking burden"

THE CROMWELLIAN
TOUCH

Those who watched the 5,000-strong marchers on a stifling day in June 1936 did so with amused benevolence, marvelled at the novelty, then went on their way. For the tithepayers, though, it was their finest hour. They could not have done better. In terms of publicity it was a triumph, and the Midsummer March lived on in the memories of thousands of farmers and farm workers long after they had left the

Lady Eve Balfour and Roderick Kedward address the crowds in Hyde Park.

baking, unfamiliar tarmac of London and returned to the haysel and the new season's harvest. They were kings and queens of the capital for a day and they made the most of it. In Hyde Park the march culminated in an unparalleled public protest and for one brief moment in time held the nation's attention.

The four platforms in Hyde Park were arranged thus:

Platform 1:

Reverend Roderick Kedward (chairman)
Sir John Prestige (proposer of the Resolution)
Lady Eve Balfour
Mr T L Butler
Mr A Turner

Platform 2:

Captain George Pitt Rivers (chairman)
A G Mobbs (proposer of the Resolution)
Mr A Maclaren, MP
F R Allen
Mr W J Rowlands
Mr H Tyler

Platform 3:

    Mr M C McCreagh (chairman)

    Doreen Wallace (proposer of the Resolution)

    Alderman George Solley

    Mr S Johns

    Mr C W Hastings

Platform 4:

    Mr C Edwards (chairman)

    Mr S Kidner (proposer of the Resolution)

    Sir Stafford Cripps, KC, MP

    Dr MacGregor Reid

    Mr W Woods

Sir John Prestige, Chairman of the Canterbury Conservative Association, took the opportunity to chastise his own Government and made a violent attack on the Tithe Bill which he declared introduced measures that prevented some 350,000 tithepayers from expressing their views in Parliament. (He did not give his source for this figure, but it is more likely to represent the number of court cases rather than the number of tithepayers, which was generally agreed to be between 80,000 and 100,000.) The Bill, said Sir John, proposed to sell them up 'stick and stone' and send them to jail if they refused to pay. The *Daily Herald* reported him as saying:

"'I want you to tell the Government, with me, that our answer is No!".
And "No" it was from a thousand throats.'

From the same platform, T L Butler from Dorset declared:

'... so long as you touch your hat to the Conservative Party, as you touch
it to the squire and the parson, so long will your loyalty be imposed upon
in this way.'

The massed gathering then united in proclaiming the Resolution watched and recorded by newsreel cameras, journalists and photographers. Doreen Wallace, standing on platform 3, made a particularly dramatic figure, one seen by her friend Dorothy L Sayers on the Pathé News. Doreen herself remembered:

'Being united in a good cause had its jolly side. The cause won the public
over. Tithepayers marched one day, several thousand strong, through
London to Hyde Park, where they addressed crowds from farm wagons.
I remember sharing a wagon with Lady Eve Balfour and Sir Stafford
Cripps – and London listened, and saw us that evening on the Pathé
News. Those were the days!'

The cry of unity was, perhaps, more valid than at first appeared. The *Daily Sketch* was almost alone in pointing out:

> 'There were many picturesque tableaux in the procession from the Embankment to the park. An historic banner, the original one designed by Joseph Arch, first champion of the rural worker, fluttered in the faint breeze as it had done at demonstrations more than 50 years ago.'

From his platform, Sir Stafford Cripps said:

> 'I know farmers are often blamed for the condition of the agricultural labourer, but you cannot blame the farmers who have to pay landlords and titheowners if they find there is insufficient left to pay an adequate wage to the agricultural labourer.'

Without the support of the farm workers there would have been no unity, and in spite of the continued misgivings of George Edwards the mid-1930s saw unprecedented accord between farmer and farm worker. There has always been more to divide than to unite the two sides of the same coin, chiefly the issue of wages, and not before or since the tithepayers' revolt has there been anything like it.

During the years of tithe protest the National Union of Agricultural Workers (NUAW) was presided over by Edwin Gooch. A member of the Union's Executive from 1926 onwards, Gooch was a Norfolk man, where his father had a blacksmith's forge. His native Wymondham is noted for being the home of Norfolk's most famous rebels, Robert and William Kett, leaders of the 1549 rebellion against enclosures, but Edwin Gooch was no rebel. *The Times* noted in his obituary:

> 'Edwin Gooch's long career in trade unionism and in the organisation of the Labour Party was solid rather than spectacular. He was generally regarded as a moderate and a man of the centre rather than the left.'

The Union supported the farmers in their objections to tithe, although support among the membership was by no means universal. At the Union's Biennial Conference in London in 1932, a Wiltshire branch had tabled a resolution demanding that all agricultural land should be freed from 'the iniquitous burden of tithe', but one speaker said:

> 'Farmers agitated against this burden, but they go to church Sunday after Sunday, and go on upholding the system.'

Another suggested that parsons should do the same amount of work as he did, and another (about farmers): *'You can fight for them but they won't do anything for you.'*

Sir George Edwards told the conference that he questioned the wisdom of the Union taking any official part in passing resolutions in reference to the tithe problem. As a Free Churchman he had always been in favour of disestablishment and thought no one should be compelled to support a church for which he had no use, but said that the resolution contained nothing about religion. All it did was to back up the present agitation by those who were not their friends, the farmers, and he joined George Middleton in propounding the old argument that many had bought their tithe-holding farms cheaply.

'There is no industry in this country,' declared Sir George, 'that has had so much done for it as agriculture, yet like Oliver Twist every time they keep asking for more.'

Edwin Gooch told delegates that he had 'not the slightest idea of supporting farmers as individuals', but he was concerned with the principle. He referred to his support for the Reverend Kedward's proposed 1931 Tithe Remission Bill, which if passed would have repealed what he considered the unjust 1925 Act. His insistence that the protest must not in any way be used as an attack on the Church was echoed in a letter to AG:

'For the sake of the Church and true religion the present position of tithe cannot be allowed to remain. I would not countenance anything that was intended as a blow against the village cleric, many of whom I esteem, and I am sure the clergymen themselves would be only too glad to get this vexed question settled.'

Although several voted against the resolution, it was carried by a good majority and marked a turning-point in the Union's support for the tithepayers. By 1934 farm workers were taking an active role in helping to thwart the bailiffs and Edwin Gooch attended anti-tithe demonstrations when he could. At Wortham the Rashes made sure that their forty-odd workers got a fair share of publicity. In *So Long to Learn*, Doreen's fictional account of the 1934 distraint, Edward addressed his men:

'So next day at midday, which was pay-time, he made his speech to his men. And a surprisingly large company they were, for he gathered-in the Ivy Farm men too. There would be trouble there soon.'

Those were the days when the men on the farms were counted in double figures, and over forty-five farm workers (the true number at Wortham) decided to march on the vicarage to make their views known, but: *'... They got no change out of the Rector, they said on their return. First he would not answer the loud batterings on the door.'*

In a retrospective article for the *East Anglian Daily Times*, Doreen wrote: *'... while the fight was on there was a wonderful solidarity among the people of the land, landowners, farmers and farm-workers, such as had never been achieved before and probably never will be again. We haggle now about a pound or two on the worker's wage. But once upon a time we were all together in adversity, fighting an anachronistic tax, the abolition of which would have helped the lot of us.'*

Writing to AG in February 1934 Edwin Gooch renewed his support for the tithepayers:

'Engagements elsewhere prevent me from attending your protest meeting at Diss tonight. I deplore greatly the proceedings at Wortham. I have not the pleasure of knowing Mr Rash personally but I know that he is making a stance on principle, and I am not surprised that the agricultural workers are supporting him ... The farm labourers are in this fight because of the effect the present position is having on them. I am concerned about their future and their position is made insecure by the non-solution of the present difficulty. Support for your movement is increasing day by day and will continue to do so while you fight on principle and carry on lawful agitation. Too much money is taken from agriculture and farmers and workers suffer.'

He numbered AG among his friends and at the Annual Meeting of the Norfolk NUAW told delegates that he entirely agreed with his 'friend' Mr AG Mobbs in deploring the steady drift of workers from the land. Mr Mobbs had suggested a united front of all sections in the industry for the formulation of a national policy for agriculture. The Union was not, he said, opposed to co-operation, but it had to be on terms. There had to be a new approach to the wages question on the part of the employers, but a united industry could accomplish much. On his platform in Hyde Park, AG drew attention to the small working farmers who, in Suffolk, were paying seven shillings an acre tithe, which equalled three to four shillings a week of the farm workers' wages. He told his audience:

'During the last ten years ten thousand agricultural workers have been driven off the land in the Eastern Counties. How can we develop agriculture with a view of bringing about increased production when the Government is placing a further burden upon us?'

In 1935 Edwin Gooch gave his support to a protest meeting over a tithe sale held at Rushmere, near Ipswich in Suffolk, where Mr J Baxter had a court order against him for two years' worth of tithe. Roderick Kedward, Doreen Wallace and AG were present and Edwin Gooch had sent a letter of encouragement:

> 'Although there has not been very much public speech-making on the subject of late, it must not be imagined for one moment that resistance to the unfair incidence of tithe is becoming less ... it is altogether too late in the day to imagine that repressive methods will kill the movement or curb the enthusiasm behind the movement. I have done my share of fighting for my own people but I have never been unmindful of the needs of the agricultural industry generally. I have taken my stand with the farmers in an endeavour to preserve the sugar beet industry ... and I gladly associate myself with other interests in the industry with the object of removing for all time the excessive burden of tithe.'

The NUAW General Secretary, W Holmes was also in support of the tithepayers. In response to H Harvey of Dame Annys Farm, Fyfield in Essex, he wrote:

Edwin Gooch addresses a public meeting in Fakenham Market Place, Norfolk in the 1940s. (Michael Gooch)

From

Councillor E. G. GOOCH, J.P., C.C.
PRESIDENT.

(To whom all replies should be sent)

Feb. 23rd 1934.

RYDAL MOUNT,

WYMONDHAM,

NORFOLK.

Dear Mr. Mobbs.

Engagements elsewhere prevent me from attending your protest meeting at Diss to-night.

I deplore greatly the proceeding at Wortham. I have not the pleasure of knowing Mr. Rash personally but I know that he is making a stand on principle, & I am not surprised that the agricultural workers are supporting him.

For the sake of the Church & true religion the present position of Tithe cannot be allowed to remain. I would not countenance anything that was intended as a blow against the village cleric, many of whom I esteem, & I am sure the clergymen themselves

Letter from Edwin Gooch to AG Mobbs, dated 23 February 1934.

'I am instructed by my Executive Committee to inform you that they are entirely in favour of the abolition of tithe charges and therefore there is no reason for you to meet them on this matter. It would be like preaching to the converted and they feel your services in this connection could be used to better advantage.'

The knock-on effect of the farming depression was keenly felt by the farm workers, who had seen their wages cut and hours of work lengthened. NUAW historian Reg Groves wrote in *Sharpen the Sickle!*:

'The lower wages and longer hours imposed in the year 1931 were followed in 1932 by pay cuts and hours extensions, in no less than thirty counties. Unemployment was high in the towns; wages in every industry were being lowered or threatened ... The union fought hard but vainly.'

In Merioneth and Montgomeryshire the wages were brought down by 1s 6d to 27 shillings for a fifty-four-hour week. Union membership plummeted, too: it fell from around 129,000 in 1919 to 30,500 by 1934.

NUAW support for farmers in the tithe war was always tentative and often given in a mood of tacit and suspicious resignation. At farm level where men worked alongside each other day after day, and where they were standing together on the front line, a certain *esprit de corps* existed. However, the *Land Worker* was able to reassure its readers that Edwin Gooch had pledged support only on a point of principle:

'The President said ... Why on earth should the burden of supporting the National Church be placed upon one industry in the land? He could not understand it. There was a lot of money that was collected in the form of tithes that did not even go to the Church; it went to the support of the Universities of Oxford and Cambridge. They were surely not going to tell him it was a right principle that the children of the high and mighty in the land should be enjoying an education that their children were denied, partly at their expense.'

NUAW historian Reg Groves voices an opinion on the subject of education and farmers:

'... farmers have long been distinguished by a persistent tendency to regard schooling as being at best a necessary evil imposed by short-sighted governments, and as an interference with the supply of cheap labour.'

When in 1934 MAFF produced figures showing how farmers paying tithe had gained substantially from the 1925 Tithe Act by a reduction in the septennial average, the point was taken up in the *Land Worker*.

'Some interesting figures were given by Mr Elliot, in the House of Commons on February 26, when he was asked what, if the Tithe Acts of 1918 and 1925 had not been passed, would have been the value in 1932 and 1933 of £100 apportioned tithe rentcharge calculated at the septennial average corn prices in accordance with the earlier Acts ... it will be seen that the farmers paying tithe have gained most substantially from the Tithe Acts. Only in 1932 and 1933 would they have paid less had there been no Acts. These facts should be borne in mind when considering this matter.'

Such consideration was, no doubt, music to the ears of George Middleton and Archbishop Cosmo Lang.

During Gooch's first speech in support of lifting tithes from the land, he told a meeting of farmers quite plainly where the Union stood. He said that it was a unique experience for him to be speaking at a meeting of farmers, and the first word he heard to the detriment of the labourers in regard to their wages and hours was the day he would walk out of the door and never return.

In spite of having been a journalist on the *Norwich Mercury* series, Gooch was not an obsessive 'Letters to the Editor' man, although he frequently used the correspondence columns to make points on behalf of the Union. Throughout his long connection with the NUAW his duties were almost exclusively honorary. He did not qualify to represent the Union at the TUC, but kept his links with other unions strong through his association with the Labour Party.

Prior to 1932, the tone of the Union had been relatively hostile to support for the tithepaying farmers, but as the agricultural depression hit harder workers had little choice other than to support their employers. Some of the old ways of thinking died with George Edwards in 1933, and the enforced letting-go of many workers from the land meant that by 1936 a number of the old prejudices and hostilities that existed between farmer and farm workers were suspended. Workers marched to Hyde Park in such unity that as far as the urban onlookers were concerned those in the column were just people from another world ... the countryside. They made no distinctions between farmers and workers.

All the old problems that existed between the two would return at the end of the Second World War, but for the purposes of demonstration against the Tithe Bill Edwin Gooch led the Union on a fairly universal road of conditional approval and support for his members' employers. At the end of the Hyde Park speeches, farmers and workers stood shoulder to shoulder and gave a hearty rendering of the National Anthem.

The final part of the Hyde Park Resolution, that it be handed to the Prime Minister and to leaders of the Labour and Liberal opposition, was an important climax to the protest. The march itself was held on the very eve of the Report Stage of the Bill due in the House of Commons two days later. However the Prime Minister, Stanley Baldwin refused to meet the deputation. The *Weekly Illustrated* said:

'Leaders, whose aim was to see Mr Baldwin, went to No 10. Were told Baldwin was in the House of Commons. Went to the House of Commons. Were told Baldwin had gone ... a little bird must have told him.'

The *News Chronicle* reported:

'When the demonstration broke up [the] resolution was taken by a small deputation to 10, Downing Street and thence to the House of Commons. Mr Baldwin sent a message that he was too busy to see them. He was dining.'

Several small groups of farmers demanded to see their MPs, and gradually the heat went out of the day in more ways than one. Several MPs had been spotted watching the procession, including Captain F F A Heilgers from the Ministry of Agriculture, which led AG to comment afterwards that there would be no excuse for the Minister of Agriculture not knowing that the procession and demonstration had been an outstanding success.

The *Farmer & Stock-Breeder* told its readers on 29 June:

'Tithepayers are incensed at the "casual" way in which Mr Baldwin treated Wednesday's impressive demonstration in London and his refusal to receive the deputation which waited upon him at 10, Downing Street. Anger was increased when the Prime Minister, replying to a question in the House of Commons, on Thursday, referred to "demonstrations of that kind".'

In the House the Prime Minister was asked if his attention had been drawn to the demonstration in Hyde Park, and whether he intended going on with the Tithe Bill in view of the tremendous opposition. Baldwin replied that his attention had been drawn to it, but *'... speaking for myself, I never find that demonstrations of that kind make me inclined to give way'.*

George Gill said that he had been 'intensely disgusted' with Mr Baldwin's behaviour:

(Above) Tithepayers' deputation to discuss tithes with the Minister of Agriculture, Walter Elliot in March 1936. (Left to right) AG Mobbs, George Solley, Roderick Kedward, V Drewitt, J E Lewis, A Turner, H Tyler, F R Allen, Rowland Rash and Makens Turner.

(Below) (Left to right) Rowland Rash, AG Mobbs and (unknown) outside NFU Headquarters in Bedford Square, London.

'Five thousand people left the fields to come to London, some of them spending all the night in trains. There never was a more thoroughly representative demonstration than that one ... We all feel very deeply at Mr Baldwin's casual attitude to such a genuine demonstration and that he should refer to it in such a way in the House of Commons.'

He wrote to the Prime Minister:

'I have to inform you that many thousands of his Majesty's loyal subjects who are seeking a precarious living by agriculture, yesterday came to London from distant and widespread areas to protest that the burdens which your Government are imposing on them in the Tithe Bill for the next 60 years are unjust and unbearable ... they deem it their duty to convey to you that such a measure will provoke rebellion in the rural areas of this country, which as peace-loving citizens they deplore and wish to prevent ... This matter, Sir, is too important to be dealt with by your secretaries and officials. I am therefore desired by the deputation which for some hours last evening sought permission to see you, to demand that you will afford them an opportunity, before the Bill is placed before the House of Commons for its third reading, to discharge the obligation which has been placed on them by this important section of the country. I am to add that in the event of your refusing to meet this deputation, its members will exercise their constitutional right to approach his Majesty the King, in order to lay before his Majesty this serious representation from this most loyal section of his subjects.'

A conference was held in London the following Wednesday with the aim of choosing two delegates from each of the twenty-five county associations to attempt a second deputation to the Prime Minister. But the organisation required proved too much and no delegation was formed. Instead the King's Petition was drawn up. Possibly because it was the brainchild of Captain George Pitt Rivers, the document was both excessively lengthy and long-winded and ran to several pages. It was divided into ten points, each starting with 'Whereas ...', the final clause being:

'Whereas former Kings of this Realm did pledge themselves and their heirs that for no business from thenceforth should be taken such manner of aids and taxes nor prises, but by the common assent of all the realm, and for the common profit thereof, and did grant that the King and his heirs would not draw such aids, tasks nor prises into a custom for

NFU Headquarters, 45 Bedford Square, London.

anything that had been done heretofore, be it by roll or any other precedent that might be founden ... We humbly pray Your Most Excellent Majesty, that in the exercise of your Royal Prerogative you summon such and so many of your Judges as you deem advisable in conjunction with representatives of tithe-payers being the aggrieved parties as well as of titheowners from whose persecutions they suffer, to enquiry into these our grievances.'

There was an official signing attended by the chief protagonists and in August it was sent to the Home Office for onward transmission to the King. Captain Pitt Rivers and George Gill received a reply to say that the Petition had been laid before the King (who might well have perused it with a furrowed brow and found it incomprehensible and impossibly legalistic). Writing afterwards, George Gill said of the Petition: *'No result followed, nor had any been expected'.*

In his epigraph to George Gill's book *A Fight Against Tithes*, Henry Williamson wrote:

'George Gill died before he could complete his story of the fight against tithes. His widow, Mrs Sarah Shorey Gill, who shared with him his hopes, frustrations, and successes, gave me his manuscript to read, because I had been a farmer and had written The Story of a Norfolk Farm ... *Yes, George Gill, of the family that produced Eric Gill and Macdonald Gill, had the right idea ... tithe, at least as it climbed as ivy upon the yeoman oak, was not honest money. It was easy money. It helped to rob the soil of its fertility. It took from the mother of all living and it gave back words which too often were a mockery of the Word ... We pay our tribute to George Gill, of yeoman farmer stock; the fields of England bore him and in due course received him back again. It is our common heritage of earth: we arise and we return, that is the balance and the harmony.'*

While the march had been a success in many ways, it remained to be seen if it had made any impact on the passage of the Bill through Parliament. Certainly many MPs had taken note of the proceedings, many of them already firmly on the side of the tithepayers and in favour of a just settlement, and protest meetings were as enthusiastic and virulent as ever. While the Commission sat distraint sales still made newspaper headlines, effigies of Queen Anne were burned, and the courts became log-jammed with distraint orders.

Deploring the indiscriminate justice of the tender sales, almost all judges had allowed a return to auctions where TPAs bought the goods and 'lent' them back to their owner. There were invariably local difficulties over the amount of auctioneers' fees, court expenses and such like, but it was all grist to the publicity mill. The value of the goods distrained was often far in excess of the amount of tithe owed. It was indeed a war, each distraint sale a battle. Writing years later, P J Butler said of the courts:

'They always took more than they really needed so that they could cover all costs and allow for low prices.'

The weeks following the London March were crucial for tithepayers. They had taken their last chance to influence those before whom the Tithe Bill would come in the House of Commons, but even as the trains and coaches took the men and women of the countryside back to their farms the distraint sales went on. The *Farmer & Stock-Breeder* reported in late June 1936:

'Following a distraint sale on the stock of three North Devon farmers, seized for non-payment of tithe, a protest meeting was held in a field at

Cartoon used on the 1936 London March.

Chilsworthy on Monday. After addresses by Mr A Turner and Mr F Chipman (hon secretary of the North Devon Tithepayers' Association) a huge bonfire was made and an effigy of Queen Anne was burnt.'

In the same issue it seemed almost certain that there would be no support in Parliament for any attempt to reject the Bill:

'Immediately after the last NFU Council meeting a letter was sent to the county branches pointing out the heavy responsibility which rested upon them in giving effect to the Council's decision that every effort should be made to get the Tithe Bill withdrawn. Many of the branches have, as a result, communicated with their MPs and the replies have been sent to Bedford Square. It is understood (writes a correspondent) that the indications are that there will be very meagre support for any motion to reject the Bill.'

~ o ~

Chapter 8

THE 1936 TITHE ACT

'The Government's scheme for abolishing tithe rent-charge, based on the report of the Royal Commission presented three months ago, has been embodied in a Tithe Bill, published today, which Mr Walter Elliot (Minister of Agriculture) hopes to rush through Parliament this summer. If the Bill passes, tithe, as such, will be abolished on Oct 2 next, the titheowners will be presented with Government-guaranteed negotiable stock to the value of £70,000,000 – and tithepayers will have to find £160,000,000 spread over 60 years, recoverable by the Inland Revenue in the manner of income-tax.'

News Chronicle, 6 May 1936

THE 1936 TITHE ACT was the final piece of legislation after what amounted to almost four thousand years of tithe history. Despite the opposition of 130 MPs the Bill was read a third time, passed in the House of Commons, and received Royal Assent in the autumn of 1936. Among those who voted against the Bill at the Third Reading on 29 June 1936 were Edgar Granville, P C Loftus, Sir Stafford Cripps and Major Reginald Dorman-Smith (President of the NFU and a future Minister of Agriculture). Dorman-Smith made what was afterwards considered to have been a brilliant speech that showed some courage, as it meant going against his own party. He said:

'I cannot support the Third Reading of the Bill. I regret that very much from a personal point of view, because I hate to be at variance with my Party and I know that, like Odysseus, the ordinary private Member who ventures to go counter to the policy of the Government is apt to run into troubled waters. I feel I have to make it clear that the organised farmers of this country will not, and cannot, accept this Measure as an equitable or final settlement of the tithe problem. If the Bill goes through as a final settlement, then, indeed, it will be one which has been forced on the farmers and not accepted by them.'

His speech was reported in the *NFU Record*:

'I do not know what this House would think if we were today passing a Measure which said to all Income Tax payers, "We are going to stabilise Income Tax once and for all, but it will not depend on whether you can pay it, on your income, or on the state of your business; if you cannot pay it out of income, then you must pay it out of capital and out of your savings". The question of personal liability is one of the worst features of the Bill and one which causes the most resentment throughout the tithepaying areas ... Because I agree with the opposition which is growing and because I believe the farmers have a good case as tithepayers, I cannot possibly support the Third Reading of the Bill.'

The position for many rural MPs had been difficult: the Tithe Bill was a major Government measure and had the result of the division been reversed the Government may well have been forced to resign. Political correspondents agreed that, for better or worse, the Bill had to prosper. Many MPs saw it as their duty to pass the Bill, since it was unlikely that better measures would be introduced. No government would make any future attempts to find a solution for a very long time to come if it failed. Opponents of the Bill also had to set the interests of tithepayers against the rest of the agricultural reform currently on the Government agenda, including help for the beef, milk and egg sections, which could have been prejudiced if they had voted against it. Walter Elliot, Minister of Agriculture, told reporters:

'I do not believe that if we ship-wreck this Bill it would be possible to bring forward a better Bill next year or within the life of this Parliament or any Parliament.'

The Editor of the *Farmer & Stock-Breeder* expressed the opinion that:

'No one could have been optimistic enough to believe that the Royal Commission on Tithe Rentcharge would be able to present a plan for

*dealing with the tithe question that would be acceptable to all concerned.
One fundamental difficulty is that there is no unanimity regarding the
nature of tithe, and, naturally, those who, rightly or wrongly, believe that
it is a tax – and an unjust and arbitrary tax – can see no equitable
solution other than the abolition of tithe.'*

Among the MPs to be censured for voting against the Government was
Edgar Granville, Member for the Eye Division, who had given wholehearted
support to the tithepayers and which he felt he owed to his constituents. As
Parliamentary Private Secretary to Sir John Simon he was widely expected to
resign, but it was appreciated that he had no alternative but to vote against the
Bill. Both Sir John Simon and the Government Whips expressed themselves
'fully appreciative' of his position, and Granville gave a 'tacit understanding' that
he would not vote against the Government again, save in an open division.

Once the terms of the Bill were announced, the First Church Estates
Commissioner and Chairman of QAB, Sir George Middleton finally agreed
publicly that tithe should go:

*'There can be no doubt that the recommendation of the Royal
Commission and the decision to extinguish tithe rentcharge under a
Government scheme meets with the approval of all reasonable people. The
existence of tithe rentcharge as part of the social and economic structure of
the country gives rise to such appalling misunderstandings and bickerings
that it is wise to get rid of it once and for all. The main difficulty is the
ascertainment of what are fair and equitable terms on which
extinguishment should be carried out.'*

This contrasted sharply with an earlier statement, when he had said that
'... *as Chairman of the tithe committee of Queen Anne's Bounty I can safely say
that the proposed settlement is entirely unsatisfactory and if there is any suggestion
that the Church will accept it as a permanent solution I can assure you that it is
quite wrong'.* Between February 1936, when the Commission Report was
published, and the subsequent July Lords debate, someone or something had
changed his mind.

Naturally he would disagree with the terms of extinction, as would many
other Church representatives, and Sir George said openly that the
Government scheme would entail considerable relief to tithepayers but
serious losses to the titheowners:

*'It is a fallacy to suppose that even incumbents of livings over £500
in value can be deprived of a large part of their tithe income*

without suffering injustice. The incumbents of many of the so-called richer livings have heavy charges to meet, including the stipends of curates and other church workers ... it would be nothing less than cruel to upset the budget of an incumbent who, through no fault of his own, is required to surrender part of his income for the benefit of landowners.'

He might have come round to calling the extinction of tithe 'a blessing', but old habits die hard. He still referred to 'landowners', never 'farmers', and refused to acknowledge tithepayers' opinion that it was the Church who should be responsible for the rural clergy, not the unfortunate few whose own living was dependent on factors beyond their control and whose liability to pay rested solely on historic roulette. He maintained to the last the official line that tithe was property and that its income should form an integral part of the Church budget for the payment of its clergymen. Taken on its merits, tithepayers agreed that incumbents should not be deprived of any part of their living and accepted it as such without reservation. They agreed with everything Sir George had to say on the subject of the plight of clergy, but in the context of twentieth-century Britain it simply was not their responsibility to prop up Church finances.

When the Bill reached the House of Lords there was little chance that anything more could be done to prevent it from becoming law, though small hope was kept alive that opposition could affect amendments. The debate began on Tuesday 7 July and went over all the old ground. Viscount Halifax, Lord Privy Seal moved the second reading of the Bill. He said that the Royal Commission recommended that the tithe should be extinguished on a tithe redemption scheme lasting forty years, and that the stabilised value of £105 should be reduced to £91 11s 2d. *The Times* reported:

'A Tithe Redemption Commission would be appointed to determine what tithe rentcharges had been extinguished by the Bill and the amount of stock to be issued as compensation. The appointed day for the scheme was April 1, 1937. The principal difference between the Royal Commission's report and the Government proposals was in the duration of the annuity period. The Commission recommended 40 years, and the Bill made it 60 years.'

With a strange mixture of passion and weariness the traditional arguments continued, but it was clear that, whatever else the Members disagreed on, it was almost universally agreed that there had to be a final solution.

Archbishop Cosmo Lang acknowledged that tithe might possibly be something of an 'issue' but remained cool under fire in the Lords debate. Lord Marley launched a long drawn-out attack on the disadvantages of the Bill to the tithepayers, to which the Archbishop replied that he was afraid that he could not follow Lord Marley into his 'history of the progressive disintegration of the Church' and asked when that 'lamentable process' had begun. He was surprised to hear that anyone should think the Church had wanted any Bill at all, since the Governors of QAB always contended that they were perfectly ready to deal with the situation on the basis of the 1925 Act, without any further legislation. *The Times* reported the Archbishop as saying:

'The noble lord [Marley] has said that tithepayers all over the country resented the payment of tithe. On the contrary, the great bulk of the tithepayers had in the past and did still pay their tithe rentcharge with the utmost willingness. It was only in certain parts of the country and in special circumstances that this resentment had appeared.'

Quite where these certain parts of the country were which saw tithepayers willingly pay tithe the Archbishop did not say. They must have been very small parts, or very small tithes, since almost every county in England had a TPA of some description. All farmers in England and Wales also had access to NFU County Executives that had barely had a meeting since 1925 where tithe had not been raised. Throughout 1935 and 1936 effigy-burning demonstrations still took place, the correspondence columns were as fiery as ever, and figures in the press showed as many as 2,000 summonses to be outstanding at any one time in several courts. There is no doubt that collection rates had improved considerably during the time the Royal Commission had been sitting, but this was due more to the war-weariness that was creeping into the movement than any willingness to pay. Many had paid up in the expectation that something was at last to be done to solve the matter. There had also been something of a 'big push' – as it was described by the NTA – to recover both current and arrears of tithe throughout 1935 when the Royal Commission had been hearing evidence.

The Bishop of Norwich took up the point about QAB readiness to carry on administering the 1925 Act and he believed that if there had been no White Paper and no Bill the Bounty would still have been able to hold the position secure. He thought that the Bill gave too much help where none was needed (tithepayers) and too little where considerable help was needed (the Church) and that seemed like a kind of terrorism.

At the end of the first day Lord Bingley summed up by saying that whatever view they might take of the Bill it was certain that they would all have great pleasure at some settlement of this 'troublesome question of tithe'. The mere fact that strong views were expressed against the Bill from both sides made him conclude that probably the ultimate solution was a good one.

The next day the debate resumed and yet more speeches were delivered on both sides, airing just about every argument on the subject of tithe, for and against, which had existed before and since 1836. (By chance, it was exactly a hundred years since Lord John Russell had introduced his Bill for the Abolition of Personal Tithes, which eventually became the Tithe Commutation Bill that converted the old tenth portion of farm produce into compulsory cash.) At the end of the second day Viscount Halifax announced to the House that the Committee stage of the Tithe Bill would be on the following Thursday.

The Bill, when it was passed, was not much different to the White Paper except in one detail. Instead of the Commission's recommended forty years for extinguishment, it was extended to sixty years. (The Bishop of Norwich had recommended 100 years.) Unless redeemed, annuities were still payable until 1996. Lord Faringdon called the new charge 'morally obsolete' and Lord Hastings asked the House to consider that tithepayers were being asked to consent to the transfer of the collection of the tithe rentcharge from the titheowner to the State. So long as tithepayers had money in their pockets from any other source, earned or unearned, they would be liable under the penalties of the law if they did not pay the rentcharge. The redemption period, said the Government, had been extended as the annuities would be 'too great' for the industry to bear and were, therefore, spread over a longer period. But sixty years was a long time for a fragile industry to continue paying a statutory tax when that a tax bore no relation to either net or gross fluctuations of income.

In *Sixty Years on Suffolk Soil*, AG Mobbs highlighted how the twenty-year extension had come about:

'A Bill was eventually drawn up and presented to Parliament in 1936, based on the general principles contained in the Commission's majority report, but with this exception, namely that the period of payment was to be extended from forty to sixty years. This was as a result of consultation between the Archbishop of Canterbury and the Minister concerned before the First Reading of the Bill. This fact was

inadvertently disclosed by the Archbishop and caused much consternation. So much so, that Mr Rash and I decided to interview our Lowestoft MP and to urge him to expose the episode by a question in the House. We arranged to meet him in the House of Commons and pressed him very hard to agree to our proposal. We, of course, knew him very well as we were all members of the County Council. Unfortunately he was a Roman Catholic and urged the danger of being accused of religious prejudice. Eventually he suggested he try and get hold of Mr Walter Elliot, the Minister in charge of the Bill and who he thought was somewhere in the House.'

AG did manage to speak to the Minister, but it was by then a 'done deal':

'The ultimate effect of the Bill was that as a result of the absolutely disgraceful intervention of the Archbishop, Parliament took over the responsibility of buying out the tithe recipients by a form of compensation equivalent to a capital sum of over 70 million pounds, with the tithepayers having to make good that sum by annual payment to the Government of the day until 1996, by which date the "ransom money" would cease to be paid and freedom bought from an age-long wrong by those whose only crime was that they chose as their form of livelihood the growing of food for their fellow human beings.'

The Government had allowed only one interested party, namely the Archbishop, to see the report before publication and in February the *Daily Herald* reported:

'The Church is mustering its forces to declare against the report of the Tithe Commission ... In the House of Commons yesterday, Mr Baldwin admitted that the withholding of the report had been prolonged, explaining that this was for the purpose of "elucidating problems for the convenience of all concerned". It is likely that the report would

"DON'T FORGET OUR SECRET TREATY."

Much was made of the fact that the Archbishop of Canterbury was allowed to see the Royal Commission's findings before other interested parties.

have been still further delayed had it not been for the Archbishop of Canterbury's statement that he already knew the findings.'

That the Archbishop let slip the fact he had seen the report appears to indicate how unimportant he considered the matter. No doubt he thought it perfectly in order that the State Church be given privileged access to a Royal Commission's findings. In the tithe debate, though, the Church was only one of many interested parties.

From within Government, Reginald Dorman-Smith wrote personally to AG explaining what had happened and confirming that neither the tithepayers' organisations nor the NFU had been consulted. He thought that calling the Archbishop into consultation was reasonable since it was the Church 'machinery' which would have to be adapted to meet the new situation. The NFU, said Sir Reginald, was often called on to give opinions about fundamental changes in government policy, but:

'... a similar course is very often adopted with the Union. We are summoned to the Ministry and are consulted in confidence about matters which have not been made known to other interested parties. The only difference is that we keep quiet about it – the Archbishop committed a distinct indiscretion!'

At a meeting of the NFU at Ashford in Kent, there was indignation at the secrecy that had surrounded the Royal Commission's findings. Representatives were sent to the House of Commons, but the *Kent Messenger* reported:

'Mr H R Hooper (Vice-Chairman) said that Captain Dykes, one of the deputation to the House of Commons, reported the Government were not legally bound to disclose a report of any Royal Commission unless they wished to do so.

"That is all very well," said Mr Hooper, "but when they publish reports of other commissions at once, it makes one think they are trying to put something over. Our opinion was that the Government wanted to get a clear line on how they were going to deal with it before making it public. Unfortunately some titheowners have had knowledge of the report, and we might presume they have been consulted. Then when the Government come out with a scheme as a bill in Parliament they will ask for the support of the members of the National Farmers' Union. That is what we feel is so unfair".'

At the start of 1936 there were between 30,000 and 40,000 tithepayers in Kent who were paying something in the region of £200,000 annual tithe and they were angry at being treated with such contempt. They considered that the report should either have been shown to none of them, or to all interested bodies. Kentish groups wanted to make more of the issue but the newspapers quickly tired of it, concentrating more on the Archbishop's insistence that his argument was not with tithepayers at all but with Government. He had, most agreed, obviously been more interested in how much the Church would get in settlement than whether or not the solution was a just one. Tithepayers, and for that matter lay impropriators, were considered irrelevant to negotiations by both Government and Church. The two institutions had carved out a Bill between them, leaving tithepayers to pay the cost for the next sixty years.

For the Church, the sticking-point was that the Government's guaranteed bonds scheme would leave them over £500,000 a year worse off in terms of money for clergy stipends. In some cases the cut in the worth of livings might be as much as one-third. The Archbishop, apparently, had not initially anticipated any kind of dip in tithe revenue and it was only when the Tithe Bill became a reality that his financiers were forced to make provision to pick up the shortfall, leaving no possibility for increasing stipends to a more dignified level. The Church was prepared to see its rural clergy reduced to intolerable levels of poverty so long as it made no appreciable difference to higher Church finance. An inquiry was appointed by the Church to investigate ways and means of promoting a more equitable distribution of tithe income, but the issues were said to be 'so complicated' that it would be a 'long time' before big changes could be made. The suggestion was made that tithe could be pooled and distributed more evenly among the recipients, but as the law stood it was 'extremely difficult' to pool tithe incomes as each living was only entitled to hold on to its own revenues. It was, therefore, impossible to take money from one stipendiary and give it to another less well-off living as no bureaucracy existed for it to happen. Such indifference appeared to bear out the suspicions of both tithepayers and the rural clergy that their plight had little impact on the administration or heart of Archbishop Cosmo Lang. The obstacles in the way of this 'more equitable distribution' appeared too difficult and complicated for the vast and powerful Church of England to tackle and it was, seemingly, unable to create the necessary bureaucracy. The Royal Commission, however, concluded that the losses caused by the terms of the Bill could be made good by a rearrangement of the Church's own finances.

Rowland Rash gave a glimpse into Church finances in one of his many Letters to the Editor on the subject, citing the opinion of one of the Royal Commission's members:

'... it is not without significance that Sir Leonard [Coates] elicited the fact that the Ecclesiastical Commissioners, mainly by a steady capitalisation of surplus income, have made increased provision for the cure of souls in necessituous parishes of a value exceeding £2,315,000 per annum, a figure which, it will be observed, exceeds the par value of the Benefice and Ecclesiastical Corporation Tithe Rentcharge combined. And all this out of surplus income! Now what about the inability of the Church to assist its poorer clergy?'

However, in October 1936 the Archbishops of Canterbury and York were prevailed upon to seek an alternative source of funding for the deprived clergy. Instead of looking to the Church's own resources, they decided to establish what was to be called "The Archbishops' Tithe Compensation Fund". It was directed towards tithepayers who were asked to voluntarily tithe the whole or part of the annual sum of which they were relieved by the provision of the Tithe Act and would *'... thus offer as a gift what they have hitherto readily acknowledged as a debt'*. They wrote in *The Times*:

'Perhaps there has never been a time when in this country, as in the whole world, there was greater need of the witness of the Church of Christ fulfilled through the ministry of all its members. But the effectiveness of that witness must necessarily largely depend on those of the members of the Church who have been specially ordained to the ministry, in other words, on the work of the clergy in the various parishes throughout the land.'

Their work, said the two Archbishops, must necessarily be affected by the Tithe Act and while it was appreciated that one advantage of the Act was a new atmosphere of harmony and good will in the countryside, *'...this advantage will be reaped at a very serious cost'*. The Fund would be administered by the Central Board of Finance of the Church of England, which Board would dole out tithepayers' gifts in the form of grants to impecunious clergy. Bending over backwards to be fair, the Archbishops added:

'For many reasons it has been thought best to collect such gifts and to administer them through a central fund, but if any of those who are willing to respond to this appeal desire to earmark their contributions for their own diocese or for any particular parish they would be at liberty to do so.'

Perhaps Archbishop Cosmo Lang thought this up in his bath, or other such moment of repose, but he could not seriously have thought that tithepayers had for almost ten years, at enormous cost to themselves, their families and their communities, fought the imposition of tithe only to pay it voluntarily at the behest of an Archbishop whose effigy they had ritually burned.

Writing in the *Kentish Express*, F R Allen replied:

'An appeal is being made for subscriptions to make good what is described as the "loss" to ecclesiastical titheowners consequent on the passing of the Tithe Act 1936 ... there is, so far as I am aware, no disposition on the part of tithepayers to deter persons having full knowledge of the facts from responding to this appeal, though many tithepayers, in view of the terms imposed on them by the Act, will probably not feel themselves under any special obligation to respond.'

Speaking in Ipswich, Roderick Kedward recalled his troops to battle:

'... this meeting of tithepayers, whilst appreciating the fact that to some extent their contentions are upheld in the report of the Royal Commission, at the same time consider that not even the Commission's proposals, much less those of the Government, in any way represents elementary justice to tithepayers, and should be strenuously opposed.'

He congratulated the efforts made by the Suffolk TPA under the *'magnificent leadership of Mr Mobbs and his associates'*, and said:

'Suffolk has been right in the forefront – in the front-line trenches – right from the start. You will soon be over the top.'

For his part, AG was still doing his best in the trenches, and said:

'There were of course cases where farmers just did not have the money to meet the demands and often an accumulation of arrears as well. One such instance occurred in the case of a small farmer in south Suffolk who, as a result of a court order, had his entire small herd of cows impounded. I had the greatest difficulty in finding his farm which was three fields away from the road and over a very bad track. When I arrived in the evening I really could have wept. It was about seven o'clock, the man was milking his cows, his wife who was shortly expecting a baby was carrying the milk into the dairy, and the eldest child was standing on a chair pumping the water for cooling the milk. In a case like this of course allowing a sale was unthinkable and the Association assisted in a settlement. I remember remarking to the farmer that he lived in a very out of the way farm. He replied that

was about the only consolation he had, as no Government Inspectors had yet been able to find him. But the Bailiff had.'

After the Lords debate, however, there was a reluctant acceptance among the parties for the main proposals of the Bill. No amount of looking back was going to change what amounted to a solution of some kind, albeit unsatisfactory to tithepayers. F R Allen wrote to AG:

'We must accept redemption of tithe in some form as an accomplished fact, on which Parliament is most unlikely ever to go back. Thus for practical purposes it becomes, as you say, a question of terms of redemption.'

The pace was beginning to tell on many, especially those working farmers who could ill afford the time or energy to fight. There were echoes of John Davies of Ruthin, who had earlier written to AG:

'... time is so short, and I am so extremely busy. This business is very near telling on me now. I sleep but little and working hard all day, writing, or at meetings at night, it all tells, but I have made up my mind to do my level best in this struggle.'

AG began to receive desperate letters about the consequences of the new 'redemption annuity' becoming a personal debt, although the general level of acceptance sapped the core of resistance. E M Fuller from Kent wrote:

'... we are arranging a Public Meeting – do hope we shall get support, the danger is that people are getting tired of it. I mean those who do not have to pay tithe or very little. If we could concentrate on a few main points that the public could understand we might still have a chance to get justice. The fact that the Government Bill will make the charge an encumbrance on the freehold is too terrible to think about. What a legacy to leave to our children!'

Public interest in tithe, however, was limited to amused witness of the Midsummer March. The *Newcastle Journal* commented:

'The Government's proposals for the extinguishment of tithe have attracted much attention from the experts and from some of those whom the proposals design to pinch, but they seem to have escaped with slight consideration from the larger public. That is no doubt in part due to the tension caused by Germany's violation of the Locarno Pact, but there are indications that it is also in part due to an impression that the proposals are fundamentally just as well as expedient.'

Somewhat surprisingly, Mr J H Squirrell wrote to AG from Stowmarket:

'I really wish you would take up a stronger line in regard to this tithe question'.

Mr Squirrell, perhaps unaware of the strenuous efforts of AG and his colleagues, was just one of many thousands of farmers who were still in arrears and consequently being pursued by QAB before the new regime came into effect. There was a complicated arrangement whereby the Inland Revenue had chosen 1935-1936 as the datum year for assessment, but due to an even more ingenious way in which the new tithe annuity would be collected there were to be huge misunderstandings about exactly what the amount of annuity should be. An Arrears Investigation Committee had been set up but it operated a muddled, inefficient procedure that made decisions blindly, having no precedent and no equivalent of George Middleton to organise it. Tithepayers were warned in the *Farmer & Stock-Breeder*:

> *'When arrears which you say are not legally due are demanded beware! Do not go near the Investigation Committee, or you will be "deemed to admit legal liability". Your only hope will be to write saying you deny liability, stating your reasons, and asking that you may have more than a month within which to apply to the Investigation Committee. Then, if necessary, dispose of the legal liability question in the courts.'*

However, many of those who could pay began to do so; they feared court proceedings and paid chiefly from weariness of the fight. Anxious that the TPAs should remain united and continue helping tithepayers unravel the implications of the legislation, Makens Turner wrote to AG:

> *'It seems to me important if it is anyhow possible to keep the united movement in being at any rate until the Bill does finally become law. To disband now would inevitably be regarded as a sign of a cave-in, besides which it looks certain that there is useful work which ought to be done, and most effectively by joint action.'*

AG observed in his autobiography:

> *'It was only natural that following an Act of Parliament which after all reduced our capital obligations by some £20 million, and annual payments by nearly 20%, our agitation to some extent died down. But we kept our tithepayers organisation in being, and in fact quite a number of distraints continued to be carried out including those on my own goods.'*

Among others, distraint sales continued at the Rash farms in Wortham. In 1936, two years after the famous distraint where nineteen Blackshirts had been arrested, yet another tithe sale was held – at Hall Farm, Wortham – after which farmers paraded with effigies of Queen Anne and Sir George Middleton, carrying placards of satirical cartoons. Following the sale, the procession wound its way to the tithe monument, unveiled at Wortham in February 1935, which bore the inscription:

'The Tithe War
134 pigs and 15 cattle
seized for tithe
Feb 22 1934'

A wreath made of carrots and other vegetables was placed on the monument and effigies were hurled onto a huge bonfire amid derisive cheers and a rendering of *Rule Britannia*. The half-mile long procession was led by Roderick Kedward and included AG, Rowland and Doreen Rash, Makens Turner and Philip Butler.

At a meeting of the East Kent Tithepayers in Sandwich, Doreen Wallace was reported urging members to keep on fighting:

'... although it had been a long and gruelling fight already. Having gone so far, however, it would not do for them to be content with less than justice. There had been a lull on both sides in tithe activity ... in her county the Queen Anne's Bounty had put plenty of men into the courts, but there had been few distraints. tithepayers had been keeping quiet, she supposed, for the production of the Royal Commission's report. She hoped it did not mean that they had got so much money in their pockets now, that they were able to pay up quietly; that they were simply longing for the end of the fight, even if it was a poor end, or that they were getting themselves in tune for giving in. That would be a sad reward for people like Kedward and Allen, who had been in it from the start.'

The fire might have died down, but the embers of dissent were still hot. Later, Doreen Wallace told reporters:

'... the Royal Commission and Government had both decided that the present figure of tithe was too high, yet Queen Anne's Bounty is making a great drive to collect arrears at the present figure. Obviously the Bounty are trying to collect in full as much as it can before anyone in authority remembers about arrears. It is a piece of immoral opportunism.'

She was making the point felt by many tithepayers in arrears. Since the Government had seen fit to reduce the annuity payments to below £100 and set up a special Committee with full powers to deal with existing arrears, many who were in arrears for the April payments felt it unfair that they should pay at the older, higher rate. The new lower annuities would not be effective until October 1936, however, and the two half-yearly payments were separate.

Not only was the arrears situation as bad as ever, but the new regime began to take effect more quickly than expected and many tithepayers who held small-value tithe were forced into redemption. With national agriculture still in depression the enforced payment of even small amounts of money brought with it yet more hardship and resentment.

There was a system of voluntary redemption but it depended on unfamiliar form-filling, as Henry Williamson pointed out:

'The Government lawyers bargained with the Church lawyers, and the bargain brought relief to some owners of poor land. If the tithe was more than a third of the annual rent, then the difference would be "subject to remission". Therefore, my rent being £105 a year, the tithe was no longer £79, but £35. However, to get this remission I had to fill in a form, asking for a Certificate of Annual Value, and send it to HM Income Tax Inspectorate. When the certificate came, I had to send it, with a letter beginning for remission of part of my tithe, to the Tithe Commission. My pleas had to be received by them by March 1st of every year. Woe betide the working farmer, doing his eighty-hour week from 1937 to 1945, if he forgot, in the rush of making seed-beds and drilling corn in a dry early spring, to apply for a Certificate, and then for remission. No mercy was shown to the delinquent fellow.'

Applicants such as Henry Williamson often found themselves a day or two out on their remission application, although few took their case to London as he did. However, his visit to *'a great white building in Finsbury Square, London, standing on several acres of land'* achieved nothing, as the official pointed to the printed rules and said that his application for remission had not been received on time and that was all there was to it. However, the matter was brought before Mr Justice Morton in the Chancery Division who was told that notices had been served a day late on some one thousand tithepayers, and therefore rendered arrears of rentcharge irrecoverable. A summons was taken out by QAB against the Tithe Redemption Commission and although the conclusion went against QAB the judge was reported as saying *'... the proceedings were perfectly friendly. The parties were both public bodies, who desired enlightenment on the construction of the [Tithe] Act'.*

The new Tithe Commission had been appointed in September with Sir Charles Howell Thomas, Permanent Secretary of the Ministry of Agriculture as Chairman. Other members were William Allen KC, A E Cutforth CBE, Edwin Fisher and Sir Norman Vernon, Bart. Their first task was to determine which titheholdings were extinguished by the Act, the amount of stock to be issued for compensation, and who was entitled to receive the stock. They also had to determine what annuities should be charged in respect of land out of which the tithe derived, to apportion the annuities where land was in the ownership of more than one person, and to manage such annuities once they were fixed. A set of rules was drawn up by MAFF prescribing the form in which particulars were to be transmitted to the Commission and the cumbersome machinery of the new bureaucracy began to turn.

On 2 October 1936 the new Act came into force. To all intents and purposes tithe rentcharge was effectively abolished, to be replaced by two annual redemption annuities paid half-yearly on 1 April and 1 October for the next sixty years. The factions in the tithe war took a few weeks to absorb and understand the implications before taking up their relative positions again.

Lay impropriators emerged from almost two years of debate aggrieved and somewhat resentful towards the Archbishop of Canterbury who, they thought, had not preserved the interests of titheowners as a whole. He had negotiated a sinking fund for the ecclesiastical tithe but there was none for the lay impropriator. Although the Church had the majority titheholding, the annual report of the land division of MAFF showed that in 1932, £583,500 of the total value of £3,163,000 tithe was held by schools, college, charities and lay owners.

As early as March 1929 AG had tried to put lay impropriators 'on the map', and wrote to F R Allen asking for information, to which he replied:

> 'The greater part of what is called lay tithe originated in the grants made by Henry VIII to his supporters and favourites at the Dissolution of the Monasteries. But both before and after that period there were instances of the alienation of tithe from the Church. A considerable amount of what is usually classed as lay tithe belongs to schools, colleges, hospitals, etc. It is difficult to state exactly how much it all amounts to, but it is probably around £780,000.'

When details of the new Bill were announced, *The Times* commented:

> 'On the side of the titheowners ... the Tithe Committee of Queen Anne's Bounty accepts the extinguishment of tithe, which is the principle of the Government's proposals, though the proposals have given the Bursar of New College a mathematician's nightmare so comprehensive that he would clearly like the proposals to be withdrawn entirely.'

The Bursar of New College, Oxford was considered by the press to be representative of the lay impropriators, Oxford and Cambridge Universities having led the attack in the past on behalf of lay owners. During an official deputation to the Minister of Agriculture in 1933, however, the Bursar, Captain G T Hutchinson represented only the Oxford and Cambridge Colleges. New College had endured much adverse publicity over its fight with the farmers of the Saffron Walden Division of Essex whose MP, 'RAB' Butler had taken up the tithepayers' cause.

The Times said:

'The Bursar argues that the proposals are a good bargain for nobody except the Government, [but] he does not take sufficient account of the fact that the Exchequer will not benefit by a single penny.'

Oxford and Cambridge Universities held the bulk of the lay tithe: Merton College had come in for considerable publicity during its fight with Roderick Kedward and the farmers of the Elham Valley in Kent. King's College, Cambridge had also been in the front line as owner of the tithe on Mrs Waspe's Ringshall farm. King's College had employed General Dealers to seize goods in Suffolk when wheat was taken from the Waspe farm to Bury St Edmunds station and sent to one of the College's Lincolnshire farms.

Car outside Parliament on the day the Tithe Bill was before the House of Lords.

Emmanuel College, Cambridge had persecuted a Norfolk farmer, E A Clarke of Little Melton, over the sum of £18. The bailiff and policeman raided Mr Clarke's farm and took away corn far in excess of the tithe arrears, and this from a farmer who had lost £600 on his farm and was facing ruin. Emmanuel College also threatened to remove all of Mr Clarke's furniture and a dramatic scene took place as Alfred Bird, a young farm hand who had worked for Mr Clarke since childhood, threw himself in front of the lorry and had to be removed by police.

There were also a number of small charity owners, such as Dr Triplet's Charity which held Lady Eve Balfour's tithe, together with private, one-man owners (or one-woman, as in the case of Mrs Sullivan, owner of the Australia Farms tithe). Their voice was not heard in the wider debate, although they made their presence felt by taking tithepayers to court on their own account.

Relatively little had been said on behalf of the lay impropriators, even when the 1925 Tithe Act made precise distinctions between ecclesiastical and lay tithe. Ecclesiastical tithe then had been fixed at £109 10s (£105 plus an additional £4 10s contribution to a sinking fund), while lay tithe was fixed at £105 with no sinking fund. In 1936, lay impropriators were subjected to the same new round of bureaucracy as the tithepayers. They were required to register their titheowning claims by means of a form, which had to be with the Tithe Redemption Commission by 31 October. The Commission required particulars of rentcharges in respect of which compensation was being claimed, and any claims for remission or merger.

Accountants across England and Wales, faced with yet more intricate and vexed dealings with tithe, rushed to get a copy of *Tithe Rent Charge and Redemption Annuity Tables* by Dr Percy Millard, a well-known authority on tithe and a former official of MAFF's Tithe Branch. It contained a summary of the Tithe Acts passed in the hundred years since the Commutation of 1836 and was an indispensable guide to many titheowners as they rushed to stake their claims.

The CLA made numerous representations on behalf of its 12,000 members, whether titheowner or tithepayer, always treading a delicate line between the two and guarding against charges of self-interest. Several CLA members took part in the Lords Debate of the Tithe Bill, including Lords Cranworth and Hastings but, just as in the NFU, there were individual hard-liners in the Association. One high-profile CLA titheowner, R S Strachey, died only a few months after the 1936 Act became law. He had long campaigned for the abolition of tithe and had written *Freedom from the Tithe*

Act 1925, the profits from which went to the Central & Associated Chambers of Agriculture in recognition of their exertions on behalf of tithepayers. He represented the small band of titheowing tithepayers who were as indignant with the system as any owner-occupier, and who offered support by way of their ability to penetrate the Establishment and speak coherently on behalf of those less able to put their case.

Compared with the slightly more dignified stance of the CLA, the hybrid membership of the NFU was struggling to accept its Executive's position and, to some extent, blamed it for the imperfections of the Tithe Act. Its most staunch supporter, AG had been left off the Union's Tithe Committee, possibly because he had told the *Farmer & Stock-Breeder* in 1934:

> 'We have given NFU Headquarters to understand that we are not going to stand any "monkeying" about over this ... After the treatment I have received from those in authority in the Farmers' Union there is only one thing that keeps me within the ranks of the Union, and that is the cause of the tithepayer. There was an alteration in the Tithe Committee at Headquarters. The conclusion they arrived at to form the basis of the evidence to put before the Royal Commission is scarcely worth the paper it is written on.'

AG said that all the Union wanted to do was to go back to the basis of the corn prices arrived at 100 years before, but he didn't want to go back, only forward. The *East Anglian Daily Times* recalled AG making a protest against the proposals of the NFU to be submitted to the Royal Commission:

> 'Mr Mobbs referred to what he termed the "unconstitutional procedure" adopted at headquarters of the NFU, and dealing with the attitude of the Council with regard to ecclesiastical tithe, said that he thought they were far more concerned for the ecclesiastical titheowner than the tithepayer within the ranks of the Union.
>
> "As to lay tithe," said Mr Mobbs, "... it is not the fault of the tithepayers that the owner has a right to collect it. It is not owners of either lay or ecclesiastical tithe that the Union should be concerned about, but those who have to pay it." Mr Mobbs concluded by saying that the only thing to do was to watch the "sort of show the Union puts up next week" and then consider the question of an application to appear before the Royal Commission on behalf of the Eastern Counties.'

In common with Lady Eve Balfour and many others, AG considered the Union's handling of the issue to be a shambles, but it was impossible for him to resign. Like it or not, the NFU was seen as the representative body for farmers and, in similar vein to Reginald Dorman-Smith's speech in the House of Commons, the ordinary member who ventured outside his party was apt to run into troubled waters. In this case it was not so much troubled waters that would damage the tithepayers' cause as their lack of credibility if they had formed a splinter or rival organisation. Those in the NTA had always been careful to point out that they were a single-issue lobby group and in no way intended to represent farming as a whole or usurp the function of the Union. There were many in the NFU who saw AG as a troublemaker with a potential for causing upsets, but good causes are not fought or won by men of pale conviction nor by those with the ability to blend into the background. AG told the *East Anglian Daily Times*:

> *'When I was a member of the Tithe Committee and wanted on one occasion to send a deputy I was told I could not do so, as it was an ad hoc Committee, but since the new Committee has been formed I find that at the last meeting at least three members attended as deputies.'*

AG always had the unanimous backing of his own Beccles Branch and was Chairman for many years, as well as becoming Suffolk Chairman. There were other, equally important, issues affecting farming – not least the setting-up of the Milk Marketing Scheme, which threatened to put small dairy producers out of business – and he was prominent in other strata of the agricultural establishment. In 1932 he succeeded in ruffling a few feathers at the annual County Show by provocatively setting up a Suffolk TPA tent next to that of the NFU. AG was only Honorary Director of the Suffolk Show for one year, but he took full advantage of the opportunity and gave Makens Turner a free hand to organise the stand. This did not go down well with others in the Suffolk Agricultural Association. At the October AGM the President, F L Bland raised the matter of the TPA tent. It was recorded in the minutes that:

> *'... a stand was allowed the Suffolk Tithepayers' Association. [The President] proposed that we do not another year accept an application from them or any other such body, intimating that should the Suffolk Show Association do so there would be a big withdrawal of support from high quarters. After discussion, Mr S R Sherwood mentioned that it was not desirable to encourage this class of Standholder, and Mr C C Smith proposed that if an application be received, the Secretary should, if he was in doubt, be allowed to take instructions from the Finance Committee.'*

Exactly who occupied the 'high quarters' was not made clear, but the county's 'gentry' were unlikely to approve such rebellion. Certainly the Church would have been the first to sit on such partisan protest, while the big guns of the NFU were outraged by the NTA tent being sited next to their own.

AG's stormy relationship with the NFU continued unabated. During the 1930s he frequently corresponded with F R Allen on the subject. While it was AG's intention always to work within the Union, F R Allen was anxious that the NTA should not be seen to be usurping the NFU's position. He thought it their moral duty to disband if it meant that the NFU would have a clearer and more unambiguous stand in the public eye. It was, though, never likely that the two organisations would agree so entirely. In 1933 the Union described NTA proposals as 'confiscatory', causing F R Allen to write hastily that '... *while so radical a difference of object exists there is a reason for the continuance of the NTA*'.

With so many demands being made on him, it seemed impossible that AG could find time to attend so many meetings, write endless letters to numerous editors, run his farm, breed awarding-winning dairy cows and attend to the everyday needs of home, family and local politics. Yet in March 1937 he was called upon to take up the Presidency of the NTA. Roderick Kedward, champion of the tithepayers since 1932, former Liberal MP for the Ashford Division and superintendent of the South London Methodist Mission for twenty years, died suddenly aged fifty-five.

The *Kentish Express* told its readers:

'*... he died unexpectedly last Friday. Although unwell on the Saturday, he went up to Bermondsey to conduct special services on the Sunday. On Monday night he was taken worse and the services of a doctor and specialist were sought as a precautionary measure. A duodenal ulcer was diagnosed; even so, it was not thought to be really serious, although Mr Kedward had a great deal of pain. But, on Friday morning he passed away in his sleep.*'

The Reverend William Solomon wrote that Methodism had lost a 'stalwart son', who was a great fighter for justice, and '*... in spite of an apparent pugnacious spirit he lived near to God*'.

The Reverend Reginald Stallard wrote:

'*After but six months' association with the Reverend R M Kedward as his colleague in the South London Mission, I would offer my tribute to the generous and magnificent qualities of Mr Kedward's sterling character. He was a born leader, and one felt intuitively the privilege of being a member of his staff.*'

Mr Sydney Sharvell wrote:

'Thinking of him now, I can see him rushing half across England at any time of the day or night at the call of a weak friend and doing it time after time, and spending his Christmas evening, as he had done for the last fifteen years, romping with the poor old folk in the local union.'

Following a service at Bermondsey's Central Hall, the funeral cortege passed through streets lined with silent mourners on its way to Kent, the *Methodist Recorder* calling it *'... a wonderful demonstration of public affection and sympathy'.* The Central Hall, seating some two thousand people, was packed, whilst mounted and foot police patrolled the pavements outside where many thousands waited patiently to pay their last respects.

At the tiny Hothfield Methodist Chapel, where he had begun his church work as a Sunday school teacher, a second service was held. The *Tuesday Express* said:

'Scores of people were unable to gain entry to the tiny Methodist chapel at Hothfield – a stone's throw from (the Rev Kedward's) Kentish home ... Farmers from counties where the agriculturalists' battle has been the hardest gathered in the daffodil-decorated chapel to pay tribute to a staunch friend and leader. As one said to the Tuesday Express, *"For us, a light has gone out; we have only the memory of his example to guide us in our future work".'*

In his address Dr Donald Soper said:

'That Roderick Kedward was a great man will be allowed by all who came into contact with him, but that he was a good man and a greatly good man was the experience not of the wide world so much as it was to ourselves. We are mourning the loss of a man nearer and dearer to us than words can express.'

Among the mourners were F R Allen, H Roseveare and Miss M K Glover (Chairman and Secretary of the Ashford TPA), Rowland and Doreen Rash, AG Mobbs, Canon Brocklehurst and A Waddell (from Ruckinge). Floral tributes came from more than twelve TPAs including East Kent, Worcester, Salisbury, Norfolk, Suffolk and Monmouthshire.

As a staunch supporter and prime mover of the tithepayers' revolt, Roderick Kedward organised protest meetings in all parts of the country and moved a Tithe Remission Bill in Parliament. By allowing the family farms at Hothfield and Westwell to be distrained on he put himself on the front line – and all this at the same time as he gave devoted service to the South London

Methodist Mission. During the First World War he had served as chaplain to the Forces in France and Egypt and, after being invalided out, returned to Bermondsey where he served on the Borough Council and Board of Guardians. Like all the other tithepayers' leaders, he had been accused of hot-headedness, law-breaking and incitement to riot; he had been called a 'stormy petrel' and a 'peripatetic agitator'. In his teenage years he had been put in gaol after holding an open-air religious meeting in Worcestershire and refusing to pay the resultant fine. (Local agitation, however, forced the Home Secretary to order his release.) Roderick Kedward was a man of the highest integrity, an ardent Liberal, and a man of God.

Donald Soper said:

'Some of you knew him as a great friend and I join myself in that company, and can testify to the qualities of courage, simplicity, kindliness and of strength which we all knew and admired in one whose personality and whole outlook on life was splendid and free.

'There are others among you whose knowledge of the one whose passing we mourn was in a wider sphere of activity and service for those who were poor and dispossessed, down-trodden, and those who were cheated, as he thought and believed, and those who needed that strength that he could so specially give. It is a great and fine thing that in this world there should have been a man like Roderick Kedward, for it is sweeter and better for his coming, and poorer and sadder for his passing.'

Mr Kedward's brothers, the Reverends H D and William Kedward, officiated and two farm wagons and a private car loaded with flowers followed the cortege to the crematorium. The *Tuesday Express* recorded:

'... as the body was being committed, heavy clouds obscuring the sun parted for a few seconds and a shaft of winter sunshine broke through the windows, touching the tulips and roses on the coffin as it disappeared.'

AG took over the NTA Presidency ably supported by those whose commitment to the abolition of tithe, in whatever form, had not wavered over the years. Doreen Wallace and her husband Rowland Rash, Makens Turner, Philip Butler and all the leaders of TPAs across England and Wales pledged to fight on. There was still work to be done on behalf of tithepayers and leadership was crucial.

~ *o* ~

Chapter 9

MARCH OF TRIUMPH
February 1939

'The Government's re-examination of their agriculture policy and the appointment of Sir Reginald Dorman-Smith, MP, a former president of the National Farmers' Union, as Minister of Agriculture were responsible yesterday for transforming what had been intended as a protest march of farmers through London into a demonstration of support of the new Minister.

'Hundreds of farmers and farm workers, many accompanied by their wives, arrived in London from East Anglia and took part in a march through the City and by way of the Embankment to Central Hall, Westminster.'

The Times, 2 February 1939

ALTHOUGH THERE WAS STILL active opposition from the leaders of the tithepayers, there was nothing that anyone could do to stop the implementation of the 1936 Tithe Act. F R Allen wrote to AG Mobbs:

'It seems to me that so large a proportion of tithepayers are so far satisfied with the present position that there are not a sufficient number of really dissatisfied ones left to make up an effective organisation concerning itself

with tithe alone. Most of those who want to continue any sort of protest will be content with the NFU ... There is of course a good deal of tithe work to do, and I have enquiries of some sort or another almost every day, but they generally relate to the personal affairs of the enquirer. There is also a great deal to be done in ascertaining the meaning of many of the clauses in the new Act which is about as badly drawn up as any Act I have come across, but tithepayers take no interest in this sort of thing until it affects them directly.'

F R Allen and AG were still writing letters to newspapers where necessary, as were Doreen and Rowland Rash, Makens Turner and other tithepayers' leaders. F R Allen told AG that he had replied to the Bishop of Gloucester's letter in *The Times* and the *East Anglian Daily Times*, and that he had heard from Mrs Rash that she had also replied to the Bishop in *The Times*. In Oxfordshire, V Drewitt was still organising meetings to discuss the new Act and making sure the correspondence columns reflected the dissent still going on in the county.

In Wales there was immense dissatisfaction with the Bill and delegates from Flintshire pressed the NFU to back a separate Tithe Bill for Wales. Cardigan put forward a resolution of strong disapproval of the increased redemption period from the Royal Commission's recommended forty to the final sixty years, but on both counts it was decided that no useful action could be taken by the Union.

The *East Anglian Daily Times* recorded:

'Tithepayers had no intention of submitting to such legislation and [Mr Mobbs] prophesied that before long the whole question would again have to be debated on the floor of Parliament.'

In spite of the eighteen-and-a-half percent decrease in payments the deep resentment at having to pay an arbitrary tax for another sixty years still had the capacity to inflame tithepayers and motivate protest. The fact that it had become a personal debt, payable on demand to the tax collector, took indignation and resentment onto a new and higher plane. Tithe was no longer a charge on the land, it was an arbitrary debt, the collection of which had the uncompromising force of the law, and arrears would not be allowed to accumulate.

Several well-publicised distraint sales took place and the press was as eager as ever for the emotive pictures of rural protest. One of the first distraint sales to take place at the beginning of 1937 was at Yaxley on the Norfolk-Suffolk border. Mr H L Newstead, whose Manor Farm was about 200 acres, paid tithe in four parishes – Mellis, Yaxley, Little Thornham and Thrandeston. It was lay tithe (although bought in 1923 by a clergyman, the Reverend W F Buttle) and handled by the Church Property Trust Limited. Mr Newstead's tithe amounted to £28 a year, and in January 1937 there were arrears amounting to about £75. He told the court that there could not be a claim for more than two years' arrears at one time, so the claim should be for the last half of 1934, the whole of 1935, and half of 1936. However, the Court ruled that the full amount was due and ordered a tender sale, although it was later agreed that a sale by auction was preferable for all parties.

Local auctioneer, Clement Gaze conducted the sale, and although forty-six pigs were up for sale only nine were purchased when the amount required was realised. The Suffolk TPA was there in force and C A West and Rowland Rash bought all nine pigs. After the sale Mr Gaze was prevailed upon to conduct a second sale, that of a young pedigree Jersey bull named Oulton Defender, bred by AG Mobbs and sold for the benefit of the TPA. Afterwards AG addressed the crowd, emphasising that although Government had set up the Arrears Investigation Committee, this particular titheowner had seen fit to press for the full amount. He said:

> 'The present distraint concerns a case of lay tithe, which has been purchased some time ago by a Church of England clergyman for the purpose of investment, but was now in the hands of a company known as the Church Property Trust Limited. Despite the fact that the average market value of lay tithe during the last twenty years is about ten years' purchase, the Government now takes over the collection of lay tithe and compensates this company and all other lay titheowners to the extent of seventeen years' purchase. One would have thought that an opportunity would have been given to Mr Newstead to appear before the Arrears Investigation Committee.'

Out in the parishes many of the rural clergy were struggling to make ends meet and tried to make the best of a bad job. QAB said that the new regime would reduce clergy incomes with yet more drastic changes and reviews being triggered each time an incumbent left and a new one was appointed. A clergyman with an income of £450, two-thirds of which is derived from tithe, would suffer a loss of £35 annually. Two years after the finalisation of the Tithe Bill, Church financiers found the situation compounded by the withdrawal of the equally controversial coal royalties. In May 1936 it was announced that arrangements were in hand to buy up the mineral royalties paid to landowners under whose property coal was mined. Mineral owners, including the Church, received an average of £5,223,000 a year from the mining industry. At the extinction of coal royalties it was estimated that the reduction in ecclesiastical income amounted to around £150,000 a year. The Government's generous buy-out terms came in for strong criticism from tithepayers, who considered that the mining industry had fared somewhat better than they had. Doreen Wallace wrote:

'... it is eminently reasonable that the value of coal royalties has been arrived at by consulting the market prices of these properties. Although the owners valued their royalties far higher, the final award turns out to be fifteen years' purchase, because that is what buyers are known to have paid when the properties have come up for sale. How different was the case of tithe rentcharge. No attempt was made to base the calculation on what the property was worth for sale ... If an award of fifteen years' purchase had been made, tithepayers would not have been ill-content. But instead, by no sort of calculation, but by an estimate of the alleged needs of the tithe-owners, a sum was arrived at which gives twenty-seven years' purchase to the Church and seventeen years' to the lay titheowner. Why this marked difference in treatment as between coal royalties and tithe rentcharge?'

Guy Mayfield comments on this:

'Nevertheless these two measures [tithe and coal] were beneficial in so far as they removed anachronisms in the sources of ecclesiastical revenue, although at a price; the cost of these benefits was reflected in the stipends of the parochial clergy.'

The man who had done his utmost for the cause of QAB, Sir George Middleton, died suddenly on 25 October 1938. Knighted in 1935, Sir George had supervised the removal of QAB from the hands of the Commissions to the State, and the fight for him was over. He collapsed and died while attending a meeting of the Corporation of Church House in Westminster. As First Church Estates Commissioner for eight years and as QAB Chairman he had countered the tithepayers' revolt in the only way he knew how – by stonewalling and maintaining a stunningly simple and consistent defence of tithe. Only in the final years, when the Tithe Act became a reality, did he allow room for discussion. His public face was one of relaxed, and often humorous, opposition to the tithepayers' leaders, his strength coming from the cold legal correctness of his case. He had always been on what he knew to be the 'right' side of the law, but tithepayers thought it was a wrong side of right. He surrounded himself with the security of the Establishment in its ultimate form, the Church of England. He was its servant, yet he used it successfully to further his own ambition. *The Times* obituary said:

> '... he assumed control of Queen Anne's Bounty also as Chairman of committees. In 1935 he became joint treasurer of the Bounty. He also flung himself into the life of the Church Assembly, and became a councillor of the Corporation of Church House. His energy was indefatigable. His first years at Queen Anne's Bounty were the years of the agitation against tithe. The organisation and system of concession to hard cases he personally instituted saved a position in danger of being lost without cause to factious agitators. The hard case he never pressed: he was against pretence.'

Thousands of hard-pressed tithepayers disagreed absolutely that his system of concession had by any means alleviated their problems. It was slow and cumbersome by any standards. In a report by QAB's Tithe Committee it was claimed that efforts were 'invariably' made by QAB to induce tithepayers to settle:

> '... in the areas of acute agricultural depression investigation of the case is offered. In certain areas over 1,700 cases have been investigated, of which 500 have been settled by payment of reduced sums or instalments. In about 150 cases no concession was considered justified, whilst negotiations are still proceeding in about 1,000 cases.'

There is overwhelming evidence, however, that where tithepayers settled it was because they were found to have assets sufficient to cover the debt, rather than an ability to pay out of income derived from the land. Even among the 500 cases where some reduction was agreed, more often than not the only 'concession' was that payment was allowed in instalments rather than a lump sum, which was no concession at all in the long term.

After the climax year of 1933 George Middleton seemed to take on board some of the strength of feeling among tithepayers, although his overall position was the same and he gave no ground in the argument. Tithe was a legal charge on a legitimate property, ordained by the legislature, and tithepayers would pay it come what may. Whether it was fair, ethical or moral was irrelevant. However, it was observed that during the negotiations over the coal royalties, Sir George appeared to have a much greater rapport with the royalty payers than he had ever had with the tithepayers and he was given much of the credit for bargaining a deal acceptable to all parties.

Only a few months before his death Sir George was crossing swords with the NTA in the press over the Archbishops' Tithe Compensation Appeal and in response to a defensive speech made by Sir George in Norwich, F R Allen wrote:

'Although the Church of England has very largely lost its hold over the people of this country, there remains among that class ... a desire, more widespread than may appear on the surface, for some form of national recognition of a Supreme Being, and a genuine, if scarcely expressed, regard to the moral responsibility which such recognition implies.'

No specific reply to this has surfaced, but it is safe to assume that Sir George Middleton had a firm and unshakeable recognition of a Supreme Being and disputed the waning influence of the Established Church. As the 1937 autumn session of the Canterbury Diocesan Conference prepared to debate the tithe issue, the *Kentish Express* had reported:

'"There is no man in England better qualified than he is to speak on this subject," said Dr Lang, introducing Sir George Middleton (First Estates Commissioner of the Ecclesiastical Commission and chairman of the Tithe Committee of the Governors of Queen Anne's Bounty) who addressed the conference on the Tithe Act.

"Nothing that has happened in the last few years has had such a pronounced effect on church finances than the passing of the 1936 Act," said Sir George Middleton opening his address.'

He went on to say that 1836 had been a very great year in the reform of the Church by making tithe payments subject to the law and gave approval to the septennial values. Outlining the history of tithe over the hundred years to 1936, he referred to the current agitation and the harm it had caused:

'Difficulties of all kinds arose, not least in this district, where even church services were boycotted, and instead of being a friend of the parish, the incumbent was an enemy of many of his parishioners.'

In what was a very long speech, Sir George went on to outline the implications of the Tithe Act for Church finances, tax assessments for the clergy, and gave the conference warning of the impending coal royalty buy-out. Briefly he referred to the burning of the effigies:

'There has been an almost complete absence of criticism against the Church since the 1936 Act. If any more effigies are to be burnt it seems

they will not be of His Grace or myself but of Mr Neville Chamberlain or Mr Morrison, and if I am anywhere near I shall hope for a front seat.'

Newspaper fashion meant that journalists no longer inserted bracketed audience reaction into their reports, but no doubt Sir George brought a smile and a few subdued expressions of amusement to the diocesan members' faces. Closing the debate, the Primate paid more tribute to the work of Sir George, referring to tithe as a 'running sore' which had at last been stopped.

Shortly before his death Sir George published *Resources of the Church*, an apologist's account of the resources of the Ecclesiastical Commissioners and QAB, saying that there were no funds available for 'fancy schemes'. The Press and Publications Board of the Church Assembly issued the booklet, although an endnote reads:

> *'This pamphlet is issued under the authority of the Defence and Instruction Committee of the Press and Publications Board, but the Author is alone responsible for the statements contained therein.'*

Sir George was more than once left to take responsibility for Church policy – a task he was apparently happy to do – and to defend QAB, but after October 1938 the voice of QAB's faithful champion fell silent. His most oft-repeated assertion was that tithepayers' agitation only came about in times of agricultural depression. That might well have been true in times gone by, but this twentieth-century agitation had stemmed from a sense of injustice.

By 1936 the depression in the country was gradually receding, but farming was still in a low state and even where marginal profits had been restored there was no extra capital for investment. AG started receiving letters again from distressed tithepayers, such as Basil Jude from Attleborough, Norfolk:

> *'I am now being fined sharp for tithe which is in arrears and I cannot possibly pay the tithe which are in arrears at present. The Bailiff came to see me yesterday and he said it must be paid next week or he must distrain my cows for same. Is there not any way to stop this in the new Tithe Act where a person can prove that he has not got the money to pay these arrears off. I should be much obliged if you could let me know if there is any way out as it will be serious to me to have my cows sold.'*

A year later there were distinct rumblings of war beyond the tithe war, when David Lloyd George wrote in the *Farmer & Stock-Breeder*:

> *'In addition to an annual increase in the ordinary annual estimates for Army, Navy and Air Force of £35,000,000, we have put our signatures to a blank cheque for a nameless amount, said to be £300,000,000, for*

a special programme of defence expenditure within the next three or four years ... Let us have national defence by all means. But the most vital of all defences is a sure food supply. If our Government really thinks there is a growing peril of war, serious enough to justify the spending of vast sums on defences, it should rank food production among those defences, alongside the Navy and Army and Air Force, as of at least equal importance.'

By the end of 1938 competition to fill the political void was as strong as ever: Mosley was still proclaiming an agricultural policy, although there were only slivers of lingering support for him in the countryside. Disillusionment had set in with regard to his future role in the nation's political life and while farmers still looked in vain for governmental support for agriculture, they knew realistically that it would not come from Mosley or the BUF.

All Farmers and those interested in Agriculture are urge[d] bring their wives, families and workers

On Wednesday, 1st February to LOND[ON]

THE CENTRAL HALL, WESTMINSTER

(Close to the House of Commons) has been booked. There will be room for al[l]

Apply for Railway Tickets (from Ipswich), including Hall Tickets (5/- post fr[ee]
V. de A. SHEPHERD, Shottisham Hall, Woodbridge. 'Phone Shottisham
A. B. JOHNSTON, 6 Princes Street, Ipswich. Phone Ipswich 3670: or fro[m]
Suffolk Farmers' Union Branch Secretaries.

Fair Play for Agriculture NOW !

Support the FARMERS'

Protest Marc[h]

Wednesday, 1st February, 1939,

Through the City of London with Bands and Banners, to a

MASS MEETING

Central Hall, Westminster,

Commencing 2.30 p.m.

A Deputation representative of all Agricultural Interests wil[l] be sent from the Meeting to the Prime Minister.

Special Train leaves Ipswich 11.5 a.m.
Arrives back Ipswich (about) 9.15 p.m.
Special Fare, 4s. 9d.

Films of the March will be taken and shown at the Hall, if possible, and afterw[ards] throughout the country. Refreshments can be obtained at the Central Hal[l]
Subscription List open at Barclays Bank, Princes Street, Ipswich. Acknowledgm[ents] will be made in the *East Anglian Daily Times.* Any surplus to Royal Agricu[ltural] Farmers' Benevolent Society.

The main political parties were, though, still largely uninterested in the desperate plight of rural England and were deaf to the warning cries coming from the run-down and neglected farms. Nor, apparently, could they detect the despondency of those who earned their living from farming voiced by Doreen Wallace in one of her many articles in the *East Anglian Daily Times*:

'... those were the days when farmers headed the weekly list of bankruptcies in the Gazette and when some were found hanging in their barns.'

In July 1938, Neville Chamberlain made his famous speech at Kettering, the *Sunday Express* reporting:

'"Why should we grow our food," asks the Premier. He believes we should let other countries feed us. "The idea that we can be starved out in a war is fallacious. We can depend upon the Royal Navy and the Mercantile Marine to keep open our trading routes and to enable us to import our food and raw materials indefinitely."'

Minister of Agriculture, W S Morrison tried to play down the effects of the speech, but it was clear that the Government was prepared to sacrifice hard-won rural votes for the more easily satisfied and accessible urban constituencies. Morrison gave the game away by commenting that the Prime Minister was '... *a townsman like ninety per cent of his fellow citizens*'.

Morrison himself came under attack in the press and was labelled 'The Man Who Failed'. What sort of return was the country getting for the £5,000 it paid W S Morrison, who became Minister in October 1936 and who had presided over the running-down of the nation's agriculture? During the 506 days of his administration over 200,000 acres of land had gone out of cultivation, 400 acres a day having been 'let go', and 13,600 agricultural workers had left the land. The need for wider debate on agriculture, its future and purpose was not to be fully appreciated for another sixty years.

The Labour Party's origins gave it an uneven preponderance of urban support, but within the Party there was a late 1930s move to target the rural seats, although it was relatively short-lived and made ineffective by the outbreak of war. In 1937 the *News Chronicle* reported the Labour Party Conference and highlighted a call from the new Chairman of the Party, George Dallas, that they should fight to get a foothold in the rural areas:

> '*[George Dallas] announced that the Party was alive to the necessity of winning the rural seats if it was ever to secure a majority in the House of Commons, and he estimated that today between 40 and 60 purely rural constituencies would have to be won. This problem was to be tackled at once. A new committee, under the chairmanship of Lord Addison, former Minister of Agriculture, would begin the task on Tuesday.*'

AG, ever apolitical on the subject of tithe, was in correspondence with the Labour Party's Agricultural Policy Committee and often attended meetings with the Secretary, Arthur Greenwood MP, at Transport House. As leader of the NTA he was still masterminding events supported as ever by the faithful F R Allen, the Rashes, Makens Turner, Philip Butler and the delegates of the Welsh Committee, but the state of the nation's agriculture was becoming so serious that tithe was a minority issue. He and others profoundly disagreed with Chamberlain's Kettering speech and began to press the NFU to make a stand. However, as always, he stood almost alone within that organisation and later wrote:

> '*Within eighteen months of [Chamberlain's] speech German submarines were sinking our food ships in the Atlantic and we farmers were called upon for the second time to stand between this country and starvation. During*

that summer I paid a short visit to Czechoslovakia, together with about a dozen East Anglian farmers. We went at the invitation of one of our sugar beet seed growing farmers. Everywhere we went, men were in uniform. It was very disturbing. We saw plenty of work going on on the farms but most of this was being done by women. At home, British agriculture had just about reached its lowest ebb. I told the Executive when reporting on my experiences that on my return I had seen more derelict land between Dover and London than during the whole of the time we had spent on the Continent. Certainly many of those engaged in our industry were nearing the end of their tether.'

Just exactly whose idea the 1939 London March was remains largely a matter of opinion, but while many laid claim to it being Mosley's there were similar claims from other parties. The British Democratic Party, sub-titled 'The Party of Tomorrow!', claimed the initiative in agitation against the Government's lack of land policy by pointing to the millions of idle acres, the continued depopulation of the countryside, the huge imports from foreign markets, the bankruptcy of farmers and the low wages of farm workers. In a pamphlet entitled *The Land Flares Up!* the BDP stated:

'... as a result of the BDP's propaganda, town workers began to take an interest in the land problem for the first time in their lives ... Major Hammond Foot, in charge of the BDP agricultural policy, was continually in touch with leaders of the National Farmers' Union ... East Anglia showed the greatest initiative in organising protests against the Government's failures, and farmers and farm workers there decided to organise a protest march to London for February 1st, 1939.'

According to the BDP, it was they who booked the Westminster Central Hall – where the meeting was eventually held – in liaison with Victor de Appleby Shepherd. It was true that de Appleby Shepherd was one of the chief organisers of the March, though his association with right-wing splinter groups was played down. Even the BDP agreed:

'The co-operation of the Fascists was refused by the march leaders and the march was agreed as a non-political demonstration.'

Fascist supporters also claimed that the March was inspired by Mosley's speech to farmers in Fakenham, Norfolk in November 1938, when he said that they should take their message to London. At the Central Cinema on 20 November he told farmers that Great Britain *'... should mind her own business and let other nations mind their own'.* Exploiting their fears over the increase in imported products, he commended to them a policy that put British farming first, the Empire farmer second, and the foreign farmer nowhere.

In Ipswich the following week, Mosley repeated an offer he made at Fakenham: he would send ten Blackshirts to march with every farmer. It was reported in the local press that Suffolk, Norfolk and Lincolnshire farmers would be accompanied by BUF members in London, Mosley urging:

'I suggest you in Suffolk go to London and march ... Agitation is the only way in which you can get things done ... You never get anything without agitation.'

At a dinner given at the Great White Horse Hotel, Mosley addressed over 200 farmers and landowners from Suffolk and north Essex, saying:

'British Fascism has no sympathy with a system which allows the tithe burden to be dumped upon the farming community. It's like asking the City of London to pay for the Army. If you want a National Church then the whole nation must pay for it.'

He urged farmers to support his view that British people should be given the opportunity to use British goods and eat British food:

'The whole aim of our system is to give to the British people for the first time in their lives the power to consume the goods which the British people produce.'

Asked what they could do to make Government take notice Mosley said:

'Go to London, where they live, and make a row.'

Scotland Yard took Mosley's pledge to send Blackshirts to join the march seriously and AG later wrote:

'When we arrived at Liverpool Street a gentleman patted me on the shoulder and said he was from Scotland Yard. The fact was that the Fascists had been some bit of trouble. They wanted to claim credit for suggesting the March. The detective said he understood I was the leader and that he was instructed to act more or less as my bodyguard, and if he was not always at my side, I need not worry. He would keep within a short distance. Photographs of the march revealed that he kept his word as he appeared in most of them, clearly indicated by his light overcoat and white silk wrapper.'

In fact, the bodyguard had little to do, although police did have to contend with a number of BUF members who joined the march. Neville Stanley was quoted in the *Morning Advertiser*:

'Mr Neville Stanley, chairman of the committee, administered a rebuke to the Fascists who had been particularly vocal during the proceedings,

East Anglian farmers arrive at
Liverpool Street Station for
the London March.

when he said "Some of you may have political views we don't agree with. Well, keep them out of this".'

Jill Goodwin, whose father W P Slater farmed at Stansfield in west Suffolk, was on the march as a young twenty-one-year-old, and remembers:

'My eldest brother and I joined the march train at Ipswich and alighted at Liverpool Street station ... The Police officers who accompanied us were all hand-picked country boys who had volunteered for the chance to see their old friends. One confided to me that they knew we should all behave well and their principal job was to prevent the Blackshirts from causing trouble as they tried to join the procession. They were eventually ejected from the Central Hall at the meeting which followed the March.'

Predictably, the NFU Executive was opposed to the march in spite of the huge strength of feeling shown by a meeting held during January in Ipswich. MPs Edgar Granville, Captain F F A Heilgers, W Ross Taylor, P C Loftus and Colonel H W Burton were on hand to give support, as were J Holt Wilson and Charles Banbury, representing the CLA, members of the Suffolk NFU, and S C Grimwade (President of the Ipswich Chamber of Commerce) in the chair. A Protest March Committee was formed and arrangements put in hand for the London March to take place on 1 February. Chairman Neville Stanley, of Felixstowe, said:

'The response to our appeal has been so colossal that we have the question of limitation of numbers under consideration.'

NFU Headquarters were horrified. At a meeting of the Parliamentary and Publicity Committee held at the end of January it was reported:

'.. [it was] made quite clear that the Council of the Union was giving no support to the proposed march and demonstration. The News Sheet item stated that the Council shares the view of the Norfolk County Branch Executive that it would be inconsistent to join such a demonstration whilst the Government are about to confer with the Union and determine what action shall be taken to restore agricultural prosperity. After some discussion, Mr H Morgan proposed that we do not in the circumstances, support our Suffolk friends. This was duly seconded and carried unanimously.'

Charles Joice of Fakenham also wrote to the newspapers:

'I should be glad if you will allow space for some comments on the suggested march in London by Norfolk farmers. This should not take place. Mr Chamberlain has given an assurance that whatever legislation *is necessary shall be brought into effect as soon as a conference has arrived at a result. This may sound like a repetition of past promises – it is something quite different.'*

So far as the farm workers were concerned, the unity of 1936 had not been preserved, and although NUAW members did go to London it was not in the same spirit or with the same purpose. Early in 1939 George Dallas withdrew from a meeting of the Suffolk NFU and sent an open letter to the press:

'I regret very much indeed that I am compelled to cancel my engagement ... the Resolution which is being submitted to the meeting calls for a united protest to impress upon the Government the necessity of doing something to achieve a measure of prosperity in the agricultural industry ... but find that the NFU, both locally in Norfolk and nationally, have officially put up a candidate in East Norfolk against the Labour candidate, who has been in the field for several years ... the NFU has decided officially to fight this splendid champion of agriculture and agricultural labour.'

In order to free some of his time AG handed over the Presidency of the the NTA to Doreen Wallace and began to concentrate on the wider farming issues and local politics. He raised the matter of the London March at the NFU's Annual Meeting, giving them one last chance to support the protest. The organisers, he said, had publicly distanced themselves from the Fascists, if that was what was worrying them, and were anxious that the Union should change its mind and take part. It did not, and the organisers decided to go ahead with the march, Union or no Union.

Anxious to claim credit for the march, the BUF put out a poster saying:

'Farmers!
You have been doped!
By the Tory bosses of the NFU.
The Tory Party is now a sub-branch of the City of London.
Do you want the NFU to be a sub-branch of the Tory Party?
If so, good-bye to British farming.
If not, say good-bye to some of the leaders of the NFU.'

However, while the Union Executive opposed the march, the members were very much for it. In his autobiography, AG wrote:

'The Committee suggested February 1st, but I visualised a number of farmers and their wives turning out into a London fog or heavy rain, and expressed my doubts. "If we get a fine February," they said, "the corn drills will be getting to work and then nothing will induce farmers to leave their fields for London."

'So February 1st it was, and the weather fortunately quite good. We had hired a band consisting of London unemployed workers who were all too plentiful at that time and they led the procession which started from Tower Hill. The 'Farmer's Boy' seemed to be one of their favourite items which received much repetition.'

This was a very different march to that of 1936. Then it had a single, unifying issue – tithe. Now it was more to do with the run-down state of the industry and how farmers would meet the challenges brought on by the possible cessation of food imports. Even as war approached Chamberlain still saw no reason to show support for home agriculture.

Victor de Appleby Shepherd and Neville Stanley made the arrangements and on the morning of the march hundreds of farmers congregated at train stations across the Eastern Counties, bound for London. The London City and Metropolitan Police were consulted and said that they would only allow a few hundred marchers, not the two or three thousand planned. Eventually it was agreed to limit the numbers and to disperse into small groups when they got to the Methodist Central Hall, since it was so close to the House of Commons. But at the very last minute, the March of Protest had to be amended. AG wrote:

'It was on the Sunday morning previous to the March that I received rather a shock in the form of an early telephone call from the Press Association. In fact I was in bed at the time. Had I heard the news, said my caller. What news, I replied. Neville Chamberlain has asked his lawyer Minister of Agriculture, W S Morrison, to resign and has replaced him with Sir Reginald Dorman-Smith.

'"My word!" I said, "that's really splendid news."

'Yes, said my pressman, but what is to happen to your protest march now?

'I was barely awake and it really made me scratch my head. I couldn't consult members of my Committee, and in fact arrangements were

already made with the Railway and tickets sold. Suddenly I had what some people would call a brainwave. I can assure you the march will take place, I told him, but with this difference. Instead of being a march of protest it will be a march of triumph.'

And so it was: it was duly reported in the national dailies and many local papers, although the *Daily Express* got its wires crossed and reported that the march had been cancelled. The *Daily Herald* said:

'The East Anglian countryside was brought to London yesterday when, carrying sheaves of corn and shepherds' crooks, sprigs of wheat in their hats, more than 1,000 farmers and their men came up to plead agriculture's cause. There were ruddy-faced youths thinking of the future and old, grey-haired men with stout sticks, thinking of the past – all marching together through the City and West End.'

The *News Chronicle* said:

'Something unusual in processions went through London yesterday. Farmers from Suffolk, Norfolk and elsewhere, many of them in working clothes, marched from Tower Hill to Temple Gardens, then attended a meeting in the Central Hall, Westminster. They carried banners and posters, and were accompanied by a band. "Justice for the Land", "Save Agriculture" were some of the slogans. And each wore an ear of wheat in his buttonhole or hat.'

The *East Anglian Daily Times* said:

'Co-operating with Suffolk farmers, hundreds from Norfolk and Essex, the home counties, as well as many from Cornwall, Devon and Somerset, made the great demonstration a complete success. A special train was run from Ipswich, which carried a strong contingent from Norfolk ... who joined the special at Colchester and journeyed to Liverpool Street. The train, which was only arranged to carry 800, landed about 1,000 at Liverpool Street.'

A few days beforehand AG had telephoned Reginald Dorman-Smith, whom he knew well from years of NFU committees, to convey his congratulations. He and Neville Stanley went to Whitehall to discuss the proposed March of Triumph. Sir Reginald gave his approval and confirmed that he was to speak as Minister for the first time in the Commons the same afternoon.

Despite the misgiving of George Dallas, a representative from the NUAW (Mr Frost of Walton-on-the-Naze) joined the speakers on the platform. The *Lincolnshire Echo* said:

'Justice for the Land' – the band lead farmers on the 1939 London March. The Scotland Yard detective can be seen on the left of the picture wearing an overcoat and white scarf.

(Above) (Left to right) Joyce Jarrold, Mrs M E Cooper, Janet Cooper and Jill Goodwin (née Slater).

(Opposite) Part of the meeting in Westminster Central Hall.

> 'Among the marchers was a party of unemployed farm workers who were included at the special request of an 81-year-old London woman sympathiser who donated £30 to the fund. "The condition that she made was that some of the money should be used to enable unemployed farm workers to go and we had no difficulty in making up that party," said Mr Stanley.'

AG, Captain Morris (a past NFU President), J O Steed (solicitor) and Doreen Wallace were on the platform. NFU member Mr E Batten represented East Sussex. Those counties who could not send men sent telegrams of support, including one from farmers in Anglesey. At the close of his address, AG quoted from a poem by Oliver Goldsmith:

> 'Ill fares the land to hastening ills a prey
> Where wealth accumulates, and men decay;
> Princes and Lords may flourish or may fade -
> A breath can make them, as a breath has made them;
> But a bold peasantry, their country's pride,
> When once destroyed, can never be supplied.'

As AG ended the quotation the audience rose as one body and cheered. In his autobiography he wrote:

'It was a really wonderful meeting and one of the proudest, if not THE proudest, moments of my life ... On reflection, after all these years, this story of one day's happenings in London reads almost like a fairly tale.

I have in my possession a very large book containing hundreds of press cuttings reporting that day's proceedings, with many illustrations and excellent photographs.'

In the House of Commons, while farmers were marching on London, Sir Reginald sat with the outgoing Minister of Agriculture and listened to what the *Daily Express* called *'one of the finest appeals ever made for agriculture in the House of Commons'*. It was made by Sir Percy Hurd, the Conservative MP for Devizes, who began:

'We have seen a melancholy procession of Ministers of Agriculture. The new Minister has special knowledge of farming which was denied to his predecessors. I should say that any man who can drive that team at Bedford Square (the headquarters of the National Farmers' Union) so successfully that he was called to the chair for two years in succession is a man of mark.'

After the speech a debate took place on a private motion by Sir Percy urging that in the national interest and as part of national defence, producers should be guaranteed a level of remuneration high enough to cover the costs of efficient production and of improved wages and conditions for agricultural workers involving a regulation of imports. All the newspapers agreed that Sir Percy, *'a small but highly determined man'*, spoke with a vehemence and conviction that reached an unusually large attendance for a private member's motion. Certainly it was the speech of his life.

AG wrote:

'All our dreams of a new agriculture emerging as a result of our efforts in 1939 were soon to be shattered. Later in the year came the declaration of a Second World War. No need then to concern ourselves with the control of food imports. Every ounce of food had to be screwed out of our sadly neglected land.'

As war approached the new Minister of Agriculture pledged government support and in December 1939, Sir Reginald wrote in the *Farmer & Stock-Breeder*:

'I want to take this opportunity of once again assuring our home producers that my every good wish goes out to them in the tremendous task which

'Save Agriculture': AG Mobbs on the 1939 London March.

they are tackling ... On December 14th I outlined in the House of Commons the general policy which the Government had decided to adopt to forward the home food production campaign – a policy which will, I am sure, indicate clearly the spirit in which we are tackling the problem and which will leave no doubt that the Government, for their part, are sparing no effort to ensure that the great resources of this country in the matter of food production are used to the full.'

A few months after the London March, NFU Headquarters were persuaded to arrange a conference of thirty-six counties to consider the operation of the 1936 tithe legislation. A resolution was unanimously accepted:

'That in the opinion of this conference, the Tithe system should be abolished at the earliest possible moment. To that end the conference urges the Council to set up an ad-hoc committee of the Parliamentary Committee to prepare the case for submission to the Minister of Agriculture and the Chancellor of the Exchequer.'

The resolution was still little more than a statement of policy, but a year later in March 1941 it was embodied in a Memorandum. AG said that it followed closely the aims and objectives of the NTA but by then the Association was barely functioning at all.

At the annual meeting of the St Alban's branch of the NFU in December 1939, an item towards the end of the agenda was entitled 'Tithe Redemption Annuity'. A letter from Headquarters giving notice of a resolution, passed by the Suffolk branch, was before the meeting. There were to be many such notices, as indeed there had been since the early 1930s, but for the moment farmers had other things on their minds. It was recorded in the minutes:

'[The tithe resolution] was allowed to lie on the table on the proposition of Major Barclay, seconded by Mr F Vigus.'

~ o ~

Chapter 10

THE FINAL STAND

'Dear Mrs Rash ... One of our tithepayers has received a letter from the solicitor to the Tithe Redemption Commission informing him that it is intended to garnishee debts due to him unless he can within seven days satisfy the Commission that the non-payment of tithe rentcharge and annuity by him is caused by conditions attributable to the present war. The solicitor does not say what debts it is proposed to garnishee, but I think it most likely that they are sums due or accruing due from the Milk Marketing Board or on account of Corn Quota. I dare say that this sort of procedure will be favoured by the Commission in the near future, as the Government have guaranteed prices and markets for next year, so that the Commission can quite easily ascertain from other Government departments particulars of sums to be paid to farmers under the various Defence of the Realm schemes.'

F R Allen to Doreen Wallace
Letter dated 9 November 1939

BY THE MIDDLE OF 1939 the size, functions and personnel of the NTA had changed, although the stalwart F R Allen was still at work in his Canterbury office. From January 1939 onwards he addressed correspondence to the new President, 'Mrs Rash'. Although still as committed as ever, he had to remind her that he had also to attend to his regular work in order to get a living. He corresponded regularly with the Tithe Commission requesting clarification on the many unclear interpretations of the Tithe Act for individual tithepayers. The claims for remission, together with anomalies that arose out of derelict or non-agricultural land classifications, were a particular headache. As late as 1952 he was still corresponding with the Tithe Redemption Commission and fighting the cause of the tithepayer.

Often Doreen would send AG a copy of F R Allen's letters:

'Here are two letters from Mr Allen which you might be interested to see ... I never know what to say to Allen that will be of any help to him, short of going to law, which I cannot authorise because there's no money for it. He gets on just as well on his own, and I can only tell him to carry on. Evidently they are having more trouble in Kent than we have had as yet, or else our Suffolk people have given up fighting and are paying without telling us!'

Although the links between the Eastern Counties and Kent were weaker than previously, Roderick Kedward's ability to lead from the front, both as NTA President and as tithe protagonist, was mirrored by Doreen Wallace in 1939 when the Wortham farms once more made the front pages. There was acceptance among tithepayers that the Tithe Act of 1936 was the final word on the subject from Government, but the insidious bankruptcy clause was deeply resented. The NTA agreed that a high-profile example had to be made, and who better than Doreen? She wrote:

'By its terms there was a 17% reduction in the annual payments. This satisfied non-farming landowners, and also a number of those farmers not burdened with high corn land tithe. These people ceased from further agitation. Those of us who believed that to support a sectarian church by a land tax regardless of the religious beliefs of the payers was illogical to the point of ridicule were not satisfied.'

She might well have crossed swords with F R Allen on her stance, which seemed to have turned from a balanced claim of injustice to one of outright attack on the Church. There is no doubt that she was by no means alone in condemning the governmental hand over of the capital sum to the Church, but by 1939 – whatever she or anyone else might have thought – what was done was done. The job in hand, as F R Allen saw it, was to mitigate the effects of the Act and continue fighting for an earlier end to annuities than the proposed 1996. The role of the Church had, as predicted, receded although the rural clergy were grappling with the effects of reduced livings. Their role in country parishes was never to hold the old authority again. The days when the local parson held sway over parish affairs were gone and the wider power and influence of the State Church was fraying at the edges. Like farming, the Second World War put a temporary stay on public debate on the role of the Church. Doreen wrote:

> '*We dourly pay, wondering why a church with capital assets of £600,000,000 (six hundred million, for those who are bad at counting noughts) needs to tax the land, when the Roman Catholic church and all the non-conformists manage on their own, often paying tithe as well if they own land. England alone pays tithe. Our European so-called brother farmers got rid of it long ago, by not paying, or by buying it out on very favourable terms (Denmark) or by having a bloody revolution as in France in 1798. The English farmer is at a disadvantage compared to any other farmer in the world, in respect of being compelled to pay a land tax for the support of religion. Those who are happy to see Royal weddings, christenings and funerals conducted by the Church of England, the 'National Church', might ask themselves why they are not all compelled by law to pay for it. Should not the whole nation be taxed for the National Church? Alternatively, it is logical for those outside the 'C of E' to regard it as a sect, and wonder why it cannot be maintained by its adherents, as the other sects are. Neither view suggests that taxing the land for religion is sensible in modern times, though taxation may have been the sole resource of Christians in AD 970.*'

Some years later she wrote to AG's daughter-in-law, Thelma Mobbs:

> '*I am a Scot, there is no tithe in Scotland, we do not have bishops living in palaces and dressed like old women. Yet no one can call the Scottish Church irreligious – it is just anti all the silly expense of public show which Jesus of Nazareth never had. (I am not religious now, but I have a bit of brain still.) The curse of Churches (all sorts) is to feel that they have to be organised in order to get money for putting on a show. Especially the RCs and the C of Es. People of good will who felt kindly towards each other could get together for ten times the beneficial work of 'the Churches'. They would find this out if they read their Bibles.*'

(Thelma Mobbs was well-versed in the subject of tithe, having been a patient listener to AG for many years and whose 'baptism of fire' into the Mobbs family was a lecture on tithe when her future husband brought her home to meet his parents for the first time!)

On 20 July 1939 tithepayers made their final stand led by their third and last President. After months of court wrangling, Doreen decided to test the bankruptcy clause. The *Eastern Daily Press* announced:

> 'Wortham, which has long been the storm centre of the tithe resistance movement in East Anglia, was the scene of a big demonstration yesterday, following a tithe bankruptcy sale at Wortham Manor of the furniture and other effects of Doreen Wallace, the novelist wife of Mr R H Rash.'

Doreen wrote:

> 'Since I could afford out of my other earnings to take financial risks which farmers could not, I decided to test whether the Act would be pushed to its extreme. I refused to pay and was made bankrupt. I proved that no farmer could be advised to take this ruinous course. But the sale of all my household goods on our lawn, in summer 1939, was the best publicity ever. The coverage by Press, Radio and Cinema of the sale in the presence of well over a thousand farmers from all the affected counties was superb.'

The sale was attended by tithepayers from Norfolk, Suffolk, Essex and Cambridgeshire, together with representatives from Kent, Dorset, Worcestershire, Oxfordshire, Wiltshire, Hampshire, Sussex, Somerset, Shropshire, Devon, Berkshire and Cornwall. Veteran campaigner A W Waddell from Kent was there, as were F R Allen and another long-time campaigner, Sam Johns from Cornwall. Before the sale Doreen took the press on a tour of her house, stripped bare of all its contents and furnishings. The *Eastern Daily Press* reporter confirmed:

> 'Mrs Rash conducted our representative through the 13 almost empty rooms of the old Manor House. All her belongings, including choice pieces of furniture, Georgian silver, framed photographs of her children, her typewriter – with which she has typed her novels – and her bed were listed for the sale. Mrs Rash remarked, "I am wondering where I am going to sleep tonight." She added that the Official Receiver seized the practically new car when she was in Ipswich and

(Above) Auction catalogue from Wortham sale, 1939.

(Below) Bill from auctioneers to AG.

drove her home in his own. The car was sold privately for £130.'

The Manor grounds were festooned with posters bearing slogans proclaiming 'Tithe – 160 millions in 60 years – the Government's tax on food', 'Tithe rent-charge or tithe annuities, a muck heap by any other name stinks as bad', and 'Land crippled by tithe for three generations – Will your grandson be free of tithe?'.

Inside was a display of photographs and memorabilia showing previous distraint sales. Had it not had a serious intent, the day could have been mistaken for the annual fete. A marquee was erected on the lawn from which Clement Gaze of local auctioneers, Thos Wm Gaze & Son of Diss, directed the bidding. He addressed the crowd:

> *'Nobody here regrets the position we are in today more than I. To me it is rather a sad job. Mrs Rash is prepared to make sacrifices in the interests of tithepayers that she would not call upon anyone else to do. She is fighting for a principle. This unfortunate bankruptcy is the result of that and the reason for the sale. Everything in the house has to be sold and paid for today ... Someone has to sell these things, and Mrs Rash expressed a wish for it to be done by someone locally rather than someone from away.'*

As in days gone by, AG (still Chairman of the Suffolk TPA) bid for each lot until the required amount was reached. When he bid for, and got, the first lot – two garden seats – loud cheers came from those crowded into the marquee. The sale realised £204 18s and, added to what had been received from her car, covered the debt plus costs. Afterwards the gathering held a protest meeting and a collection towards the sale costs raised £45. A procession was made to the Tithe Memorial at the Rashes' Hall Farm. F R Allen made a short speech and Doreen Wallace laid a wreath of field peas on the monument in memory of the fifteen cattle and 134 pigs seized in 1934.

Eighty-year-old Harry Roseveare, of Ashford, spoke on behalf of the tithepayers of Kent and as Vice Chairman of the NTA. He paid tribute to Doreen Wallace and referred to two tithe bankruptcy cases in Kent. The first was A W Waddell, who had been sold up for tithe three times and was the first farmer to be made bankrupt in Kent. The second was a sick man in a sanatorium who had a wife and young family. They were to be turned out of their home farm and lose their means of livelihood for tithe arrears. He said:

> *'I move that this mass meeting of tithepayers calls upon the Government immediately to amend the present tithe legislation, which is an insult to British justice.'*

'Homes are sold up for tithe' – Doreen Wallace chaired by supporters in 1939 after the bankruptcy sale at Wortham Manor.

Immediately after the sale Clement Gaze wrote to AG:

'I enclose detailed receipts for your purchases today. I think Mrs Rash may feel gratified at the way her friends turned up to support her. I am very much obliged for your help which I think went a long way towards the orderly nature of the proceedings.'

This was the last time that tithepayers' protest hit the headlines. In the presence of many of the old campaigners, their enthusiasm for the fight hardly dimmed by ten years of war, a bonfire was lit beneath a gallows from which hung a copy of the 1936 Tithe Act. Had Roderick Kedward been there he would have stood proud and stubborn on a farm cart, berating the perpetrators of injustice and rallying the troops. His spirit, and that of the thousands of tithepayers in England and Wales who still carried the burden of tithe, was unbroken but as frustrated as ever by what they saw as blatant injustice.

Twenty years later, Doreen Wallace wrote:

'The Tithe War was toil, tears and sweat – until Hitler made a worse one including blood, and we all had to submerge our own troubles to save our country. We tithepayers had to be careful, under AG's guidance, to keep the peace, bash nobody, use no guns, our only weapon publicity. And how right he was. Publicity was a most effective weapon, until Hitler stole it!'

Within weeks of the Wortham bankruptcy sale the tithe war more or less ended. The following March the Executive Committee of the Suffolk NFU prepared a memorandum of individual cases of tithe distress for submission to Headquarters. Sixty-five individual cases were compiled from individual tithepayers but were typical of many more which were excluded in order to keep the document within reasonable limits. It showed farmers being asked to pay tithe at the very time they were also being asked to increase productivity. This meant not only capital investment but also a requirement for greater cash flow for wages and general running costs. Farm buildings and field gates were derelict, hedges were overgrown through years of neglect, ditches were in urgent need of cleaning out and field drainage had lapsed dramatically during the depression years. Farm machinery was in need of repair and replacement, while stock and seed had to be bought. Where old grassland was being converted to arable, extra finance was not available to those who already had mortgages and overdrafts. Government was expecting increased home food production to occur with no investment other than wishing. As Sir Percy Hurd told the House of Commons in his speech in February 1939:

> *'I am sure the Prime Minister knows that you cannot plough the land by turning things over in your mind.'*

On and on went the instances of farmers being put under severe strain by the Tithe Commission, which pursued tithepayers to practically every court in the land. Again and again, tithe was described as a 'millstone round the

Painting (1941) by Philip Butler of the distraint sale at his farm at Barking in 1936, where some of his livestock was forcibly sold up to pay tithe. In the foreground are some of the leaders of the Suffolk Tithepayers' Association: Lady Eve Balfour, AG Mobbs, Makens Turner and Rowland Rash. (Museum of Rural Life, Stowmarket, Suffolk)

neck of farmers and agriculture'. One farmer lost his flock of Blackface ewes in tithe raids by the Commission, and later his pig herd went too. Another had a visit from the Tithe Redemption Commission officers, who pressed him to pay the £60 owing or lose his stock. In conclusion:

'This Memorandum compiled at the request of Headquarters, strengthens the views held by this County Branch for a very long time, namely that tithe charges constitute an unfair burden on agriculture generally, and more particularly where they relate to those lands which produced heavy crops of wheat at the time of the commutation, but which today are often the least remunerative.

'A year ago this Branch carried out an intensive survey of the parishes comprising the County of Suffolk, where tithe charges average between 6s and 7s per acre. This survey revealed an appalling state of affairs – 15,853 acres of derelict land, 22,800 acres of semi-derelict land, 105,344 acres requiring draining, and 1,232 sets of farm buildings badly in need of repair.

'This Branch is convinced that heavy tithe demands over a period of years have in a large measure contributed to these deplorable conditions. Such a state of affairs constitutes a National Tragedy even in peacetime. How much more is this the case when our country is fighting for its very existence, and when every available acre is required to produce to its maximum capacity. To that end this Branch recently expressed the opinion that the Government would be well advised to order a tithe moratorium for the period of hostilities, and at the same time to drastically amend the present legislation with the object of bringing the anachronistic tithe system to an end at the earliest possible moment.'

No moratorium was granted or ever likely to be granted.

British farmers, notwithstanding the poor state of their industry, raised their game yet again as they did in 1914. On 1 September 1939 Sir Reginald Dorman-Smith was given wide power under the Defence of the Realm regulations and set up the County War Agricultural Executive Committees, known popularly as 'War Ags'. With the country dependent for over 60% of its food on imports, the 'Dig for Victory' campaign was launched and the need for home food production was notched back up to the top of the nation's agenda.

~ o ~

POSTSCRIPT

EVEN DURING THE WAR, when home food production was of national importance, the Tithe Redemption Commission went about its business. The work of re-surveying the 13,000 tithepaying districts went on slowly throughout the war, often held up by construction work and service camps operating on tithed land that made assessment difficult.

In 1940 an Oxfordshire farmer told his TPA how the Commission had taken £270 from his bank account for tithe and the following June grabbed his milk cheque. Other farmers, too, found that the Commission could take money paid to them by the Milk Marketing Board directly from their bank accounts. Money paid out by the Wheat Commission was snatched, as were rents paid on land commandeered by the military in Kent. In 1944 the War Office agreed to divert one farmer's War Compensation payment to the Tithe Commission until a debt of £599 11s 10d tithe arrears was cleared, without discussion with the tithepayer or any investigation into the circumstances.

In 1945 the NFU issued a comprehensive Statement of General Policy in a booklet entitled 'A Policy for the Nation's Greatest Industry' and stated:

'The tithe system operates as a tax upon agricultural production and accordingly the Union argues that amending legislation be introduced to provide for the extinguishment of the system at the earliest possible moment.'

Also in 1945, a Wiltshire farmer over sixty years of age became the first twentieth-century man to be put in prison for tithe arrears. The *News Chronicle* reported:

'The question of tithes, kept in the background by the war, has arisen again. Hundreds of landowners will soon be faced with claims for arrears dating back to pre-war years. Today farmers from Wiltshire, Hampshire and Dorset are driving to Winchester Prison to secure the release of Mr Ernest John Thorne ... who was taken to the prison yesterday in default of

paying £37 7s 6d tithe arrears. The Tithe Redemption Commission took proceedings in Salisbury County Court, and a committal order for 14 days was made in Mr Thorne's absence failing payment by July 19. Yesterday a Bailiff called ... and took Mr Thorne, who was busy harvesting, to Winchester by car.'

Ernest Thorne was a Council member of the NTA, which was still nominally functioning with Doreen Wallace at the helm. Mr Thorne told the *Wiltshire Gazette* that he was treated with every courtesy in prison and when he was not in his cell he lectured the warders on tithes!

Shortly afterwards, a Kent farmer was committed to prison for seven days for non-payment of tithe.

The old warrior, AG Mobbs was himself threatened with prison in 1947. He came before Judge Carey Evans at Lowestoft County Court for tithe worth £1 14s 2d. Judgement had been made the previous November and as the amount had not been paid Mr W Boycott, acting for the Tithe Commission, applied for a committal order. The Judge declined to make AG either 'a martyr or a hero' and said he would find other ways to make him pay. The sixty-year-old veteran campaigner was disappointed: he had fought the tithe war for twenty years *'... and I shall continue to fight until a reasonable measure of justice is meted out to tithepayers,'* he told the Judge.

The case made international news: one of AG's newspaper clippings is from a South African paper, the *Natal Daily News*, which carried the headline 'Farmer Tells Judge to Jail Him, But Judge Says: "A Respectable Citizen Like You – No"'.

Perhaps to encourage AG, a member of the Ashford (Kent) Tithepayers' Association sent him an article from a Bath newspaper concerning a Somerset tithe case of the seventeenth century. One William Goodridge had been a prisoner in the Fleet for thirteen years on account of unpaid tithes and had petitioned the House of Lords to take up his case with the Commissioners of Sequestration. The Vicar of Banwell insisted on pressing his case for the £2 worth of Small Tithe 'because he was entitled by law'. The appeal was dismissed but Mr Goodridge was eventually released from prison. It occurred to many tithepayers in the 1940s that things had barely moved on from 1689, since men were still being sent to prison for non-payment.

In the years following the 1936 Tithe Act there were to be various 'interpretations' and 'adjustments' made by MAFF and the Inland Revenue. Archbishop Cosmo Lang's description of tithe as 'a running sore' proved apt. Every so often headlines would appear in the press asking 'Another Tithe

AG Mobbs leaving Lowestoft County Court in March 1947.

War?', 'Landowners and Tithe – Bill as Indigestible as Ill Conceived' and countless others. One or two tithepayers, including AG, never gave up the fight. Doreen Wallace remembered that he went on having household goods distrained upon for redemption annuities. It was all good-tempered: the County Court judge would say "Our friend Mr Mobbs again?" and a lawn-mower or something would be confiscated. The following day it would be headlines in the papers and invariably AG would get a letter or two from those who remembered the fighting years of the 1930s.

In 1971 AG again made the national dailies when a bailiff with a distraint warrant collected two guns and a silver cup. The cup was one of his prized possessions and had been for almost forty years since he had won the Championship of England and Wales for the best British Friesian bull in the days when the Mobbs' Oulton herd was famous throughout the land.

In 1962 another twist in tithe legislation was embodied in the Finance Act of that year, which compelled immediate redemption of the tithe, of whatever amount, each time land changed ownership. By the terms of the 1936 Act there were still thirty-four years of tithe annuities left and tithepayers were paying well over a million pounds annually. After 1962 the dwindling number of tithepayers felt even more beleaguered and embittered as compulsory redemption could still cause hardship, the cost being approximately seven times the annuity liability.

All during the 1960s and 1970s AG continued to hear from distressed tithepayers from Lancashire and Yorkshire to Cornwall, and from Lampeter to East Anglia and the south east of England. By then many were addressed simply to 'AG', even from men and women who knew him only by repute. He had a long correspondence in 1969, stretching over several months, with a farmer in Surrey whose farm was being sliced in two by the building of the new M3 motorway. The Tithe Redemption Committee had no regard to the disastrous effect that the motorway would have on the farm business, but with AG's help they did finally suspend payments until such time as the compensation money was paid.

The new Farmers' Union of Wales kept in close touch with AG, writing to congratulate him whenever he appeared in the press and updating him on the Welsh fight to hasten abolition which was accelerated in 1969.

In 1970 AG again addressed the Lowestoft County Court in answer to his twentieth court application for the recovery of tithe redemption annuities:

> *'I cannot willingly pay this demand ... You have the right to order distraint on my goods, and if you so choose commit me to prison ... I have with me information received from the House of Lords and the Public Records Office, which I maintain proves conclusively that practically all sections of the community are in law, still liable to tithe payments. Yet we of the land are alone compelled by law to meet that liability. The fact is that the farming community have paid over £1,000 million in tithe in different forms since all other sections of the community have repudiated their legal obligations. It is really a fantastic situation when you and I are equally legally liable to pay tithe, and yet it is your duty to sit in judgement on me and enforce payment if necessary by a prison sentence.'*

A resolution was sent to the Minister of Agriculture in 1972, drawn up by the Suffolk NFU and eleven MPs, asking for immediate legislation for the abolition of tithe. It was unsuccessful.

In the same year a Farmers' Federation was formed in Birmingham, led by Mr Wallace Day. The *East Anglian Daily Times* said:

> *'The Federation, led by the indefatigable Mr Wallace Day, seems not to be a breakaway from the NFU but a ginger group working within it. It is*

the desperate and despairing child born out of the hard times, whose harshness is likely to increase in the coming months. Mr Day has gone so far as to say that there is going to be more distress among farmers this winter than during the pre-war depression.'

Wallace Day and the tithepayers of England and Wales had much in common: they too had tried to fight a cause from within the NFU, with questionable success.

But if the label 'indefatigable' fits anybody, it must surely be F R Allen. In 1951 he was still formulating resolutions for a meeting of a Special Committee on a policy for tithepayers. He pointed to the violations of the 1936 Act and recommended that tithepayers continue pressing for the removal of this 'inequitable tax'. It was, he said again, an intolerable burden. The final letter from F R Allen in the Mobbs Collection is dated 15 March 1952 and was written not from his office in Canterbury but from his home in Blean. He continued to despair of the way in which the Tithe Redemption Commission carried out its ever-changing duties. He ends one of his hundreds, if not thousands, of letters (this only to an anonymous 'Dear Sir'):

'To the best of my observation, the number of those disposed to take an active interest in the matter is small, but I take this opportunity of reminding you that the tithepayers' committee has not met for a long time, and there is some business to clear up. In view of the lack of interest, however, I do not propose to call a meeting unless I receive from the majority of the members a request to do so. Should I receive such a request, I shall, of course be pleased to do what is necessary.'

Over twenty years before, in 1929, he had written to AG saying that he had *'already been fighting tithe for thirty years'*: by the 1950s he would have been fighting it for more than fifty.

When negotiations over the Common Market came into play during the late 1960s, threatening to distance individual farmers from control of their own destinies, the matter of tithe was infinitesimally small – except to those still paying it. It was AG's hope that Europe would 'do' for tithe. The *East Anglian Daily Times* said:

'It is the tragedy of British agriculture that efficient farmers, driven by dwindling incomes and despair can make only angry noises in the impotence of their predicament.'

The rest of Europe, it seemed, had no interest in tithe since, without exception, it had ceased to exist in all countries bar England and Wales, where farmers still paid tithe annuities or were forced to pay by the Courts, year after year. Some hoped that the NFU would call attention to the fact that, as all Europe was free from tithe, it would be in the interests of equality that it should disappear from England and Wales. But although the Union did make certain representations, the reply came back that there was nothing in the Treaty of Rome to justify that line of action. AG wrote to the Minister of Agriculture, the Rt Hon James Prior (later Lord Prior), who replied that he saw no prospect of any change and he had no evidence of any *support from the National Farmers' Union, who would have to consider this change along with other matters which in their view might have a higher priority*.

As his constituency MP, Mr Prior was the patient recipient of numerous late-night telephone calls from AG on the subject of tithe and agriculture-related subjects. AG was never the kind of man who 'sat quietly at the back of the hall', as one contemporary put it.

In a letter to the *Eastern Daily Press* a Norfolk farmer asked:

'I have just received my annual demand for tithe – have our prospective brothers-in-law in Europe received theirs yet? Of course not, their legislators have long since abolished such an archaic injustice. How much longer must British farmers tolerate the indignity of meeting demands which are invalid ... If Mr Heath, Mr Prior and their colleagues are so determined to join Europe then they must not condone this singular outrageous demand, thus enabling Britain's premier industry to compete as a viable entity.'

AG followed this up in the *Farmers Weekly* at the end of 1971 with:

'Britain is the only country where the injustice of tithe payment continues to be enforced ... A few months ago Suffolk farmers were told by a representative from NFU Headquarters that "if the Government were pressed to abolish tithe redemption annuities, they would almost certainly require the industry to foot the bill" ... What utter twaddle! ... Is it not high time we realised that this wretched business could be wiped out with the stroke of a pen ... Has our union so little sense of justice that it can stand by and display such indifference and ignorance?'

Finally, in 1976 the Government gave in. Five lines of print forming Clause 45 of the Finance Bill of 1977 put an end to agricultural tithe (though not rentcharges such as corn rents, corn rent annuities and chancel repairs). After October that year no further notices of compulsory redemption of annuities would be issued. The Inland Revenue press release (17 June 1976) read:

'In reply to the Parliamentary Question from Mr Christopher Price
(Lewisham West): "To ask the Chancellor of the Exchequer what is the
present position on tithe redemption annuities, and whether he will make
a statement" the Minister of State, Treasury, Mr Denzil Davies, today
gave the following Written Answer: "Under the Tithe Act 1936, Tithe
Redemption Annuities are payable until 1996, unless terminated earlier
because the Treasury are satisfied that there are sufficient funds in the
Account to service existing Redemption Stocks and meet the eventual costs
of redemption. Annuities are compulsorily redeemed if the land is sold or
divided ... the Government have decided that steps should now be taken
to speed the extinguishment of Tithe Redemption Annuities. It is proposed
therefore that there should be only two further annuity payments – a
normal payment in October 1976, followed by a final payment in
October 1977, equal to twice the normal payment on the basis of
ownership of land at that time."'

The reason given was that the administrative costs of the scheme had
increased with inflation and it had been decided that steps should be taken to
speed up extinguishment of tithe annuities. It was hoped that by doubling the
final payment there would be sufficient funds to service and ultimately
redeem the outstanding redemption stock. If there was a shortfall it was to be
met by the Exchequer.

Looking at a copy of Percy Millard's Tithe Rentcharge Table for 1926, it is
astounding how complicated and fantastically minute the calculations were during
the hundred years of tithe rentcharge. The practicalities of splitting tithe rental on
one farthing (as was the case in the 1920s) would have been as good a reason as any
for questioning its continuance. The booklet contains such sentences as:

'Table VI – For ascertaining the amount of the yearly payments which, if
accumulated at compound interest at each of the under-mentioned rates
and for each of the under-mentioned periods of years, would be sufficient
to produce an amount equal to the consideration money for redemption
at the end of each such period, respectively.'

AG was ninety years old when in October 1977 he paid his final tithe
demand of £87.28. On the receipt he wrote: Final Payment to end a great
injustice well nigh 4,000 years old.

When he heard the news he wrote a five-page memorandum which began:
'It is with the greatest possible gratification that I read the Treasury
announcement to the effect that the present unredeemed annual tithe

AG Mobbs' final tithe annuity payment in 1977 'to end a great injustice well night 4,000 years old'. In 1964 AG was offered voluntary redemption of annuities in the sum of £658 17s 10d, which were costing £46 2s 5d annually, after yet more 'tinkering' of the Tithe Acts 1936 and 1951.

> *payments, now known as tithe redemption annuities, are to end next year instead of 1996. It is almost unbelievable that this ancient system, for centuries an outstanding injustice, has been continued for well nigh 4,000 years.'*

Not only AG, but also Lady Eve Balfour and Doreen Wallace lived to see the end. They were the last of a dying breed – men and women of ordinary means whose strength of conviction gave them the courage to take on the Establishment in times when unquestioned deference and automatic respect for one's 'elders and betters' ruled supreme. They learned to rise above the intensity of their anger and frustration that their case was not listened to by successive Governments and coped, too, with a burning, unquenchable sense of injustice. Lady Eve 's achievements are widely known and numerous. As a member of staff at the Soil Association headquarters (at Haughley, Suffolk) during the 1970s this author experienced the ripple of excitement when news came that Lady Eve was expected on one of her occasional visits. She took part in the BBC's *Yesterday's Witness* programme, broadcast in 1972, as did AG and the Rashes.

The Tithe Redemption Office (TRO) had, for a small fee, answered postal enquiries about whether or not particular land was subject to other tithe charges (corn rents, corn rent annuities and chancel repairs), but discontinued this after December 1978 and the office closed the following January. There were many tithe anomalies that were not extinguished by the 1936 Act, or by the 1977 Finance Act, and special redemption arrangements

'Guardians of the Corn', a composite painting by P J Butler (in 1941) of Roderick Kedward, AG and Doreen Wallace. (A A Mobbs)

had to be negotiated. In 1973 it was costing almost £300,000 a year to run the TRO, which employed ninety-one staff (there had been over 200 staff in 1965) plus a few ancillary staff in other branches of the department. The new Tithe Records Office operated out of the Inland Revenue offices in Thames Ditton but it, too, was closed in 1981 when all records were transferred to the Public Record Office.

Three permanent reminders of the tithe war still stand: at Elmsett in Suffolk, parishioners walk and drive past the Tithe Memorial daily. As the Westren family planned, it is sited opposite the church entrance as a visible reminder of the harsh, dark days of the 1930s when a family's goods could be sold to pay tithe. Miss Janet Cooper, who still lives in the village, remembers:

> *'I have very vivid memories of the tithe war. We farmed Manor Farm, Elmsett at the time (my family still does) so we were neighbours of the Westrens ... My mother was one of the local farmers' wives who rang the church bells after the failure of the bailiffs to take away the barley stacks ... the Rev Haslewood's reaction to the ringing of the bells was to lock up*

the church, almost unheard of in those days. My father had been churchwarden, but took a rest during the tithe war!'

Miss Cooper, together with her mother and cousin, Joyce Jarrold, went on the 1939 Farmers' March and were pictured in all the national and provincial newspapers. She also remembers:

'There was much bad feeling between the Rev Haslewood and the local farmers. He had come to Elmsett from a mining area, and had no understanding of rural Suffolk and the problems farmers were facing at that time ... and there was a very fiery letter sent to those farmers wives who had rung the bells. I remember my father telling me once there was a feeling that he (the Bishop) would have done better to have ignored the whole thing. By sending such letters he only added fuel to the fire. It made my mother very angry.'

(Above) Elmsett memorial sited opposite the parish church, where the message is more important than the spelling.

(Below) Wortham tithe memorial pictured in the 1940s.

The Wortham monument is covered with lichen and stands on a bank beside the site of the old farmyard from where there is a commanding view across the Waveney valley. It is there to remind those who seek it out of the days when the men of the parish, supported by hundreds of farmers and farm workers from all over England, held off the bailiffs for eighteen days. In 1992 agricultural journalist Herman Simper wrote:

'I met up with Rowland Rash when I joined the Eye NFU Committee ... a nice, quiet, unassuming man was Rash. A fighter and well respected for it ... I had to redeem the tithe when I bought the Depperhaugh Estate at Hoxne in 1968 ... My father's farm at Charsfield had always been tithe-free for some reason unknown to me. But, being a Non-conformist, he was totally behind the campaigners. Perhaps that was easy,

seeing that he had no tithe to pay! ... Many of the farms where we had to pay off the tithe have changed hands two or three times since. Some of the younger farmers (with that outgoing not on the sale particulars) are not aware of what battles there may well have been over that overhead in earlier years. No one should grudge them that. But the Wortham Memorial should remind us of the humiliations suffered by brave, fighting farmers of the 1920s and 30s, seeing their stock or implements forcibly auctioned by what was the Law.'

Doreen Wallace died in 1989, aged 92 (Rowland had died in 1977 only a few weeks after the cessation of redemption annuities). A few months before her death she was writing letters railing against the way farming was going within the EEC and leading a revolt of Diss residents, organising a protest group against the local council who wanted to change the numbers of her and her neighbours' homes. The Eastern Angles Theatre Company brought the story of the Wortham distraints to life in 2001 with Ivan Cutting's play *Tithe War!* which had its premiere that autumn at the Sir John Mills Theatre, Ipswich.

In Kent the Tithe Memorial to Roderick Kedward, erected by the NTA by subscription, stood for many years in a corner of what was once Beechbrook Farm, Westwell, the stage on which much of the Kent protest was performed. It was there that anger and bitterness burst into flames as bonfires devoured the effigies of an Archbishop and a long-dead Queen of England. The money for the monument was raised by the NTA (masterminded by Doreen Wallace) and what funds were left over were donated to the Royal Agricultural Benevolent Institution. The modern landscape of Kent is being radically altered and in 1993 Roderick Kedward's son Philip feared for the monument's safety and

(Above) Kedward Monument, Ashford Market (old site) (Hobbs Parker) and (below) new site.

suggested it be moved to the new Ashford Market, which it was in 1998. So now office workers and visitors to the market can sit beside a beautifully cleaned memorial to the Reverend Kedward, and perhaps wonder what tithe was all about. It was a different Ashford Market where, in December 1932, Kedward had addressed hundreds of placard-bearing farmers at an auction gift sale organised by the Ashford and East Kent TPA. He spoke from an auctioneer's stand, the words delivered with his usual fire and conviction underwritten by his Kentish accent:

> *I want to say emphatically that we are not here in the interests of any party or any religious denomination. We have no quarrel whatever with the Church, and when Sir William Wayland said, the other day, that I was attacking the Church, he never made a greater mistake in his life. I don't want to attack the Church: I attack excessive tithe ... tithe will do more damage to religion than anything else ... you can never maintain a spiritual religion by compulsory payments. You cannot maintain either the Established Church or any other church by the aid of the Sheriff's officer.'*

He urged them to stand together, because the inherent justice of their cause would win through, he said, and it was the spirit of the Men of Kent that would lead the movement for liberty and freedom.

The Kedward Memorial looks right in its new setting and surprisingly contemporary – with its very own water feature!

In the years since 1936 the rural clergy have fared badly and a crisis exists within the Church of England about how it will meet the £12 million shortfall in clergy pensions. Links between church and farm are all but dead, too, since the Church Commissioners now own a mere 125,000 acres of agricultural land. During 1999 sales of church land totalled £27 million, including development land, and the Commissioners acquired, amongst other investments, an indirect interest in the Bluewater Shopping Centre in Kent. In July 2001 *The Times* reported:

> *'Nearly £4 million is to be slashed from the budgets of 13 dioceses in the Church of England, leaving them struggling to pay their clergy.'*

The Church is appealing to worshippers who, they say, must increase giving if current clergy are to be looked after in their retirement. Such news, comments *The Times*:

> *'... could hardly have come at a worse time for parishes. Rural dioceses in particular have seen incomes slump because of foot-and-mouth as regular worshippers are forced to stay at home. Even before foot-and-mouth,*

several dioceses had moved from positions of surplus to barely breaking even, with some in debt.'

Voluntarily tithed income is one remedy – a very different proposition to compulsory tithe – and has proved popular in America with many of the 'new' church congregations. A modern exponent of tithing, Dr R T Kendall writes in his book *The Gift of Giving*:

> *'I doubt that there is a more threatening subject than that of tithing. That which touches our wallets and purses taps a very sensitive nerve ... it is strange how uneasy we feel when the matter of giving emerges. Many of us, however, would prefer to speak of giving than of tithing. Talk of giving makes us nervous but the idea of tithing arouses feelings of hostility in us.'*

The freedom to choose whether or not to tithe was not given to the tithepayers who are the subject of this book, but in 2001 the courage and rightness of their cause was vindicated by the 1998 European Convention on Human Rights. Extraordinarily, in 1994 a notice was served on landowners Gail and Andrew Wallbank demanding that they repair the chancel of the parish church of Aston Cantlow in Warwickshire to the tune of an estimated £95,000. The Parochial Church Council claimed the cost of repairs under the provisions of the Chancel Repairs Act 1932 from the owners (as so-called 'lay rectors') of Glebe Farm, Aston Cantlow. Bruce Dear and Robert Hill wrote in the *Estates Gazette*:

> *'Historically, the rector of a church has been obliged to repair the chancel, a duty supported by the produce of the rectorial property (the glebe) and parish tithes. However, tithes were abolished in 1936, and the duty on the owner of rectorial glebe to repair the chancel has gone. None the less, the liability to contribute to chancel repairs has vested in the lay owners (or lay rectors) of glebe land since the dissolution of the monasteries.'*

With a not inconsiderable measure of disbelief, Andrew and Gail Wallbank heard parts of the sixteenth-century Act of Succession read out in court. Echoes of a past age resounded ominously into the twenty-first century, sending a shiver down the

Andrew and Gail Wallbank in their garden at Carno, mid Wales. (Richard Stanton)

spine of other landowners liable under the 1932 Act. It seemed that the Wallbanks would need to consider selling their property in order to meet the cost of their legal obligations, by now amounting to a staggering £100,000.

In May 2000, the *Country Landowner* reported:

'In 1985, on submissions from the CLA, NFU and others, the Law Commission report condemned the liability as "anachronistic and capricious in its modern application" and argued for its abolition after a ten-year period. However, the Government rejected the proposals, saying that abolition might contravene the European Convention. Once rejected, the Law Commission has confirmed that they cannot raise the issue for review again.'

Following in the footsteps of the valiant tithepayers of the 1930s and 1940s, Andrew Wallbank prepared his own legal defence. Methods of appeal not open to the tithepayers of the inter-war years were employed – namely the 1989 Human Rights Act – and in May 2001, a judge finally allowed the Wallbanks' appeal. The judgement decreed that legitimate taxation in the public interest had to be pursued by means that were not completely arbitrary or out of all proportion to their purpose. The liability for chancel repairs attaching to former rectorial land was entirely arbitrary, and therefore violated the European Convention on Human Rights. In his conclusion the judge said:

'To summarise what has been a long judgement, this appeal succeeds on each of two alternative grounds. The first is that the modern liability of lay owners of what was once the glebe land of a rectory to defray the unmet cost of repairs to the chancel of the parish church is a form of taxation which does not meet the basic standards set by Article 1 of the First Protocol for the protection of citizens' possessions from the demands of the

Cast of Eastern Angles' play *Tithe War!*, premiered in Ipswich in 2001, which dramatised the story of the Wortham distraints.

state, because it operates arbitrarily. The second is that the way in which the common law singles out the owners of such land from other landowners is unjustifiably discriminatory and so contrary to Article 14. By virtue of s.6 of the Human Rights Act 1998 the Parochial Church Council, as a public authority acting otherwise than under the compulsion of primary legislation, may therefore not lawfully recover the cost of chancel repairs from Mr and Mrs Wallbank.'

How those protagonists Roderick Kedward, F R Allen, AG, Doreen and Rowland Rash, Lady Eve Balfour, P J Butler and the thousands of other English and Welsh tithepayers would have devoured the words 'arbitrary tax' and 'legitimate taxation in the public interest'.

The dawn of the twenty-first century sees agriculture plunged yet again into turmoil – the countryside marches, the fuel protests and the harrowing accounts of the prolonged Foot and Mouth outbreak that has dramatically affected rural communities. Newspaper reports read uncannily like those of the 1930s when some of the finest herds of dairy cattle in the country were broken up, firstly for tithe, and secondly when the effects of the new Milk Marketing Scheme came into play. Writing about the sale of the famous Saracen herd of Friesians in Berkshire during the 1900s, the *News Chronicle* reported:

'The invasion of the farmyard by auctioneers and the crowds of dealers, farmers and idle onlookers, for the sale of a herd carefully built up over many years, is one of the tragedies of farming. Cattle, with their pet names, their special mannerisms, and their capacity for large-eyed sympathy, are regarded as valued friends on the farm. I have seen farmers, dairymaids and stockmen weep unashamedly when their favourite cows have been sold under the auctioneer's hammer.'

In 2001 the world saw herds and flocks upended onto funeral pyres, and families appeared on television ashen-faced and the air behind them thick with smoke as they spoke about the sound of slaughterers' guns. All this combines with the wider significance of what was once called the Common Market to raise the ghost of the 1930s depression when the countryside was in revolt.

There are many injustices left in the world to fight, but agricultural tithe is no longer one of them. The effects of the Chancel Repair Act are, though still being challenged. The Aston Cantlow PCC is seeking leave to appeal against the 2001 Judgement.

~ *o* ~

Appendix I
SELECTED CHRONOLOGY

Based on 'A Chronological Review of the well nigh 4000-year-old Tithe System' compiled by A G Mobbs

AD 33 St Matthew 23:23 & St Luke 11.42 'Woe unto you, Scribes and Parisees, hypocrites; for ye pay tithes of mint and anise and cummin, and have omitted the weightier matters of the law, judgement, mercy and faith'.

794 Offa, King of Mercia, made over to the Church (by law) the tithe from his entire kingdom. For the first time, the Church had a civil right, by way of property and inheritance, to enforce tithe as its legal due.

1086 Canute II, King of Denmark and England, martyred by opponents to his laws for the enforcement to pay tithe.

1274 Pope Gregory X decreed that tithe payment be made compulsory throughout Europe.

1547 Henry VIII removes tithe from the Roman Catholic Church, handing its revenue to the new English Church, with some to lay impropriators. Tithe abolished in Scotland. Introduction also of a distinction between Predial (referred to land tithe) and Personal Tithe representing the payment of a tenth of the clear gains of various other sections of the community.

1704 Establishment of Queen Anne's Bounty for the Augmentation of the Maintenance of the Poor Clergy.

1744 Bohun's Law of Tithes defines Personal Tithes: *'For as they arise from the clear gains made by honest labour, art or industry, it will include not only all kinds of trades and manual occupations, but also all other lawful employment and professions of life, whereby any clear gain or profit is made.'*

1779 William Cowper writes *The Yearly Distress, or Tithing Time at Stock in Essex*, published in *The Gentleman's Magazine* in 1783.

1789 Tithe abolished in France without compensation.

1823 An Act allows for the voluntary commutation of tithes in Ireland, followed in 1838 by a reduction of 25 percent. (Tithes finally abolished in Ireland in 1869.)

1825 The Potato Riots took place in the Isle of Man. At the end of the 18th century the increased cultivation of the potato inspired the introduction of a new Potato Tithe.

1836 The Tithe Commutation Act converted the old tenth portion of farm produce, i.e. tithe, and converted it into a compulsory annual cash payment under its new title, Tithe Rentcharge. The value of this payment was to be assessed on the 7-year average price of corn and applied to titheable land in England and Wales. (This Act was amended in 1837, 1840, 1846 and 1878.) A special body, known as the Tithe Commissioners, administered the Act and were given powers to fix an extra tithe on any land newly cultivated as fruit or hop plantations, to be called an Extraordinary Tithe, and a survey undertaken to map and record every titheable asset. The 1836 Bill replaced an earlier one by Lord John Russell and the Chancellor of the Exchequer proposing the abolition of all personal tithes except those on mills and fishing. The Bill passed the Commons but was dropped after a first reading in the Lords. In its place came the Tithe Commutation Act.

1836   Tithe abolished in Spain and in Switzerland where the Grand Council announced a vote to accept total abolition.

1837   Tithe Act allowed landowners to merge tithes on their land, thus extinguishing rentcharge altogether on some farms.

1838   Rebecca Riots occurred briefly, then again between 1842 and 1844, in south-western Wales. Although rioting was in protest against tollgate charges on public roads, it was caused by the wider grievances of agrarian distress and increased tithe charges.

1846   QAB Governors became (under statute and for the first time) the trustees of tithe rentcharge moneys belonging to benefices.

1869   Tithe abolished in Ireland.

1878   The Tithe Act of 1878 allowed redemption of tithe on land required for public purposes, e.g. the building of a church, or place of public workshop, a town hall, school, or other public building. However, on any land which had been charged with a rentcharge exceeding twenty shillings, the Commissioners were entitled to set the redemption charge at twenty-five times the amount.

1882   The Tithe Commissioners assumed the title and functions of the Land Commissioners, later to be absorbed into the newly created Board of Agriculture (1889).

1886   David Lloyd George becomes Secretary of the South Caernarvonshire branch of the newly formed Anti-Tithe League. Riotous opposition to tithe in Wales and the first Anti-Tithe League was formed. The Extraordinary Tithe Redemption Act was passed.

1887   Tithe riots at Mockdre Clwyd, Wales, which were suppressed by military and police. A Welsh Clergy Defence Association was formed. At a public meeting held in Colchester Public Hall on 15 January, farmers and politicians met to consider the Tithe Question. It was reported in the local press that 'the tithe war was breaking out again'. Tithe abolished in Italy and the clergy paid by the State.

1891   A Royal Commission on Tithe Redemption was nominated and a new Tithe Act subsequently passed. Its prime object was to reduce the number of tithepayers by making the landowner responsible for payment, not the occupier. The landowner would collect it from his tenant, thus emphasising that the tithe was a charge on the land itself and not a personal liability of the owner.

1899   Ecclesiastical titheowners exempted from half of their rate burden, the shortfall to be taken up by the general ratepayers.

1903   Tithe abolished in Denmark, the State contributing an amount equal to seven times the annual value of tithe.

1918   Tithe Act provided that for the period 1 January 1918 to 1 January 1926 (i.e. seven years), the value of tithe rentcharge should be stabilised at £109 3s 11d. for every £100 of tithe. The Act also prescribed reversion to a 15-year average of the price of the three cereals (wheat, barley, oats) in 1926.

1922   Commission appointed by the Archbishops to enquire into the Property and Revenues of the Church. Its report (in 1924) recommended the 'remodelling' of the constitution of QAB but no action was taken.

1925   Tithe Act increased £100 of tithe to £109 10s, to be stabilised for a period of 84 years to replace the seven-year period laid down in the 1918 Act. Tithe rentcharge was made payable half-yearly, the 1 April and 1 October to be the due dates. Recovery of unpaid tithe could only be effected through the County Court, and no proceedings were to be instituted until the rentcharge had been at least three months in arrears. The Act imposed on QAB the duty of collection for the whole of the ecclesiastical tithe rentcharge of England, then about £2,000,000 annually.

1930   Kent Tithepayers' Defence Association formed, in opposition to hop tithe.

1931   Suffolk Tithepayers' Association formed, followed by Norfolk and Essex. During the year nearly 50 similar associations were formed in England and Wales, all eventually linking to the National Tithepayers' Association.

1932   Church Assembly asked the Archbishops to appoint a Commission to investigate the relationship between QAB and the Ecclesiastical Commissioners. Roderick Kedward becomes President of the newly formed National Tithepayers' Association.

1934   Tithe Bill dropped and Government appoints a Royal Commission to enquire into the question of tithe rentcharge in England and Wales. Enquiry lasts for 18 months.

1936   A Tithe Bill is introduced which makes tithe rentcharge a personal debt, thus making the tithe-resisting farmers liable to bankruptcy and imprisonment. Although tithe was effectively abolished there were to be redemption payments over a 60-year period, the final redemption date being 1996.

1945   Tithe abolished in the Isle of Man by the Tynwald (the Manx Parliament).

1948   Ecclesiastical Commissioners and QAB merged to form the Church Commissioners.

1960   The functions of the Tithe Redemption Commission, set up in 1936, were transferred to the Board of Inland Revenue.

1962   Tithe legislation embodied in Finance Act compels immediate redemption of tithe rentcharge annuities when land changes ownership.

1976   Government announced sufficient funds in the tithe account to allow full redemption to take place. Administrative costs of collection were high and opposition in some quarters as strong as ever.

1977   Section 56 Finance Act orders final annuities for tithe rentcharge (though not Corn Rents, corn rent annuities or Chancel Repairs liability).

1978   Tithe Redemption Office closed.

1981   Tithe records moved from Board of Inland Revenue to the Public Record Office.

1994   A Parochial Parish Council applies to a Lay Rector for £95,000 under the Chancel Repairs Act 1932.

1996   Date set for final redemption in the 1936 Tithe Act.

2001   Judgement brought in the Supreme Court of Judicature Court of Appeal (Civil Division) upheld an appeal against the respondents in regard to the Chancel Repairs Act 1932.

2009   The original date set in the 1925 Tithe Act for the final extinguishment of ecclesiastical tithe.

Appendix II
SELECTED BIOGRAPHIES

ALLEN, Frank R – Secretary of the NTA and its 'legal' voice (although he was not a lawyer). He was a house agent, tithe expert and rent collector (*Kelly's Directory of Kent 1925-1940*) which gave him an 'insider's' view of the distraint system. From his office at 19 St Margaret's Street, Canterbury he gave unstinting service to hard-pressed tithepayers and travelled extensively to support burgeoning TPAs and to speak at public meetings. He was always known as F R Allen and lived at Damian Cottage, Tyler Hill Road, Blean.

BALFOUR, Lady Eve (1893-1990) – niece of the Conservative Prime Minister, Arthur Balfour, Lady Eve spent the First World War as a bailiff on a farm in Wales, training land girls, and later went to Reading University where she gained a Diploma in Agriculture in 1916. As a tithepayer she became involved in the tithe disputes in the early 1930s and gave evidence to the Royal Commission in 1934. She was also one of a number of farmers whose dairy herd was broken up soon after the Milk Marketing Scheme was introduced. A pioneer of Grade A milk supply and the carton system of distributing it, Lady Eve had lost some of her best cows to tithe distraint sales. She blamed tithe, plus the levies of the Milk Board, for the eventual dispersal of the herd. She formed the Soil Association in 1938 and was awarded the OBE in 1990. As well as being a farmer (at New Bells Farm, Haughley, Suffolk) and activist, she was also a crime novelist, musician and licensed pilot. Her classic work *The Living Soil* was published in 1943.

GOOCH, Edwin (1889-1964) – started life as a blacksmith, moved into printing and then into journalism, becoming Chief Sub-Editor of the *Norwich Mercury* series. '*He was born, lived and died in Wymondham, where 400 years earlier there was the Kett Rebellion against the injustices of the times. The Kett Rebellion was a bloody affair, but Edwin was a peaceable man, and when he espoused the farmworkers' cause he did so peacefully, and perhaps in the long run, more effectively than Kett'* (Wynn, 1993).

Gooch was political agent for George Edwards in 1923, became MP for North Norfolk in 1945 and was President of the National Union of Agricultural Workers from 1928-64. He was a supporter of the anti-tithe movement, but only as a matter of principle. The Union's backing was always conditional on the behaviour of the farmers towards their workers. He was created CBE in 1944 and was a member of the Norfolk War Agricultural Executive Committee.

'*He always believed that only a prosperous agricultural industry could pay the workers well, and was ever ready to spring to the defence of the industry and welcomed the growing prosperity of the farmers. Little enough of this prosperity rubbed off on the workers as was his wish, and although he often expressed disappointment at what the farmers offered in the way of wages, he never changed his idea of co-operating with them'* (Wynn, 1993).

GRANVILLE, Edgar Louis (1898-1998) – elected Liberal Member for Eye, Suffolk in 1929 and remained in the House of Commons until defeated by a Conservative opponent in 1951, switching to the Labour Party the following year. Harold Wilson created him a life peer in 1967 when he took the title Lord Granville of Eye. Edgar Granville became an ardent supporter of the anti-tithe movement and in the 1930s made several tithe remission proposals including a Private Members' Bill in the House of Commons (supported by Dr J H Morris-Jones, Nat Lib, Denbighshire). The main provision of the Bill would have been to reduce the amount of tithe recoverable in the courts and to allow for remission in respect of land washed away or destroyed. In May 1931 he took part in a wide-ranging (but 'almost deserted') Commons debate on agriculture during which Roderick Kedward (Liberal, Ashford) raised the question of tithe rentcharge and George Middleton (Labour, Carlisle) answered in his capacity as First Church Estate Commissioner. Edgar Granville and Roderick Kedward were together frequently on public platforms on the subject of tithe. Granville voted against the Tithe Bill at its Third Reading in 1936.

KEDWARD, Rev Roderick Morris (1881-1937) – born at Beechbrook Farm, Westwell, Kent, where his father William Wesley Kedward had farmed since the 1880s. He was the Liberal MP for Bermondsey West from 1923-24 and from 1929-31 the Member for the Ashford Division. In 1931 he unsuccessfully introduced a Bill for Tithe Remission but lost his seat to Captain Michael Knatchbull later that year. He contested the 1933 by-election (precipitated by Captain Knatchbull succeeding his father as Lord Brabourne) but was beaten by W P Spens. He took over the NTA Presidency in 1932, a post he held until his early death on 5 March 1937.

A Non-conformist Minister, he spent the last 20 years of his life as Superintendent of Great Central Hall, Bermondsey (South London Methodist Mission) as well as owning the family farms in Kent (which carried tithe liability). It was when he began preaching in the local chapels that he met hard-pressed tithepaying farmers. As a man of influence, with an acute nose for injustice, Roderick Kedward took up their cause. He was a small, rotund figure, capable of great indignation, and gave his 'all' to those causes close to his heart. His numerous speeches on behalf of tithepayers were delivered with high emotion in his native Kentish tones and with the ease of a natural speaker.

A monument was erected to his memory by tithepayers in a corner of Beechbrook Farm, which was sold shortly after his death. In 1998 the monument was removed from beside the A20 to Ashford Market at the suggestion of his son, Philip Kedward. Ashford Market was relocated from its town centre site, where it had been situated for 142 years. On 12 May 1998 the New Ashford Market was opened by the Rt Hon the Lord Ampthill.

LANG, Cosmo Gordon (1864-1945) – enthroned as Archbishop of Canterbury in 1928, Cosmo Lang was to preside over the Church of England during the most turbulent years of the tithe dispute. His effigy – dressed in distinctive gaiters and top hat – was burned in Kent during the 1930s, alongside one of Queen Anne. He was inevitably prominent during the parliamentary debates of the tithe bills introduced during his time as Archbishop. He resigned in 1942 and was succeeded by Dr William Temple who held the post for only a short time – both men died in 1945.

MIDDLETON, Sir George (1876-1938) – born at Ramsey, Huntingdonshire. Educated at the Church Elementary School in Ramsey, he started work in the Post Office as a boy. He rose within the ranks of the Union of Post Office Workers and moved to Crewe (where he married). He became editor of the UPOW magazine *The Post* and later the *Postal Clerks' Herald* and *Postal and Telegraph Record*. He became a JP for Cheshire and a member of the Advisory Committee for making magistrates for the Knutsford Division of Cheshire.

After unsuccessfully contesting the Altrincham division of Cheshire in 1918 he was returned MP for Carlisle in 1922. He continued to contest for Labour until his rejection in 1931. In 1929 he was elected Parliamentary Church Estates Commissioner and in 1931 became First Church Estate Commissioner. In 1932 he assumed control of QAB as Chairman of Committees. In 1935 he became joint treasurer of QAB and was knighted in the same year. Tithe was only one of QAB's duties, which included administration of the Parsonage Measure (relating to the sale by an incumbent of a parsonage house) and a group of Acts generally known as the Gilbert Acts which made loans to incumbents for various purposes. He collapsed and died while attending a meeting of the Corporation of Church House in Westminster.

Middleton had his first public fight with A G Mobbs in 1933 and never wavered in his defence of tithe. Although a Labour MP and defender of the rights of the Post Office clerks, he was never able to identify with the tithepayers. He was said to come from 'yeoman stock' (*The Times* obituary, 26 October 1938) but he did not come from farming stock and appeared to carry a prejudice against farmers whom he could only identify as being a privileged class. He grew up in Ramsey, on the edge of the flat, reclaimed fen land, where a fragment remained of the great Benedictine establishment that was founded there in the 10th century. Cromwell was also born in Huntingdonshire and it is tempting to speculate that Middleton was the model for more than one character in Doreen Wallace's novel *Land from the Waters*, the story of the 17th-century draining of the Fens. After a tithe sale at Hall Farm, Wortham in March 1936, an effigy of Queen Anne was burnt along with one of her 'boyfriend' Sir George Middleton.

MOBBS, Albert 'AG' George (1887-1978) – a Suffolk farmer who first began his fight against tithe in 1924 and continued the struggle for 60 years. Besides devoting astounding amounts of time and effort in organising and supporting the tithepayers' revolt, he was also a successful farmer and local councillor. Aged 21 he began managing the 500-acre family farm before taking on the 330-acre Laurel Farm on his own account, where he built an award-winning pedigree Friesian herd. He was a firm supporter of the Milk Marketing Scheme brought in during the 1930s and was always in the forefront of agricultural progress and controversy. He was, though, considered a 'thorn in the side' by some NFU colleagues on account of the tithe war, but nonetheless gave a lifetime of loyal service to the Union. He was Chairman of the Beccles Branch from 1925-1946, County Chairman from 1936-1938 and County Delegate to Headquarters until 1948.

AG was a man of high integrity, born into the staunch Suffolk tradition of Non-conformity, and his family numbered among their acquaintances many well-known political figures. He was supported by his wife, Dorothy (nee Bond), who in 1935 was asked by Rowland and Doreen Rash to unveil the Wortham tithe memorial (at Hall Farm) which she did, addressing the gathering beforehand. The Bond family farmed at nearby Carlton Colville and Dorothy's father, Arthur Harper Bond was founder of the Swanley Horticultural College, which went on to become the first such body to admit women students. (*The History of the Bond Family 1761-1940*, Neal Harper Williams, 1993)

Dorothy Mobbs was supportive of AG's stand, although her interest in tithe, unlike her husband's, was finite and she understandably got tired of the subject on more than one occasion. AG's habit of rehearsing his endless and countless speeches meant hours of being a one-woman audience. She was, though, deaf in one ear and would indulgently 'listen' to the speech with a book in one hand and a finger in the good ear. To AG's 'What did you think of that, dear?' she would smile and say 'Very good, dear'!

In tribute to AG, Doreen Wallace wrote: *'To work in harness with AG, to share the fun as well as the ardours of a political struggle, had been a great experience for us all. I never managed to count the thousands who were with us, drawn and encouraged by the personality and eloquence of a man committed to the hope of getting justice in the end.'*

She also wrote in the Introduction to *Eighty Years on Suffolk Soil*: *'I did not enter the already wide orbit of AG Mobbs until the outbreak of the Tithe War. By then, he was known beyond East Anglia as a keen and far-sighted breeder of Friesian cattle: and my husband had met him on the East Suffolk County Council ... it was not long before he and I were working, together and separately, on the job of organising Tithepayers' Associations all over East Anglia, the Midlands, the south and west of England as far as Cornwall, and parts of Wales. AG was a compelling speaker, easy to listen to, and endowed with endless energy and fire ... AG is now a very old man if one reckons by years, months and days: but not in terms of the spirit. When we oldies depart from this scene, I wonder if anyone will take up the cause of justice for the land, or will they all be too busy "getting and spending" to notice such minor matters as history and principle? Those of us who are friends of AG can congratulate ourselves on having known someone whose view of life extended beyond his own personal advantage. Large abstract ideas like Justice mean something to him.'*

The Mobbs and Rash families were close, but not familiar. While AG referred to Doreen as 'Mrs Rash' even after many years' acquaintance, she quickly and happily fell into the habit of calling him 'AG'. Christmas cards – which from the Wortham end took the form of charming watercolour sketches executed by Doreen – were signed 'Mr & Mrs R H Rash' or 'From the Rashes'.

PITT RIVERS, Captain George H L F (1890-1966) – had land in Dorset and Wiltshire and played a prominent role in the anti-tithe movement as both a titheowner and tithepayer. In 1933 he told an audience at Tollard Royal: *'We are not here to talk about our personal interests. Some of us may have conflicting interests. Some of us may be titheowners ... I happen myself to be a titheowner. But here we are fighting for the industry, not for one partner, and we want to put as far as we can our personal interest on one side and fight for farming'.*

He was Chairman of the Wessex Association and regularly attended meetings of the Wessex and Southern Counties Tithepayers' and Common Law Defence Association (to which body he donated the annual value of the tithe rentcharge that he received as titheowner). He was also a member of the CLA and together with R S Strachey did much to form the Association's tithe policy, although he constantly challenged the Association's executive decisions. Many protest meetings were held at his home village of Hinton St Mary, Dorset, in a tithe barn that he had converted to a theatre in 1939, where Oswald Mosley once addressed an audience.

He wrote *Revolt Against Tithe* (1934) and other exposures of the tithe system. He was the grandson of the explorer and anthropologist Lt-General Pitt Rivers and was, for a time, owner-director of the Pitt Rivers Museum at Farnham, Dorset. In 1935 he contested the North Dorset Constituency as an Independent Agriculturist. In *Who's Who* he listed 'refuting politicians' as one of his recreations.

TURNER, Makens (1890-1978) – unfailing in his support for the tithepayers, he was Vice-Chairman of the Suffolk Tithepayers' Association and right-hand-man to AG Mobbs from 1930 until after the 1936 Act became law. He manned the Suffolk TPA stand at the 1932 Suffolk Show, and like AG was a farmer and prominent NFU member. He was also Churchwarden at Elmsett and on the Parish Council (Elmsett Parish Council Minute Book, EG 541, Bury St Edmunds Record Office). On one occasion he made representation to Bishop Whittingham (St Edmundsbury & Ipswich), but came back disgusted with his attitude. He is buried in Elmsett churchyard, within sight of the Tithe Memorial.

WALLACE, Doreen (1897-1989) – was born in Cumbria of Scottish parents and after gaining an Honours Degree at Oxford University taught in a secondary school for three years before marrying Rowland H Rash, a farmer at Wortham on the Norfolk-Suffolk border. She wrote 47 novels (also several non-fiction works, some with R Bagnall-Oakeley) and in 1934 published *The Tithe War*. She was involved in the tithe dispute from 1931 onwards and in 1939 became the NTA's third and last President. She used her novels to make political points and her name as a writer to attract publicity for the cause, the two being mutually beneficial. She enjoyed, too, the racy excitement of being a woman in a man's world, which agriculture was – and to some extent remains.

In February 1935 a Tithe War Memorial was unveiled at Wortham to commemorate the 1934 tithe seizure (where it still stands). In 1979 Doreen wrote to AG Mobbs' son and daughter-in-law enclosing material she thought would be of value to anyone writing a history of the tithe war. She said that she would do it herself, but *'... I'm too old, most people think I am dead ... Tithe is dead now because we made it too difficult to collect! But it is a big part of agriculture history'.* A biography *Doreen Wallace (1897-1989), Writer and Social Campaigner* by June Shepherd was published in 2000. In 2001 the Eastern Angles Theatre Company performed *TitheWar!*, a play based on the Wortham tithe distraint sales of the 1930s.

Appendix III
SIMPLE GLOSSARY

Alterage – tithes paid by medieval parishioners on important occasions.

Annates – like 'first fruits', annates were Papal in origin and at the Reformation were diverted to the Crown. It was the 'first fruits and annates' which Queen Anne restored to the Church in 1704 to found the Bounty. Annates, like 'first fruits', are not strictly the same as tithe.

Annuity – the 1936 Tithe Act replaced rentcharge with a 'terminable redemption annuity' payable for 60 years.

Apportionment – MAFF held the definitive maps showing the tithe apportionment (i.e. each parcel of land and its tithe liability), together with records of where tithes had been redeemed, merged or re-apportioned (in cases where farms had been split up). Although it was often necessary to refer to these maps where a dispute arose, their accuracy was by no means guaranteed and therefore created further problems that rumbled on for years. After 1936 land that was divided often had to be re-apportioned which invariably raised an Order of Redemption if the divided rentcharge value fell below a certain amount.

Agistment – tithe on grass or herbage eaten by (usually barren) cattle at pasture.

Augmentation – literally, an increase or enlargement. The original brief for the QAB Commissioners from 1704 onwards was to use the revenue of the Bounty to increase the livings of the rural clergy. It took ten years or so after QAB was first established to begin augmentation.

Central Landowners' Association (CLA) – founded in 1907 as the Central Land Association it became the Central Landowners' Association in 1918, changing again to the Country Landowners' Association in 1949. In 2000 it became the Country Land & Business Association. The CLA's current 50,000 members own 60 percent of the countryside in England and Wales.

Chancel Repairs – in 2001 it was estimated by the Law Commission that some 5,200 churches and 3,780,500 acres of land are still liable for this ancient part of tithe, namely a liability for Chancel Repair as laid down in the Chancel Repairs Act of 1932. In 1994 a Parochial Church Council presented a lay rector with a liability for chancel repair in the sum of £95,000. (See also Chancel Repairs, Legal Records Information Leaflet 33, PRO.)

Church Commissioners – formed in 1948 as an amalgamation of the Ecclesiastical Commissioners and the Governors of Queen Anne's Bounty. It consists of Archbishops and Bishops of England, lay Church Estates Commissioners, and other clerical and lay members. Up-to-date information about the Church Commissioners and the estates and revenues of the Church of England can be found on the Church of England website (see below) or from 1 Millbank, London SW1P 3JZ.

Church of England – the Established or State Church that has the sovereign as its titular head. By the Act of Supremacy, 1534, Henry VIII and his successors took the title of 'the only supreme head on earth of the Church of England'. The Church, prior to the 1530s, had been under the authority of the Pope. As part of the English Reformation, Henry VIII removed tithe ownership from ecclesiastical to lay impropriators for the first time in its history. Its website is www.england.anglican.org.

Church in Wales – In 1894 a committee was appointed to protect QAB's Welsh revenues. After a long and complicated procedure, much of the Bounty land was transferred to the Welsh Church Representative Body (in 1912) and at disestablishment (1919-1920) it was secularised. The Church Acts of 1914 and 1919 did not abolish Welsh tithe, but ownership of tithe rentcharge in Wales and Monmouthshire was for the most part vested in the Welsh Church Commissioners.

Commutation – in 1836 the Tithe Commutation Act abolished all payment in kind and made compulsory the payment of annual tithe in cash. Tithe Commissioners were appointed to draw up a complete list of all tithes payable in every parish in England and Wales (apportionment), and by means of local valuers commute them into a money payment called Tithe Rentcharge.

A large number of tithes had been commuted in the 18th century (as a result of the Enclosure Acts) and a 'rent' in lieu of tithes substituted, based on corn prices (see Corn rents), or a gift of land given in lieu of tithes. In some counties, Northamptonshire in particular, large areas of land were commuted during the 18th century. In 1836 the newly appointed Commissioners had first to document tithes already commuted. All early commutations had been subject to local variation, while the 1836 Act used an average price for the whole country. The Act also made it possible to redeem tithe by payment of a capital sum where the land was sold for building purposes (see also Tithe barns).

Corn rents – variable charges outside the scope of the 1836 Tithe Commutation Act which resulted from individual commutation of tithe during the 17th, 18th and early part of the 19th centuries. Certain tithes were commuted to monetary payments and were tied to the average price of corn, many such arrangements taking place under the Enclosure Acts of the 18th century. Corn rents differed from tithe in that they were not necessarily subject to the same rates and taxes and were dependent on local legislation.

Deeds of Merger – where a tithepayer was also the titheowner, a Deed of Merger was possible, thus annihilating tithe liability.

'Degwm' – the old Welsh word which described the substance of a tithe – one thing out of every ten.

Ecclesiastical Commissioners – appointed by Parliament in 1835 to manage the estates and revenues of the Church of England. It consisted chiefly of archbishops, bishops, deans and canons of the Church of England, and included the Governors of QAB, the Tithe Commissioners and others. Their capital derived from tithes, lands given in lieu of tithe, tithe redemption monies, etc. In 1948 the Ecclesiastical Commissioners were amalgamated with QAB to form the Church Commissioners for England.

Ecclesiastical Tithe – tithes payable to ecclesiastical persons and bodies, as opposed to lay impropriators.

Exemptions – although tithes were primarily payable in respect of productive land there were exemptions, including forest lands while in the occupation of the Crown (or its lessee); glebe or church lands in a parish in the occupancy of the parson or incumbent; lands owned by those deriving title from one of the privileged orders (Cistercians, Templars, Hospitallers), and others. Some land was discharged from tithe by the greater monasteries at the time of their dissolution.

Extraordinary Tithe – after 1836 the Commissioners had the power to fix an extra tithe on any newly cultivated land which had on it fruit or hop plantations. It was considered that the profit on hops and fruit per acre was not 'ordinary' but 'extraordinary'. Compared with a profit of, say, £3 per acre on arable land, profits of between £30 and £60 were possible from an acre of hops or fruit trees. In 1881 there was considerable agitation against Extraordinary Tithe and in 1882 an Anti-Extraordinary Association was formed. In 1886 the Extraordinary Tithe Redemption Act abolished the power to create Extraordinary Tithe, but converted the existing charge into a fixed and permanent rentcharge not liable to variation and payable whether or not the special cultivation continued. By the 1930s much of the land bearing Extraordinary Tithe had long since ceased to be used for hop-growing, thus Kent was one of the counties most affected by Extraordinary Tithe (almost half of the total). Sussex and Herefordshire were similarly affected.

'First fruits' – the 'first fruits and tenths' of a benefice were originally paid to the Pope's representative in England but transferred to the Crown at the Reformation. The nature and entitlement was not strictly the same as tithe and should be considered separately. Following the 1836 Tithe Act, a Select Committee of the House of Commons was ordered to report on 'First Fruits and Tenths and Administration of Queen Anne's Bounty', but they were not extinguished until 1926, under the First Fruits and Tenths Measure.

Fish Tithe – due to the difficulties of collection, and because the fish were taken from the sea or a common river, there was little tithing of fish. However, special and ancient local customs existed in Wales, Yarmouth (Norfolk), Scarborough and a few other places.

Glebe – from the Latin *glaeba* meaning soil, glebe land is that which has been given in entirety by a landowner to the Church, or that purchased by the Church with money belonging to it. In most parishes glebe land was bequeathed over the centuries and came mostly in small strips, but occasionally there was sufficient to amass a Glebe Farm. Income from glebe land belonged to the incumbent, or other ecclesiastic body, for whose benefit the original gift was made. A survey of the profits and possession of benefices was undertaken in 1571, and the resulting documents called Glebe Terriers. These terriers continue as Diocesan Records and often contain details of tithe collection.

Great Tithe – a tenth portion of corn, hay or wood. Also known as Predial Tithe (qv), and Rectorial Tithe because rectors usually had rights to them. It was these Great Tithes which formed the bulk of what became known as 'agricultural tithe'.

Lay impropriator – titheholders who are lay owners and hold entitlement to tithe income that had originally belonged to the monasteries. At the Reformation some Rectorial Tithes became the personal property of new owners who were outside the Church. Some of these were institutions, such as universities and charities, which kept ownership from the 16th century to final redemption in 1996 and were the target for the protestors.

London – there were numerous ancient tithe liabilities on property in the City that became a source of annoyance to urban tithepayers. Houses belonging to, or built on, parts of the old country estates, broken up in 1918-1920, often carried outstanding tithe. The estates were often so divided that it was impossible to assess individual liability.

Ministry of Agriculture, Fisheries and Food – 'MAFF' came into existence in 1919 as the new version of the old Board of Agriculture. The role of MAFF in the collection and administration of tithe increased after the 1936 Act. In 2001 MAFF was abolished almost overnight and became the Department for Environment, Food & Rural Affairs (DEFRA), which the farming press immediately dubbed the Department for the Eradication of Farming and Real Agriculture.

Mixed Tithe – defined as the tenth, not of the immediate produce of the ground, but of animals receiving their nourishment from the soil, e.g. milk, lambs, wool, eggs, etc.. Also known as Small Tithe.

Modus (*modus decimandi*) – an arrangement whereby a tithepayer and titheowner agreed to commute payment into cash. A large number of moduses relate to hay and were contracted between 1189 and 1570. Where the parson could not, or was not able to, make his hay at the same time as the parishioner (thereby impeding farming practice) the parishioner had to agree a modus in lieu of his tenth share. The legality of such arrangements was continually challenged in the courts, since to verify a modus it was necessary to prove that the arrangement had existed 'since time immemorial'. In 1570 an Act prohibited further moduses, chiefly due to the compounded depreciation due to inflation. After 1836 land subject to a modus was charged at a separate rate and objectors could make representation to the Commissioners.

Parson – the Rector, or incumbent of a benefice, who is the local representative of the Church and has full possession of any inherited rights belonging to the parish. The word Parson is more readily associated with those such as Parson Woodforde, and its use has declined of late.

Personal Tithe – a tenth part of the profits of trade and industry arising out of the labour of the parishioners. By 1830 there were only two Personal Tithes left, those for mills and fish.

Peter's Pence (also Romescot, Rome Fee, Rome Penny, Hearthpenny) – obscure origins and invariably confused with tithe as a result of its presumed link with St Peter and, therefore, the Church of Rome. Peter's Pence was only one part of the revenue collected in England by the Pope's agent and with the removal of papal authority at the Reformation, Peter's Pence was abolished. Henry VIII made no provision to retain it, as he did tithe. (See *English Parish Church*, Stephen Friar.)

Predial/Praedial – the Great Tithes, being a tenth part of the actual produce of the soil, such as wheat, oats or barley. From the Latin *praedium*, an estate.

Public Record Office (PRO) – a vast collection of tithe-related material is housed at the PRO in Kew. A copy of *Domestic Information Leaflet 41 Tithe Records: A Detailed Examination* can be downloaded from its website: www.pro.gov.uk. Instances of tithe disputes are evidence of its turbulent history and documentation offers a glimpse into the uneasy co-existence of Church and farm. A man is accused of removing his sheep from one parish to another to avoid tithe; men are found to have broken into tithe barns; there are endless wrangles over sheep clipped and fed in different parishes (and therefore subject to more than one tithe); and there are disputes over tithe of cheese, teasles and other Small Tithes. The PRO also holds files relating to the 1836 Tithe Commutation Act, and the Tithe Maps, together with Deeds of Merger and Redemptions.

Queen Anne's Bounty (QAB) – corporation formed in 1704 as 'Queen Anne's Bounty for the Augmentation of the Maintenance of the Poor Clergy'. Governors were set up to administer an annual income of around £15,000 that derived from 'first fruits and annates'. QAB Acts of 1715 and 1717 attempted to improve collection of the 'bounty' and embarked on the first augmentation of poor benefices.

'In 1846 [QAB] Governors became under Statute the trustees of moneys received for the redemption of tithe rentcharge belonging to benefices, and such moneys were invested for the benefit of successive incumbents. The Governors hold in this way redemption funds of tithe rentcharge redeemed prior to the passing of the recent Tithe Act 1936 totalling nearly £7,000,000. The duties under the earlier Acts were, however, slight compared with those imposed on QAB by the Tithe Act,

1925, under which the whole of the ecclesiastical tithe rentcharge of England (about £2,000,000 yearly) became vested in them in trust for incumbents and ecclesiastical corporations.' (George Middleton, *Resources of the Church*, 1937)

QAB was a quasi-legal, quasi-ecclesiastical body whose work previous to 1925 was concerned mainly with the Church's 'first fruits and tenths' and redemption moneys. In addition to its collection responsibilities for tithe rentcharge imposed under the 1925 Tithe Act, QAB also had independent management of various Extraordinary Tithes, corn rents, payments in lieu of tithes, tithes on gated or stinted pasture, cattle on common land, etc.

After 1925 QAB had an apparatus of fifteen regional committees and, for the first time, *'a burden of administration and, as it turned out, litigation, far beyond anything it had experienced hitherto'* (G F A Best, *Temporal Pillars*). After 1919 the Welsh tithes no longer fell within the description of ecclesiastical tithes and were therefore not collected by QAB. Although there were between 80,000 and 100,000 tithepayers in England there were only four investigators appointed to mitigate the effects of the 1925 Act and rule on hardship cases. By 1933 they had dealt with only about 2,000, with thousands more pending.

The Governors of QAB included the Archbishops of Canterbury and York, the English diocesan bishops, the Speaker of the House of Commons, the Master of the Rolls, Privy Councillors, deans of cathedral churches, the Attorney-General and Solicitor-General, the Lord Mayor and Aldermen of the City of London, the Lord Mayor of York and Mayors of English cities, and King's Counsel. The bishops attended meetings according to rota, and on an average from five to twelve lay Governors attended. (W G Hannah, Principal Assistant Secretary of QAB, 1934)

In evidence submitted to the Royal Commission in 1935, QAB revealed that as regards 1,137 livings, the income of which did not exceed £300 per annum, no less than 66 percent of the total income was provided by tithe, while as regard 3,829 livings exceeding £300 per annum but not exceeding £500 per annum, approximately 55 percent of the total income was derived from tithe. (*The Times*, 28 February 1936)

In 1948 QAB was amalgamated with the Ecclesiastical Commissioners to form the Church Commissioners. This process was begun in 1932 when the Earl of Selborne was appointed to investigate the property and revenues of the Church.

Rector – originally appointed to serve a parish and in receipt of the parishioners' tithes. Rectors were responsible for the church services and the spiritual welfare of their parishioners (see also Parson). Lay rectors are those who hold the responsibilities of rectorship when and where that office was separated from the Church at the Reformation and removed to lay ownership.

Rectorial Tithe – Predial or Great Tithe, so named because rectors usually had rights to them.

Redemption – tithe rentcharge could be redeemed by the payment of a lump sum in compensation to the titheowner. Between 1836 and 1918 redemption consideration was not less than 25 times the par value of the rentcharge. Redemption of £100 rentcharge would, therefore, mean a payment of £2,500. Only about 1.7 percent of the total tithe rentcharge was redeemed between 1836 and 1918. After 1918 redemption was made easier and was determined in accordance with rules administered by MAFF and the old minimum of 25 years' purchase of the par value was abolished. (Lawrance, 1926)

The *NFU Record* gives the number of tithe redemption cases completed in 1932 as 1,436, representing about £3,163,000. Of that, approximately £2,002,100 was vested in QAB and £96,000 for ecclesiastical corporations. The Ecclesiastical Commissioners owned £276,000 and the Welsh Church Commissioners £206,000. Various lay owners held the balance of £583,500. (Annual Report on the work of the Land Division of the Ministry of Agriculture for 1932, HM Stationery Office.)

The 1936 Tithe Act ordered compulsory redemption for annuities of £1 or under, extended to £3 in 1958. In 1962 the Finance Act ordered compulsory redemption when land changed ownership.

Figures relating to redemption numbers can be found in Lord Ernle's *English Farming Past and Present.*

Redemption Annuities – the 1936 Tithe Act replaced rentcharge with a 'redemption annuity', payable until 1996. Not all tithes were included, however, and part of the Tithe Redemption Commission's duties was to determine which tithe liabilities were covered by the Act.

Regium Donum – a grant made originally in 1672 by Charles II to the Presbyterian Clergy in Ireland to pacify Dissenters. This 'king's gift' was abolished within a few years, but was resurrected and then quickly abolished again several times before final abolition in 1852. Non-conformist Dissenters strenuously objected to *regium donum* as it was considered a sop to take the sting out of their opposition, and a salve to the conscience of government. Sir Robert Walpole brought it back to the statute books in 1723, outraging the Dissenters by his maxim 'Every man has his price'. It was finally abolished in 1852.

Rentcharge – the name given to tithe in the 1836 Commutation Act, although it was shortened back to 'tithe' by its opponents. The sum of rentcharge originally apportioned to a particular piece of land was referred to as the 'commuted' amount. Tithe rentcharge was abolished in 1936 and replaced with redemption annuities. During the 1930s, the rentcharge averaged out at around seven shillings an acre, although some Essex land paid 18 shillings.

Royal Agricultural Benevolent Institution (RABI) – charity formed in 1860 by a group of Essex farmers who were concerned about the overwhelming hardships suffered by many farmers. A donation was made to RABI as part of the memorial to Roderick Kedward, and both the Mobbs and Rash families supported its work. It is likely that RABI was called on to help distressed tithepayers but when it moved from London to Oxford most of its records were destroyed. The present Welfare Secretary emphasises that the assistance they give to working farmers is to help in an unforeseen emergency. It is possible, therefore, that distress brought on by non-payment of tithe might not have qualified tithepayers for help, although the support shown by the NTA indicates that it was not entirely immune to requests for help from tithepayers.

Scotland – Scottish tithe, under the name of 'teinds', was commuted in 1633 (see Venn, Second Edition 1933).

Small Tithe – deemed to be livestock, wool and non-cereal crops, although Small and Mixed Tithe are indivisible. Products such as beans, peas, potatoes, turnips, hops, mustard seed, apples, herbs, wax, honey, hemp, etc. were considered Small Tithe, as were windfall apples, cuttings or lopping from scrubs or small trees, coppice-wood, and all garden produce. Even saffron, though gathered only once in three years, was tithable. Practices and traditions often varied from one parish to another, but Small Tithes were invariably paid at certain times of the year. The tithe goose, for example, was payable at Lammas and store pigs between Ash Wednesday and 1 July. Very small tithes were often carried forward to succeeding years to make up a decent tithe amount.

'Time immemorial' – tithes were said to have existed since 'time immemorial', or 'time out of mind', or 'time whereof the memory of man runneth not to the contrary'. In 1275 'legal memory' was arbitrarily fixed in English law and has never been changed. A right was considered to be immemorial if it could be proved to have commenced before 3 September, 1189, the beginning of the reign of Richard I, by which reasoning tithe had been paid since time immemorial.

Tithe – in its simplest form, a tenth part of the annual produce of land or labour, made compulsory in the 10th century. No tithes were payable on coal, turf, tin, lead, brick, tiles, earthen pots, lime, chalk, etc., because they were not the increase of the earth but were the substance of it. In principle, tithe could not be paid twice on the same crop in a single year, but where grass, clover and the like were mown twice in the same year, tithes could be taken twice. Similarly where animals have young more than once in the year, such as pigeons, hens, etc., they were also liable for secondary tithe. There were broadly three types – pradial tithes, mixed tithes, and personal tithes – and were paid 'in kind' until 1836.

Tithe barns – although most parishes would once have possessed a tithe barn, few have survived, but those that do were originally built by medieval monastic communities to store the tithed produce of their estates. Provision was made in the 1836 Tithe Act for the sale of barns or buildings that had been used to house tithes paid in kind and were, therefore, made reduudant by commutation. With consent from the Commissioners barns could be pulled down and disposed of or sold. Tithe files held at the PRO contain specific correspondence and drafts relating to the sale of title barns. (See *Local and Family History*, David Hey)

Tithe impropriates – payments severed from the Church altogether and payable to a lay person or institution (lay impropriators).

Tithe maps – produced for England and Wales between 1838 and 1854 as a result of the 1836 Tithe Commutation Act. Maps were drawn up in triplicate, one each for the tithe office, the parish clerk and the diocese. In addition to those in the PRO, some Record Offices may hold the maps for their areas. Maps and apportionment schedules relating to Wales are held in the National Library of Wales. Unlike enclosure maps, tithe maps show the whole parish. Their drawback is that they were not drawn to a uniform scale, not all of them received the seal of the Commissioners (guaranteeing accuracy), and the numbers corresponding to the tithe apportionment do not always follow those of the maps themselves. The 1936 Tithe Act necessitated a programme of new maps, based on Ordnance Survey, but the process was never completed. After interruption by the Second World War, the project was finally abandoned in the 1950s, with only about half the tithe districts being mapped.

Tithe Redemption Committee – government-created body established in 1936 to execute the provisions of the 1936 Tithe Act. It consisted of a Chairman and up to four other Commissioners appointed by the Treasury in consultation with MAFF. The Tithe Redemption Office was closed in December 1979 and the records deposited at the PRO.

Tithe Rent Charge (Rates) Act (1898) – the 1925 Tithe Act completed a process begun in 1898 when 10,000 clergy were relieved of their remaining rate burden. The total amount of rate relief was around £600,000 annually and in some parishes the rates question was as tricky as tithe itself. After a complicate two-step rating concession had been applied, the shortfall had to be met by the general body of ratepayers. Farmers were granted similar rating concessions in 1923 and 1925, when farm buildings became derated altogether. (See *The Church of England*, Mayfield)

Tithe Rentcharge – the Tithe Commutation Act of 1836 converted the old tenth portion of farm produce in kind (as previously demanded and enforced by law) into a compulsory cash payment. This new Rentcharge was payable by the tenant and was to be assessed on the average corn price every seven years. In general parlance, it was shorted back to 'tithe'.

Tithe values – the 1836 Tithe Act laid down procedure for converting payment in kind to cash. The first scale was fixed in December 1836 when £100 would purchase 94.95 bushels of wheat, 168.42 of barley, and 242.42 of oats. The prices were those published annually in the *London Gazette*. These figures were used by valuers nationwide to calculate the initial amount of rentcharge.

Vicar – from the Latin *vicarius*, meaning substitute or proxy. If a parish is, or was, served by a vicar it generally meant that at some time the benefice was administered by a monastic or collegiate foundation who appointed a vicar to administer the parish on their behalf. The monastery kept the Great (or Rectorial) Tithes, and used the Small (or Vicarial) Tithes to pay a vicar who served the parish in their place. In the 14th century Parliament endorsed the practice and made legal provision in the form of Vicarial Tithe.

Wales – under the Welsh Church Acts, 1914 and 1919, the argument of Welsh tithepayers ceased to be with the Church (see The Church in Wales). The obligation to pay, however, remained the same, so while the targets for protest were slightly different from those in England the principle of hostility was the same. Much of the agitation against tithe had taken place in Wales during the 1880s and stood as an example to the protestors of the 1930s. It was estimated that at the time of commutation in 1836 about 22.8 percent of the net value of Welsh tithe was held by lay impropriators.

The Tithe Maps of Wales are at the National Library of Wales. The National Library Database of Welsh Tithe Apportionment Maps and Schedules is currently in preparation.

Appendix IV
TITHEPAYERS' AND TITHEOWNERS' ASSOCIATIONS

Throughout the 1930s and 1940s there were many local committees and groups which organised protest on both sides of the argument and most NFU county branches had a Tithe Committee of some description. The branch TPAs operated under the umbrella of the County Association, which in turn was affiliated to the National Tithepayers' Association. The list is by no means complete. Where possible officers' names are given.

Anti-Extraordinary Association – existed from 1882 until the passing of the Extraordinary Tithe Redemption Act in 1886.

Anti-Tithe League – formed in Wales (Ruthin) during 1886 after intimidation of tithepayers who refused to pay.

Berkshire – in a letter from the NTA dated April 1931, F R Allen refers to *'a flourishing association going in Berkshire ... the Berkshire people are very keen'*. Much wider support was also given to the Oxford, Berkshire & Buckinghamshire TPA where the combined strength was thought to be better used. The association was variously entitled and often appears in press cuttings as the Berkshire, Bucks & Oxon TPA. Mr V Drewitt played a leading role in the TPA and was also on the NFU Tithe Committee.

The **Wallingford & District** TPA covered a considerable part of Berkshire and Oxfordshire.

Brecon – the **Builth** TPA was formed at the end of 1931, with Mr W Moore of Breviton as Secretary.

The **Hay** TPA was formed in December 1932, with Mr W Prosser of Fordfawr, Mr Powell of Glasburg, and Mr Meredith of Clyro as Honorary Secretaries.

Buckinghamshire – see Oxford, Berkshire & Buckinghamshire TPA.

Cambridgeshire – the Cambridge and District TPA was formed during 1930. The Hon Secretary was H W Game of Burwell.

Caernarvonshire, South – this branch of the Anti-Tithe League of 1887 had, briefly, David Lloyd George as its Secretary.

Cheshire – although tithe was not acute, the county gave strong support to the tithepayers cause where it could.

Churchmen's Defence Union – operated from 229 Strand, London, its Secretary E W I Peterson. The CDU seems to have combined with the **Tithe Owners' Union** with Mr Peterson as joint Secretary. There was also a body called **Central Church Committee for Defence and Instruction** which published leaflets in defence of tithe.

Cornwall – several local TPAs formed during the early 1930s, but in January 1934 a meeting was held in **Bodmin** for representatives of the several groups to band together in a single TPA for Cornwall.

Cumberland – no TPA as such was formed, but several cases of tithe distraint were put through the Penrith County Court on behalf of QAB.

Denbighshire – the farm of Richard Edwards at Gwersyllt Hall Farm, near Wrexham, was the scene of numerous demonstrations and tithe distraint orders. Farms in **Ruthin** were badly affected. In 1932, the NFU estimated that £1,000,000 went out of Wales every four years in the form of ecclesiastical and lay tithes.

Devon – the county TPA was formed at Tiverton in January 1933 and included representatives from other local associations (at **Barnstaple, Bideford, Tiverton, Newton Abbot** and **Wiveliscombe** in Somerset). Mr W A Down was Chairman, Mr John Lewis Vice-Chairman and Mr James Lewis Secretary.

    Barnstaple – the Chairman of the Barnstaple TPA, Mr A Turner of Goodleigh, was elected Chairman of the county TPA, with Mr Chipman of Bideford as Secretary. Mr Turner had livestock seized by the bailiff at his farm in September 1934.

    Exeter – in 1933 it was decided to form a TPA for Devon.

    Newton Abbot – the TPA was involved in skirmishes with Mosley's Blackshirts when the BUF interested themselves in a tithe distraint sale where the Association bought goods and returned them to the farmer.

    North Devon – a TPA formed in Barnstaple in February 1933, with Mr A Turner as Chairman and Mr F Chapman as Secretary.

Wytheridge – a TPA was formed at the end of 1931 with Mr B Cox as Secretary.

Dorset – this county TPA was dominated by Captain George Pitt Rivers, who was both a tithepayer and titheowner, and who lived at Hinton St Mary. The Association worked closely with the TPAs in South Wiltshire and Hampshire.

Durham – see Yorkshire

Essex – F C Krailing, who was also on the NFU Tithe Committee as well as the Halstead TPA, headed the County TPA.

    Colchester – the Main Hall in Colchester was chosen to inaugurate the TPA and echoed a previous public meeting in 1887 held to protest against tithe. Only a few months after inauguration, the TPA numbered nearly 1,000 members.

    Halstead & District – administered from Great Yeldham, the Chairman (and Treasurer) was F C Krailing and the Secretary W R Cohen.

    Saffron Walden – by April 1933 there was a strong district group who formed a TPA and were affiliated to other Associations in Essex.

Farmers' Tithe Defence League – '*... formed in the autumn of 1886, positively contributed by organizing, first, refusals to pay tithe rent-charge, and second, when the non-payers' goods were distrained on, demonstrations of solidarity in their support. At first peaceful enough, despite the occasional appearances of gangs of quarrymen (who, having no direct concern in the dispute, were premonitory of the bands of Blackshirts who tended mysteriously to turn up on similar occasions after the First World War), these demonstrations soon became more menacing.*' (*Temporal Pillars*, G F A Best)

Gloucestershire – formed in January 1933 at the Bell Hotel, Gloucester. Gloucestershire was one of the counties where the local branch of the NFU was 'diametrically opposed' to TPAs and considered the NFU capable of looking after the tithepayers' interests.

Hampshire – the TPA operated jointly with the **South Wiltshire** TPA.

Herefordshire – following a public meeting at Hereford in December 1932, the TPA was operating by January 1933 and was closely associated with the **South Herefordshire** TPA. E C Andrews was Chairman. Tithe was a most contentious issue in Herefordshire where the Bishop of Hereford was one of the principal recipients of tithe.

Hertfordshire – the **Bishop's Stortford & District** TPA was formed by disillusioned members of the NFU who felt that the Union did not represent the interests of tithepayers. The Chairman was H T Cox, JP CC, and P Coleman was Secretary. The Labour MP J A Seddon was a supporter.

Isle of Man – the IOM Government, the Tynwald, extinguished tithe in 1945 and although there were no protest sales or demonstrations there was a deep loathing of tithe. Mr Harvey Briggs, whose father was a tenant in **Onchan** during the 1930s, paid annual tithe of £6 12s 11d on 100 acres. The sum quoted for redemption was £199 7s 6d. In due course the landlord did redeem it, but Mr Briggs had to pay an annuity of £6 a year – leaving him just 12s 11d better off.

Kent – there were at least six local Tithepayers' Associations in Kent, as well as a Joint Committee representative of all the Associations in Kent and Sussex. Because of the hop tithe it had one of the most active and vociferous roles in the protest. Kent TPA was inaugurated on 17 December 1930, at the Guildhall in Sandwich; F R Allen addressed the meeting. The meeting had to decide what action to take and decided on a policy of refusal to pay. Thus began the unanimous policy of 'passive resistance'.

The **Kent Tithepayers' Defence Association** was formed early in 1930 in opposition to hop tithe.

Ashford – in September 1931 a Joint Committee was formed of all the Tithepayers' Associations in Kent (6) and Sussex (2). Mr J H Cooke from Udimore was Treasurer. Its special province was the collection and administration of a Defence Fund in the two counties. In the 1950s there was still a nucleus of revolt in the form of the Ashford, Kent & Sussex TPA, who published *Facts and Incidents of an Unequal Struggle* and continued to lobby Parliament on behalf of tithepayers under the Chairmanship of Thomas Pendry. Mr C Davison was Vice-Chairman, and the Secretaries were Miss M K Glover and Miss W E Pendry. Among its most ardent supporters was H Roseveare, JP, who was Chairman of the Ashford TPA in 1932. In 1935, H Roseveare told the press that in the district of Ashford alone there were between 700 and 800 distraint orders outstanding.

Elham – a very active branch, having a high number of tithepayers in its area, which did battle with the Elham District Council for a reduction of valuation for rating purposes, and defended tithepayers against the distraint activities of Merton College, Oxford.

Paddock Wood – the TPA came into being on 19 December 1933, when Mr P Morphett was elected Hon Secretary.

Sandwich – this was one of the first associations to be formed in Kent, on 17 December 1930, the members of which went on to become the Kent TPA. Alderman G C Solley, JP, of

Richborough near Sandwich was Chairman, with Mr Coleman as Treasurer and Mr F R Allen as Secretary. By 1934 the paid-up membership was 189. The Sandwich TPA was one of the first to adopt the Non-Payment Campaign. Alderman Solley, an ex-Mayor of Sandwich, was distrained upon for tithe arrears and as an Alderman was a Governor of QAB.

Stansted – a TPA was formed here at the beginning of 1934, with the Baroness Meyern Hohenberg as Chairman.

Weald District – branch operating from 1932 onwards.

Kent & Sussex TPA – Mr H Roseveare formed the joint TPA when the pressure on the two counties became intense.

Lancashire – while there appears to have been no TPA as such, a group of farmers in the Culcheth district between Leigh and Warrington were served with notices to redeem tithe during 1932. Tithe liability was not acute in the county, but its farming leaders gave full support to the tithepayers' cause.

Leicestershire – representatives of Leicestershire tithepayers formed part of the NFU discussion group which advised the Deputation to the Minister of Agriculture re Tithe in April 1931.

Lincolnshire – in January 1933 a TPA was formed in **Peterborough**.

Monmouthshire – a TPA was formed in **Abergavenny** during 1933, with Mr J Griffiths as Secretary.

Montgomeryshire – a TPA was formed at **Llanfair Caereinion** in April 1933. They passed the resolution: *'That in view of the present depressed state of agriculture we find it impossible to pay the present rate of tithe, and implore the Government to take immediate action for the amendment of the Tithe Acts to save the industry from ruin and the farm labourer from dismissal'.* Chairman was Mr J P Jones and the Secretary Mr W H Davies.

National Tithepayers' Association – an early version of the later NTA was already having some effect in the 1920s, under the leadership of A J Burrows (Kent Land Agent Alfred J Burrows who later amalgamated with Knight, Frank & Rutley). In December 1924 a preliminary meeting was held and on 6 January 1925 the Tithepayers' Association (TA) was formally constituted. In 1925, shortly before his death, NTA Chairman Sir Henry Rew published tithepayers' dissatisfaction in *The Times*. In 1920 Sir Henry had been on the same Committee as Mr Le Fanu, Treasurer of QAB, to investigate future cereal prices. Differences of opinion arose and Sir Henry took the side of the tithepayers.

After 1925 the TA became more effective and in 1929 F R Allen of Canterbury drew up their objective as being: *'... to secure statutory protection from excessive tithe – not for some tithepayers, but for all tithepayers; not temporarily, but permanently; not by favour, but of right; not merely as to arrears, but as to tithe which, looming in the future, threatens still further to drive away capital and destroy enterprise. For the sake, not only of this generation of tithepayers, but also of the children and grandchildren of this generation, the claws of the extortioners must be drawn, once and for all.'*

At the beginning of 1929 the subscription was 5s and the AGM was held in London during January.

In 1931 the TA was administered from F R Allen's offices in St Margaret's Street, Canterbury; Viscount Lymington, MP was President, and A J Burrows was Chairman of Council. Mr A Blomfield was Hon Treasurer. F C Krailing was a one-time Council member. In 1932, both Lord Lymington and A J Burrows resigned, leaving the way open for the TA to become the National Tithepayers' Association. In that year the Chairman, Reverend Kedward, became President, a post he held until his death in 1937, when A G Mobbs took over.

In July 1933 the *Daily Herald* reported that more than 11,000 farmers had pledged themselves as members of the NTA.

Norfolk – one of the largest of the TPAs, it was also one of the first to be founded in 1930 and by 1934 had over 500 members. Its Chairman was Mr Stanley Kidner, whose family was in the forefront of anti-tithe protest. Secretary was Edwin Clarke, whose land at Hethersett and Little Melton carried tithe owing to Emmanuel College, Cambridge.

Throughout Norfolk there were various District Committees, which invariably entitled themselves TPA, including those at **Harleston** and **Long Stratton**.

In 1936 and again in 1939 there is mention of the **Norfolk League of Tithepayers' Association** whose Secretary was E A Clarke.

Northumberland – tithe was not a big issue in the county, but there were many small liabilities amounting to as little as 3 pence an acre.

Oxford, Berkshire & Buckinghamshire – members from all three counties operated under the one Association, although there were several local branches. In 1933 Mr A T Carr was Honorary Secretary. The **Wallingford & District** branch TPA, which covered parts of Berkshire and Oxfordshire, was particularly strong and well organised.

Shropshire – the Shropshire Association, with Mr J Hamer as the Hon Secretary, held numerous meetings across the county and neighbouring counties to support the anti-tithe movement. Gatherings were held at Minsterley, Bishops Castle, Westbury, Llanfair, Middletown, Wem, Dorrington, Wellington, Oswestry, Llanidloes, Shrewsbury, Guilsford, Ellesmere, Craven Arms, and Bridgenorth.

Wellington – a TPA was formed here, the Secretary of which was Mr F H Davies of Sugden Hill.

In 1932 a TPA was formed at **Bishops Castle** and embraced farmers in Minsterley.

In April 1933 a TPA was formed at **Ludlow**, T W Howard as Chairman and L H Davies as Secretary.

Somerset – the County TPA threw its lot in with Associations in Dorset, Wiltshire and Hampshire and was included variously in the resulting umbrella association. R S Strachey was Chairman of the Somerset branch of the CLA and liaised closely with the TPA in the county.

Wiveliscombe TPA – formed at a meeting of about 80 farmers held in the White Hart Hotel, Wiveliscombe on 5 December 1933. The Chairman was Furze Jewell and the Secretary Mr H Burnell.

Yeovil TPA – organised public meetings in Yeovil and Crewkerne. Mr A W James was Chairman with Mr Chinnock as Secretary.

South Wiltshire – while operating in its own right throughout the 1930s, its officers operated under the wider title of **South Wiltshire, Hampshire & Dorset TPA**. (See also Wiltshire)

Suffolk – founded in February 1931 at a meeting at the Crown and Anchor Hotel in Ipswich. The Committee was AG Mobbs (Chairman), Mr Makens Turner (Vice-Chairman and also a member of the Suffolk NFU Executive), Mr Philip Butler (Secretary), R H Rash, and his wife, Doreen Wallace.

In March 1933, AG Mobbs was invited to address the **Bury St Edmunds** District Branch with a view to forming a separate committee to deal with lay tithe.

Sussex – two TPAs functioned in Sussex but their main contribution was on the Joint Committee of the Defence Fund that worked in association with the Kent TPAs.

The Tithe League – administered from London by Mr C McCreagh and seems to have been something of a one-man-band. Mr McCreagh later joined the Council of the NTA as Treasurer.

Tithe Committee (NFU) – almost all County Executives had a tithe sub-committee, the national Tithe Committee being formed in 1933.

Tithe Owners' Association – not all titheowners were opposed to eventual abolition, and during 1924 members of the NFU attended a meeting of the TOA which agreed that an attempt be made to look at redemption 'on fair and equitable terms'. It was, however, the 'terms' which divided the owners and the payers. In 1925 it was reported at a meeting of the NFU Taxation Committee that consideration was being given to a report of the CLA, the Land Union and the NFU '... *appointed on 9th October, 1923, to negotiate on behalf of tithe payers with a Committee representing Tithe Owners appointed by the National Assembly of the Church of England'*.

Tithe Owners' Union – it is not clear if this was the same body as the Tithe Owners' Association, as in 1925 there was also a **Tithe Owners' Union and Church Property Defence Association** in consultation with the NFU. One such-named Union joined with the **Churchmen's Defence Union** with E W I Peterson as Secretary.

Urban Tithepayers' Association – in August 1935 a small group of suburban house owners in **Carlton Colville**, near Lowestoft in Suffolk, formed themselves into what is thought to be the first and only UTA. An unexpected demand for the redemption of tithes on their garden plots was made by MAFF at the request of QAB. The official demand was for over £155 on an area of four acres which had been divided into house plots. The new house owners had been forced out of condemned housing in Lowestoft and they were already paying more than they could afford to building societies. In spite of the fact that some men were earning only 28s a week and paying out 18s a week in mortgage repayments and rates, QAB were adamant that they would pay tithe on their gardens. Secretary Robert Jarper named his new home 'Nil Desperandum'.

Warwickshire – in 1994 the Parochial Church Council of **Aston Cantlow and Wilmcote with Billesley** invoked the 1932 Chancel Repair Act to require lay rectors of Aston Cantlow to defray the cost of repairing the chancel of the parish church.

Welsh Clergy Defence Association – formed in November 1887 after tithe riots at Mochdre, Clwyd, when 84 people were injured and the Riot Act had to be read.

Wessex – called the **Wessex & Southern Counties Tithepayers' and Common Law Defence Association**, it was formed in Wincanton on 2 December 1932 and administered from Salisbury in Wiltshire. The Committee was: Mr F J Farquharson (President), Mr C L Rutter (Secretary and Treasurer), Mr E H Dyke, Miss M Guest, Captain John Bailward, Mr G Barnes (Hon Secretary of the Wincanton Branch of the NFU), Mr J G Inglis (Chairman-elect of the NFU), and Mr Tozer. The TPA worked closed with the Wessex Association, whose Chairman was Captain G H L F Pitt Rivers. Captain Pitt Rivers became Chairman of the Wessex and Southern Counties TPA, with Mr O Griffin as Vice-Chairman, H C Knapman, N P & D J Read as joint Hon Treasurers.

Wiltshire – the **Wessex & Southern Counties TPA** was administered from Salisbury and many Wiltshire farmers were members of the umbrella TPA that organised meetings throughout the region.

The **South Wiltshire TPA** was supported by the Mayor of Andover, Councillor E C Lovell (himself a tithepayer). The scale of subscription was from 1s up to £2, according to tithe payable.

The **Warminster** Branch of the NFU disagreed with the Wiltshire TPA, maintaining that the solution was to make farming more profitable.

During 1933 the **Salisbury & District** Branch of the NTA advertised for new members.

Women's Branch of the NTA – operating mainly in Norfolk and Suffolk, this was started and organised by Doreen Wallace from Wortham in July 1934. In November 1934, the first general meeting of the Norfolk Women TPAs was held at the YMCA Rooms, **Norwich**.

Worcestershire – the County Branch of the Worcester NFU lobbied the Worcestershire MPs on behalf of the tithepayers and eventually a TPA was formed in September 1932. Members of the Worcestershire TPA drove to Suffolk to support Doreen Wallace in her distraint sale in 1934. In 1932 the amateur boxer and 'Squire of Hanbury Hall' Sir George Vernon became President under the 'don't-pay' banner and quickly affiliated the Worcestershire TPA to the NTA. Mr H Tyler of Martin Hussingtree was elected Chairman. Sir George's interest was sparked when he discovered that he was still deemed responsible for tithe on half an acre he had presented to the parish of Hanbury near Droitwich and was called upon to pay the 2s 3d annual rentcharge. Sir George, also Chairman of the Droitwich magistrates, had a tithe burden amounting to £900 a year on the land belonging to Hanbury Hall.

Prime Minister Stanley Baldwin was a Worcestershire MP and consistently dismissed the TPA as 'unconstitutional'.

There was a branch TPA in **Tenbury**.

Yorkshire – the North Riding of Yorkshire & South Durham County Branch of the NFU made representation on behalf of the tithepayers. Although not severe, there were curious anomalies in the interpretation of the tithe maps, and many of these cases came to court as errors in collection. The County Secretary F C Johnson of Stapleton, **Darlington** ran a campaign to lobby local MPs.

Appendix V
EDITED SELECTION OF NEWSPAPER
AND JOURNAL REFERENCES

This is not a complete list, but is intended to illustrate the level and content of press coverage generated by the tithe dispute. Many of the publications are no longer in print. Articles and letters appearing in *Farmer & Stock-Breeder, Farmers Weekly, NFU Record* and the *Church Times* are too numerous to list, and only a sample is included from the *East Anglian Daily Times, Eastern Daily Press, Kentish Express, Kent Messenger*, etc. There were, of course, thousands more articles, letters and reports in hundreds more publications.

Andover Advertiser
Mass Meeting in the Guildhall, Andover – Chairman: The Mayor of Andover – Viscount Lymington, MP and F R Allen invited to speak (30.10.1931)
The Tithe Burden to the Farmer – in 1932 (1.4.1932)

Berkshire Chronicle
Berks NFU ... the Wallingford Branch wrote welcoming the tithe policy of the union, and urging that the latter should work in close co-operation with all bodies anxious to alleviate the present unjust burden of tithe, and to secure a settlement founded upon the principle of the land's capacity to produce the tithe demanded. (18.11.1932)

Berrows Worcester Journal
W'shire Farmers' Attitude (26.11.1932)
Payment of Tithe – Mr Baldwin's views (9.1.1933)
Tithe Payers' Meeting at Bromyard – 'Immediate Redress' Demanded (4.3.1933)
Policy on the Tithe Question – Tithe Committee's Report (11.3.1933)
Tenbury Farmers' Union – Discussion on the Tithe Question (18.3.1933)

Birmingham Gazette
Tithe-Fighting Spirit Develops – Don't-Pay Policy Adopted at Meeting of New Worcestershire Association (22.11.1932)
Farmers March in London (2.2.1939)

Birmingham Post
Tithe Rents – Mr Denman answered in the negative the question whether the Ecclesiastical Commissioners, having regard to agricultural losses, would consider the cancellation of tithe rent for a period of five years. (13.12.1932)
Mr Baldwin's Views on Tithe (9.1.1933)
Farmers' Union Annual Meeting – Tithe Question to be Discussed (12.1.1933)
Abortive Tithe Sale Near Wrexham – Why a Farmer has Decided to Pay (21.3.1933)
Tithe Protests by Welsh Farmers (28.3.1933)
Speech in Defence of Queen Anne's Bounty – Meeting in Dorset Creates a Precedent (10.4.1933)
Tithe Acts Protest – An Address to Farmers at Gloucester (24.4.1933)
Farmers' March and Mass Meeting (2.2.1939)

Cambridge Daily News
(original title of *Cambridge Evening News*)
(The cartoonist Sid Moon worked for the *Cambridge Daily News* until 1935 and the NTA commissioned a series of his cartoons which were used for posters and banners at demonstrations.)
Tithe and the parsons – 'Clergy Should Help Payers' (10.1.1933)

Cardiff Weekly Mail
Farmers' Refusal to Pay Tithe – 'Burden is More Than We Can Bear' (14.1.1933)
Tithe Rent Sales to be by Tender – County Court Judge's Order in North Wales (11.3.1933)
Welsh Farmer and his Tithe – Offer to Pay Made in High Court (25.3.1933)

Church Times
Tithe (18 November 1932)
Mr Kedward and the Tithe Act (17.3.1933)
Tithe – Churchmen's Defence Union (24.3.1933)
The Tithe Problem ... it is absurd to treat the present dispute as a struggle between the

Church and the agricultural interests – Letter from AG Mobbs (15.9.1933)
Tithe (22.9.1933)
Tithe – George Middleton – T Bennett – AG Mobbs – Howard Dobson – H D Lockett (6.10.1933)

Cork Examiner

Farmers' Revolt – Tithe War ... *"but I know all about this. This what happened in the tithe war in Ireland a hundred years ago". This is so, but what my friend was telling me about was the struggle that is going on in many places in England at the present moment ... law-abiding fellows, who would hate to be thought to have anything Irish in their make up ... when you get down to the elemental things human nature in Kent is very like human nature in Tipperary'* (19.11.1932)

Daily Dispatch

Farmers' "Victory" at Tithe Sale – "Hymn of Hat" and Oratory – How Sale was Held up – Lively Farm Scenes in Wrexham (23.2.1933)
Tithe Suit in High Court – Farmer Decides to Pay (21.3.1933)

Daily Express

'I manage a very poor farm in Kent. The house and buildings are practically uninhabitable, and the land unlettable. Yet the tithe is 8s 6d per acre – just about the value of the land if I could let it. Beyond this there is land tax, quit rent, and fee farm rents' – E E Cockett (24.12.1932)
100 Policeman in Farm Tithe Raids Comedy – Only Two Hens 'Arrested' (22.12.1932)
Though Queen Anne is Dead – Fenland still pays taxes to her Ghost (14.1.1933)
County Condemns Tithe Law – Protest Meeting (21.3.1933)
Judge Says Household Goods Can Be Seized To Pay Tithes – Farmer's Test Case Plea Fails – Decision to be Fought on Appeal (7.4.1933)
'Sir, The agitation against payment of tithe is spreading, and I am not surprised when I take into consideration figures relating to a farm near Doncaster ...' (11.4.1933)
Trousered Daughter of Peer in Farmers' War – "Tithes are a Racket on Chicago Scale" – Lady Eve Balfour, Milkmaid and Ploughman – She Shuns Society (1.8.1933)
Harvest Interrupts A Tithe War Charge Against 36 Farmers – Lady Eve Balfour in The Dock – Solicitor tells of "Imprisonment" in a

Barn – Pelted with Eggs (4.8.1933)
Farmers Win Tithe Victory – Unconditional Surrender of Mrs Waspe's Crops (10.8.1933)
Woman Laments her Home Stripped for Tithes – 'I shall not have the courage to begin again' (5.6.1934)
Government Bid to Save Little Man £40,000,000 – Fight Over Mine Royalties Begins (4.5.1936)
Country Came to London – With Tithe Grievance (25.6.1936)
Sir Reginald Promises "A Square Deal" by William Barkley (2.2.1939)

Daily Herald

Tyranny of the Tithe – 'Agricultural land paid nearly £3,000,000 in ecclesiastical tithe in the year 1928-29' (5.4.1930)
Scots best at Making Farm Profits – Heavy tithes and mortgage charges (28.12.1932)
Signs of a Truce in the Tithe War – Putting an End to Farcical Auctions (26.12.1933)
Children "For Sale" – 2,000 Farmers Stop Tithe Sale – auctioneer signs "No More" Pledge (23.2.1933)
Preparing Plans for Tithe War (15.3.1933)
Farmers Want New Tithe Bill (16.3.1933)
Tithe Sheep Sent Across Country For Sale – Herded in 40-acre Clearing Station – Chipping Norton, Oxfordshire (12.7.1933)
Tithe War to the Death – No Quarter Pledge by 11,000 Farmers (19.7.1933)
MP's Bill to Cut Tithes – A Sliding Scale Based on Profit (20.7.1933)
The Inside Story of The Tithe War by A W Rapley (2.8.1933)
A Bishop Defends Tithes – Dr Albert A David, Bishop of Liverpool, here presents the Churchman's side of the Tithe War – 'In Ancient times the only way of investment was in land ...' (10.8.1933)
Tithe was £20: £2,000 Wanted Now – Farmer told he should sell his Land (21.8.1933)
Tithe Muzzle on Clergy – Must Not Make Public Their Grievances – Bishop stops Vicars' "Justice" Protest ... An "order" to the Chelmsford Diocesan Conference not to discuss its tithe troubles in public was given yesterday by Mr George Middleton, chairman of QAB Tithe Committee (12.10.1933)
Tithe War to Start Again – Farmers Threatened with Mass Offensive (9.11.1933)
Scenes at Tithe Distraint – How villagers and

local farmers attended a tithe sale at Standlake, Oxon (10.4.1935)

Church May War with State – Report on Tithe Next Week – £500,000 Loss Feared (20.2.1936)

London Tithe March – Rebel Farmers Chained to Banner – Victim of Forced Sale in Repurchased Chair (25.6.1936)

Daily Mail
Socialist MP's £2,200 job – Local Party Rift – Mr George Middleton (19 June 1931)

Farmers Expect Home Market Help (19.1.1933)

350 Farmers Prevent Tithe Distraint Against a Widow – Men Besieged in Barn for Hours – Hive of Bees and Bad Eggs (23.5.1933)

The Tithe Revolt: Police Court Proceedings Adjourned (4.8.1933)

Farmers' Victory in Tithe Dispute (11.8.1933)

Day of Dramatic Moves in Tithe War – Wheatfield Bailiff Called Off – Legal Advice before Police left Camp (15.8.1933)

Paupers of the Church by F G Prince-White (15.3.1934)

Farmers March in London To-day by Percy W D Izzard (1.2.1939)

Tithe battle flares up again (8.9.1969)

Daily Mirror
Starving Ex-Wife (24.3.1933)

Mr Ashton Seimes, a farmer of Kingfield near Rye, Sussex, beside railway trucks loaded with property, sold out of his stock for tithe arrears, which was collected while he was away. A man lay across the railway line as a protest (25.3.1933)

Take the Pylon! – Court Rejects Bailiff's Suggestion for Tithes Distraint (31.3.1933)

Fear of a Conflict in Tithe War – Fascists Camp beside Two Bailiffs (9.8.1933)

Tithe Plight of Aged Couple – Furniture seized for £2 17s Debt (11.8.1934)

Human Barrier in Kent Tithe Raid – Drama at a Tithe Raid – Demonstrators Prone on the Ground (7.9.1934)

Primate's Effigy burnt as Protest – Farmers Join in Tithe Seizure Scene – 'Just Death' Verdict at Mock Inquest (6.4.1935)

And they call it ... Queen Anne's Bounty! by A E Waddell, the Kentish farmer who is leading the war against tithes (30.10.1935)

£70,000,000 Tithe Relief Scheme – No Extra Charge on the Exchequer (28.2.1936)

Farmer Giles Comes to Town – The March of the Yeomen of England (2.2.1939)

Why Albert Mobbs of Laurel Farm wants to escape from the Dark Ages (19.9.1969)

Daily Sketch
Novel Tithe Case (31.3.1933)

Women in Barrier of Bodies at Tithe Raid – Lie in Track of Lorries at Farm – Wild Scenes (7.9.1934)

Primate's Effigy in a Bonfire – Fireworks at an Amazing Tithe Sale Protest (6.4.1935)

London Sees Men 'In Chains' – Mass Demonstration Against Tithe Bill (25.6.1936)

5,000 Farmers come to Town (2.2.1939)

Daily Telegraph (The)
Tithes Injustice Averted – Sequel to Exposure by "The Daily Telegraph" – Canvey Island Man's Goods Returned – Thanks to the prompt action of The Daily Telegraph, the grave injustice which threatened Mr Arthur J Groves, the 70-year-old pensioner, of Canvey Island, has been averted (20.5.1931)

Resistance Campaign to Continue ... the Rev R M Kedward, the former MP ... said he was determined to continue his resistance campaign to relieve agriculture (30.11.1932)

Farm Tithe Comedy – Sixty Police in a Raid – Booty, Two Fowls and an Egg. (22.12.1932)

50 Per Cent Tithe Offer (25 January 1933)

Ashford By-Election – The Tithe Dispute (4.3.1933)

Eve of Poll at Ashford – Tithe Promise (14.3.1933)

Farm Politics at Ashford (15.3.1933)

Tithe Grievances – Government Inquiry Recommended (22.3.1933)

Tithe dispute – Writ of Attachment Superseded (28.3.1933)

Furniture Sales for Tithes (7.4.1933)

Burdens on British Farmers – J W Whittome (15.4.1933)

Still Another Tithe Battle – Men and Women lie in Front of Lorries (7.9.1934)

Tithe Abolition Recommended in Unanimous Report – "In Interests of All Parties and Country as a Whole" (28.2.1936)

Denbighshire Free Press
The Tithe Question (26.11.1932)

Farmers and Burden of Tithe – Judge Orders Payment of Amounts Due (14.1.1933)

Ruthin Farmers at Dinner – The Tithe

Problem Discussed (18.3.1933)
Wrexham Farmer and his Tithe (25.3.1933)
More Tithe-Payers in Court (8.4.1933)

Denbighshire Herald
Denbighshire Farmers – Union and Payment
of Tithes (24.12.1932)

Devon Gazette
Why Farmers cannot Compete with the
Foreigner (23.12.1932)
Exeter Farmers and the Position – The Tithe
Question (30.12.1932)
Farmers' Union – Demand for Inquiry into
Tithe Acts (24.3.1933)

Dorset Daily Echo
Dorset and Tithes (18.3.1933)
Tithes Chairman faces His Opponents – Keen
Debate at Unique Dorset Meeting
(10.4.1933)

Dover Express
County Court – When applications for tithe
came before Judge Clements at Ashford
county Court on Monday, his Honour
declined to make any orders. The applications
were by the Church Property Trust Ltd. And
no reason for this decision as given
(10.3.1933)

East Anglian Daily Times
Colchester Public Hall – testimony of
Churchwarden Gardiner (17.1.1887)
Agricultural Burdens – Sir Walter Guinness
and the Governments pledges (11.1.1928)
Farm, Field & Garden – Tithe Owners
Concessions (7.1.1933)
Taxes on Unpaid Tithes – County Court
Judge's Remarks at Diss (19.1.1933)
Tithe Settlement in Sight? – Suffolk
Chairman's Optimism at Colchester
(30.1.1933)
Brighter Prospect for Agriculture – Hardships
of Tithepayers (9.4.1933)
Blackshirts Committed for Trial at Old Bailey
– Story of trenches and alleged obstructions
on Wortham Farms (2.2.1934)
'Clergy Cannot Live on Fresh Air' – Bishop of
Chelmsford on Tithe (2.5.1934)
The Royal Commission on tithe – To inquire
into and report upon whole question of
Rentcharge – Names of Personnel – Sir John
Fischer Williams, K.C., appointed Chairman
(28.8.1934)

Eastern Counties and Tithe – Evidence before
Royal Commission (22.12.1934)
Amazing Tithe Sale Scenes – Effigies Burnt at
Wortham (17.3.1936)
Great Anti-Tithe Bill Demonstration in
London (25.6.1936)
(During April 1936, the EADT ran a ' Tithe
Platform' series of articles by Sir George
Middleton, Reverend George Wilkes, J O
Steed, AG Mobbs, Doreen Wallace, 'A Lay
Observer', F A Girling, the National
Tithepayers' Association, the Churchmen's
Defence Union, and others.)
Yaxley – Some scenes at the tithe sale ... for the
benefit of the Suffolk Tithepayers' Association
(2.2.1937)
(During 1938 the EADT ran a 'How
Agriculture Could be Restored' series of
articles by W E Sherston, AG Mobbs, W J
Shingfield, Charles Goddard, Mr Somerset de
Chair (MP), and others)
Will Farmers do the Mosley March?
(13.12.1938)
Suffolk Farmers' Threat to Government
(10.1.1939)
Farmers' Great London Rally (2.2.1939)
Farmers Burn Tithe Act (21.7.1939)
When farmers fought the tithe war – Doreen
Wallace (14.10.1974)
Prolific author fought for farmers' rights –
Doreen Wallace has died aged 92
(25.10.1989)
The Gentlemanly distraint at Laurel Farm
(1.4.1971)
End of an Injustice (23.9.1977)

Eastern Daily Press
New turn to Controversy at Church Assembly
– Canon G Brocklehurst raises tithe
rentcharge at (3.2.1932)
Rates on Tithe – District Council's
Application at Diss (18.1.1933)
Suffolk Tithe Resolution Carried (19.1.1933)
Tithe Gift Sale at Ipswich (8.4.1933)
Tithepayers' Meeting at Lynn (12.4.1933)
To-day's Tithe Meeting in Norwich
(10.6.1933)
Tithe 'War' Memorial Unveiled near Diss
(23.2.1935)
Wortham Tithe Distraint (5.6.1935)
Tithe Sale at Rushmere – No Bids for Cows or
Furniture (1.7.1935)

Norfolk NFU Discuss Tithe Bill – Why Mr
Alfred Lewis is in Favour of it (22.6.1936)
Blackshirt Support Offered (22.11.1938)
Farmers Demonstrate in London (2.2.1939)
Tithe Sale at Wortham Manor (21.7.1939)
Farmers urge tithe abolition (21.7.1972)
The End of the Tithe (28.9.1977)

Eastern Evening News
Suffolk Tithepayers' Association – To the
Editor, George Middleton (8.3.1933)
Tithepayers' Meeting at Lynn (17.3.1933)
West Norfolk Farmers' Losses – Claims for
Tithe at Wisbech County Court (27.4.1933)
Bitter war fought in field and farmhouse
(5.12.1968)

Essex Chronicle
The Tithe Question – A meeting of farmers
was held in the Congregational Schoolroom at
Dunmow to consider the question of tithe.
(16.12.1932)
Farmers' Meeting at Great Yeldham – Address
by Mr R A Butler, MP (27.1.1933)

Estates Gazette
Norfolk – Our duties as tithe agents and
collectors for and on behalf of Queen Anne's
Bounty keep us in close touch with the
agricultural situation ... (21.1.1933)
Distraint for Tithe (15.4.1933)
Parochial Church Council of the Parish of
Aston Cantlow (26.5.2001)
Beyond the call of duty ... Human Rights Act
1998 looks set to have a considerable impact
on real property law (23.6.2001)

Evening Standard
Readjustment of ordinary tithes 'Lady of the
Manor' (1.1.1886)
London Tithe-payers – The farcical climax to
the police raid on ten Kent farms, which
resulted in two fowls and one egg being seized
in lieu of tithes, prompts a correspondent to
call attention to irritating anomalies on the
tithe system in and near London (22.12.1932)
How the tithe Trouble Arose – It is becoming
increasingly clear that, whatever may be the
merits of the case, the tithe system is
producing such result as to make it a source of
public scandal (28.7.1933)

Evesham Standard
Pershore Farmers' Union – The Tithe

Question (24.12.1932)
Payment of Tithe – Mr Baldwin's Views
(13.1.1933)

Farmer & Stock-Breeder
Sequel to Anti-tithe Meetings – Governors of
QAB emphasise that their rights rest upon
perfectly firm legal basis (3.8.1931)
Tithe Revision Due – A Reply by the
Wallingford & District Tithepayers' Association to the Governors of QAB (24.8.1931)
*'Sir – I understand that the Bishop of
Chelmsford has said that in no paying tithe to
the Church we are not paying our just debts. I
beg to differ.'* Geo J Hook. (14.11.1932)
The 1925 Tithe Act – *'Sir ... A tithepayer has
been paying tithe on four acres thirty-one poles of
land, which was commuted in 1836 at £3 13s
1d. This year Queen Anne's Bounty are
demanding from him £4 in tithes ...'*
(19.12.1932)
Farmers and Tithe – Gloucester NFU
Member's Attitude to Proposed Association
(16.1.1933)
A Tithe Discussion (23.1.1933)
Tithe Payers Denounce New Bill –
'Parliament Should Justify Debt Before
Arranging for Collection' says Mr Mobbs
(16.4.1934)
NFU Faces a Tithe Crisis – Report of its
Committee Referred Back at council –
Meeting by Three to One Majority –
Tithepayers Refuse to Accept Government's
Bill – Headquarters in a Dilemma (23.4.1934)
A Royal Commission on Tithe (11.6.1934)
When Tithe Bill Becomes Law, Richard
Acland, MP, Barnstaple Division of Devon
(20.7.1936)
Rousing Call from East Anglia (17.1.1939)
NFU battle over tithes (16.9.1969)

Farmers Weekly
Ipswich raises £78 (22.6.1934)
Time to Sweep Away Tithe (13.12.1935)
Another Tithe War? (16.11.1945)
New Tithe Act Wanted (30.11. 1945)
Tithe and Tax – Letters to the Editor
(7.12.1945)
Battle to end tithe flares again (8.8.1969)
Well, does your lawyer pay tithe? By Frank
Butcher (2.1.1970)
Tithe Battle Flares as Bailiffs Act (16.10.1970)

Flintshire Observer
Denbighshire Branch and Tithe Question
(24.12.1932)
Farmer Tithe-Payers in County Court
(12.1.1933)

Folkestone Herald
Protest Against tithe Payments – Resolution
Passed at Folkestone Meeting – Rev Kedward's
Vigorous Attack (21.1.1933)
Non-Payment of Tithe (8.4.1933)

Guardian (The)
A 14th century Tithe Barn – a writer expresses
the opinion of the tithepayer (13.11.1931)
Tithe – H Hugh Breton, South Molton – W
H Harvey, Essex County Tithepayers'
Association (11.12.1931)
The Attacks on Tithe (18.8.1933)

Hampshire Chronicle
*'Sir, Landowners in Hampshire are not refusing
to pay Tithes. There is no case for confiscation,
nor is there for redemption; but there is for
conversion. War Loan Stock has been converted.
Why not Tithe?'* L G Richards. (19.11.1932)
Farmers' Topics – The Tithe Committee
(17.3.1933)
Hampshire Farmers' Union (15.4.1933)

Hampshire Telegraph
The National Farmers' Union – and the Tithe
Question (24.3.1933)

Harrow Observer
Tithe Farm Estate (17.3.1933)

Hereford Times
Farmers and tithe – Hay Branch of the
Association to be Formed (24.12.1932)
Salop Farmers – Discussions at Craven Arms
Meeting – Tithe Matters (31.12.1932)
Farmers' Union – The Tithe Question
(7.1.1933)
Tithe – Sir ... in 1925 the Tithe Act was
passed to secure the tithes (14.1.1933)
Tithe on Chapel – Kingstone Methodists
Refuse to Pay (11.3.1933)
Tithe at Ludlow – Branch of Association
formed (15.4.1933)
Facing disaster ... Dr Pearce, the Bishop of
Derby ... Cathedral revenue at Hereford is
derivable from tithes (17.2.1934)
Tithe Questions & Herefordshire Tithepayers
– A Challenge to the Bishop (24.2.1934)
Farmers and the New Tithe Bill – Hereford

Protest Meeting – Lady Evelyn Balfour and
The Church (14.4.1934)

Hull Times
*'I am surprised that both the NFU and the
Landowners' Association have decided not to co-
operative with the Tithepayers' Association. I
think the view is gaining ground among farmers
that the best way to deal with the hard cases that
undoubtedly exist is to approach the
Commissioners in a friendly spirit.'* (10.12.1932)
In Farming Circles – A Tithe Inquiry
(24.12.1932)

Ipswich Evening Star
Judge on Suffolk and Essex Tithepayers
(10.1.1933)
Annual Assembly of NFU – Suffolk Branch's
Tithe Resolution Carried (19.1.1933)
Tithepayers' Association for Eye – Mr Mobbs'
Invitation to the Clergy (22.3.1933)
Suffolk Tithepayers' Association (29.3.1933)
Furniture Seized for Tithe (7.4.1933)
Tithe Cases at Beccles County Court
(11.4.1933)
A Tithepayer consults his Conscience
(12.4.1933)

Isle of Thanet Gazette
Farmers Protests Against tithe – Alderman G
C Solley's Remarks at Folkestone (21.1.1933)
Minster Farmer's Tithes (8.4.1933)

John Bull
The Terrible Tenth – *'When sane and
substantial citizens declare – as they are doing
today – that they will go to prison rather than
pay a debt which the law demands of them, it is
evident that they are suffering from a rankling
sense of injustice ...'* (4.7.1931)

The Journal
Black Shirts at Wortham, 'Purely Defensive
Action' against Tithe Distraint, says National
Political Officer (17.2.1934)

Kent Messenger
Tithe Payer & the Law (19 July 1930)
Sir A Geddes and Mr Kedward – 'Trying to
Poison the Minds of the People' (24.10.1931)
What our Readers Think – Farmers and the
Tithe (26.11.1932)
Tithe Resisters' New Move (3.12.1932)
Police Ambush for Tithe Payers – Attempted
March on Rectory frustrated (30.3.1935)
How Far is the Primate involved in the Tithe

Problem? (20.4.1935)

News and Views for Farmers – 'An Intolerable Position' (15.2.1936)

Tithe 'War' Ends in Farmers' Favour (29.2.1936)

News & Views for Farmers – Tithe Bill Action – Ashford Demand for Withdrawal of the Tithe Bill (6.6.1936)

230 Tithe Orders (6.3.1937)

Death of Rev R M Kedward (6.3.1937)

Kentish Express (see also **Tuesday Express**)

The Pluckley Tithe Demonstration – F R Allen (19.7.1930)

Farmers' Gifts for Tithe Campaign – £173 realised in Ashford Market (2.12.1932)

The First Gift Auction Sale (31.12.1932)

The Elham Tithe Sale (13.1.1933)

Farmers' Union and tithe (25.2.1933)

'86 Tithe Agitation – Reminiscences of those who Remember the Scenes (3.3.1933)

Tithe Deadlock – Judge Refuses Orders (10.3.1933)

Elham Tithe Question – Unsuccessful Attempt towards Settlement (21.4.1933)

New Decision in tithe War – Judge Urges Compromise (5.5.1933)

Farmers' Evidence Before Tithe Commission (30.11.1934)

Rector and Tithe Redemption – Canon Brocklehurst's Evidence Before Commission (1.3.1935)

Tithepayers Burn Primate's Effigy – Scenes at Westwell Tithe Sale – Three Donkeys in Procession (April 1935)

MPs and Tithe Scenes – 'Insult to Head of the Church' (12.4.1935)

Sheep Seized for Tithe – Distraint at Charing (5.6.1936)

Letters to the Editor – Replies to "A Parson's Daughter" – H Roseveare (21.8.1936)

Unexpected Death of the Rev R M Kedward (12.3.1937)

Archbishop Reviews Re-Call to Religion – Tithe Discussion (29.10.1937)

Kentish Gazette

The Elham Tithe War – Sir Wm Wayland Gives his Views (19.11.1932)

Tithe (18.2.1933)

Critical Stage in Tithe Campaign (28.4.1933)

Kidderminster Shuttle

Markets and Tithes – Captain H Tyler (a member of the County Union), speaking as a

representative of Worcester Tithe Payers' Association, addressed the meeting on the militant steps being taken to bring about repeal of the 1925 Tithe Act. (17.12.1932)

Leighton Buzzard Observer

Tithe Rent Tax – 'The Chairman said the tax on the tithe rent charge on the Rye allotments amounted to £20 13s 9d. This amount included £11 13s 3d due from Mr Labrum, and he wondered whether they could be made to collect Mr Labrum's portion.' (7.3.1933)

Lincolnshire Echo

Lincolnshire Chambers of Agriculture – Tithes (10.3.1933)

Welsh Farmer's Tithe Protest (27.3.1933)

Liverpool Echo

Welsh Tithe Dispute – Alleged Contempt of Court (6.3.1933)

'I Can't Alter the Law' – Judge Whitmore Richards at Cheshire County Court (7.3.1933)

Sequel to Welsh Tithe Dispute (27.3.1933)

Defaulting Farmers – Judge on Sympathetic Treatment (4.4.1933)

Liverpool Post

Distraint for Tithe – Order Allowing Sale by Tender – Judge and the Farmers' Agitation (8.3.1933)

The Church and Tithe (10.3.1933)

North Wales Farm Tithe Protest – Wrexham Farmer in High Court (20.3.1933)

Tithe Payments – Montgomeryshire Farmer's Suggestion (22.3.1933)

Tithe Payments – Sir, S Aurelius Jones, Vicar of Gwersyllt (23.3.1933)

Tithe Collection Anomaly (28.3.1933)

Welsh Tithe Cases (5.4.1933)

Lynn Advertiser

An Agricultural Survey for 1932 – by Sir Richard Wintrey (30.12.1932)

Tithe and the Farmer – Protest Meeting at Lynn (14.4.1933)

Malvern Gazette

Payment of tithe – Mr Baldwin's Views (13.1.1933)

Manchester Evening News

Tithe Rent Notices Sent Out by Trustee after Thirty Years – For the first time for about 30 years notices have been sent out to the several hundred people in the parish of New Church,

Culcheth, near Leigh, of a proposed tithe rent charge (20.12.1932)
Farmers of North Eager for Fight – Though in Lancashire and Cheshire the position is not so acute it was stated by farmers of both counties today that any action decided upon by the NFU to end the tithe system would receive their support (23.2.1933)
Tithe Warning (8.3.1933)
Tithe Writ Case Ended – Farmer Pays Full Rent Charge (27.3.1933)

Manchester Guardian
Carlisle Labour and Mr Middleton, MP (22.6.1931)
Farmers Sued for Tithe – £600 involved – Many cases at Ruthin (11.1.1933)
Tithe Campaign – Preliminary Steps in Anglesey (24.3.1933)
Welsh Farmer's Tithe Paid – Writ Superseded (28.3.1933)
Tithe Critics – Bounty Chairman Heckled at Meeting/Welsh Farmers and Tithe (10.4.1933)
Obituary – Sir George Middleton (26.10.1938)
The Farmers' March (2.2.1939)

Morning Post
Socialist MP's £1,200 a Year – Sir George Middleton (22.6.1931)
Ashford Awakens – Beer, Tithes and Employment (10.3.1933)
Political Notes – Tithe Grievances (22.3.1933)
Tithe Collection by Ruse – Farmers Outwitted (24.3.1933)
Puzzled Cheam Residents (3.4.1933)
Furniture for Tithe Rents – Distraint Held to be Legal (7.4.1933)
Tithe war in Kent (2.5.1933)

New Statesman
Mr Keynes's Proposals (1.4.1933)

Newcastle Journal
More About the Tithe Proposals (21.3.1936)
"A Square Deal" for Agriculture (2.2.1939)

News Chronicle
Tithe Raid Comedy – 100 Police Escort Two Hens – Runaway Van Adventure (22.12.1932)
Tithe-payers Support Mr Kedward (14.3.1933)
By-Election Apathy Scares Tories – The Angry Farmers of Ashford (15.3.1933)
Rector Says Clergy are Living on the Dole (9.9.1934)
Three New Counties joint Revolt on Tithes –

Attack on NFU Policy (19.9.1934)
600 Farmers at Tithe War Debate – *'Six hundred farmers from all parts of Devon and Cornwall crowded Bude Picture Theatre today to hear a debate between Mr George Middleton, Chairman of the Tithe Committee of QAB and Mr A G Mobbs'* (28.9.1934)
Tithepayers Offer to Settle but Deny Liability (7.12.1934)
State Funds to Wind up Tithe – 'Only Way to Avoid Conflict' (8.12.1934)
A Townsman's View of Agriculture by Sir Walter Layton (5.2.1935)
Open War on Tithes – Protest to Premier at 'Gross Extortion' (28.8.1935)
Government Loan to End Tithe System – Mr Elliot's Offer to Primate (14.2.1936)
£70,000,000 Scheme to End All Tithe – Payment Spread over 60 Years (28.2.1936)
New Tithe Battle – Both Sides Attack Settlement – Farmers Will Fill Gaols, Mr Kedward – Church Loses £13,500,000, Queen's Bounty (29.2.1936)
Surprises of New Tithe Bill (6.5.1936)
Tithe Bill Survives Heavy Fire – Opponents Will Fight on (23.5.1936)
5,000 Farmers' Protest March Through West End – "Drop The Tithe Bill" call – The Cromwellian Touch (25.6.1936)
Farmers Come to Town (2.2.1939)
Tussle over Tithes is Starting Again (9.8.1945)

News of the World
Tithe Sale Scenes – Story of a Notice in Verse – Contempt of Court alleged (12.3.1933)
Tithe Protest – Sequel to a Farmers' Agitation (26.3.1933)
Tithe War Truce – QAB and the Payers (30.4.1933)

Northampton Evening Telegraph
Farmers' Tithe Grievance – Tax Fixed When Corn Prices were Higher (20.3.1933)
Matters of Moment to Farmers – Tithe Payments (4.4.1933)
Farmers Invade London (1.2.1939)

Observer (The)
Mobbs Comes to Town by J W Murray (21.9.1969)

Oxford Mail
Clergy Case in Tithe Dispute (28.11.1932)
Fight Against Tithes (20.1.1933)

Tithe Peace Hope (17.2.1933)
'Scandal of the Tithe is Still with Us' – Bishop
Shedden's Remarkable Sermon at Cuddesdon
College Festival (18.6.1935)

Oxfordshire Times

*'There is not a shadow of doubt but that the
discontent and friction which the 1925 Act has
fomented will increase unless steps are taken by
the Government to amend the Act upon terms
that are equitable to both tithe owners and
payers.'* (18.11.1932)
'Grave Injustice' of Tithe – Novel Sale in
Oxford (26.11.1932)
Tithe Proposals Attacked – "Entirely
Unacceptable" – Oxford Protest at 'Mortgage'
on Agriculture (7.3.1936)

Oxon Advertiser

Cholsey Farmer's Early Callers – Bailiff
Demands £31 for Tithes – Auctioneer takes
inventory of furniture (27.4.1934)

Peterborough Advertiser (The)

Animated Anti-Tithe Demonstration at
Peterborough – Vigorous Speakers from the
Southern Battle-Front – Why the 1925 Act
should be Repealed! – The Scandal of Church
Gifts in Perpetuity – Relic of an Easy-Going
Age (27.1.1933)
Peterborough's Anti-Tithe Meeting – a Reply
to Some of the Speakers by Queen Anne's
Bounty's Tithe Chairman (10.2.1933)

Post and Weekly News (The)

The Tithe War – Farmers hear Debate at Bude
– Two Sides of the Question Explained
(6.10.1934)

Press and News

Tithe Chief Faces Heckling Essex Farmers –
Lively Reception at Saffron Walden Meeting –
Bounty an 'Innocent Instrument' – No Mercy
for the "Cans" Who Won't (1.9.1933)

Reading Mail

*'Livestock and goods of all kinds given by farmers
were sold at Oxford Cattle Market on Wednesday
to raise money for propaganda for a revision of
the Tithe Laws and to protect those whose goods
are sold by distraint for tithe.'* (26.11.1932)

Reading Mercury

Tithe Policy – Wallingford (19.11.1932)
Berks Executive, National Farmers' Union –
The Tithe and Milk Questions (24.12.1932)

Country – with the Farmers – Views at
Oxford NFU Meeting – Minister and the
Tithe Problem (14.1.1933)

Reynold's Illustrated News

Merger of Tithe and Rent-Roll –
£250,000,000 Capital – The Church of
England is taking a leaf out of the Big Business
Bible. The organisations which look after its
material affairs are likely to become
rationalised (5.11.1933)
Mystery Owner of a Great Derelict Estate –
Tithe Problems (27.9.1936)

Salisbury & Winchester Journal, and General Advertiser (The)

The Tithe Question – Condemnation of
Compulsory Redemption (20.1.1933)
The Tithe Question – The Case for Queen
Anne's Bounty – Interested Parties meet at
Hinton St Mary (14.4.1933)
Wiltshire Landowner's Survey – Tithes in the
County (14.4.1933)

Shrewsbury Chronicle

The Tithe Act Problem – Mr R S Strachey's
Views (30.12.1932)
Readers' Views on Tithe, Police and Motorists
(3.3.1933)
Tithe Act Amendment Urged (24.3.1933)

Southern Daily Echo

Talking Over Tithe Question – Meeting ' To
See Rights and Wrongs' (10.4.1933)

Spectator (The)

The Revolt Against Tithe by R C K Ensor
(4.8.1933)
The Tithe Question in England and in Wales
(24.3.1933)
The Tithe Bill – *'Sir, Many will regret that The
Spectator (hitherto a source of "sweetness and
light" on the tithe problem) erroneously regards
the dead Bill as a compromise"* (and, implicitly, a
fair one) ...' (22.6.1934)

Suffolk Chronicle

Suffolk Tithepayers' Association – Next week's
Sale at Ipswich for Funds (31.3.1933)
Remarkable Tithe Sale Scenes – Ipswich
market Inundated with Gifts – Stock Realises
£750 – Buyers attend from all part of the
country (7.4.1933)
A Living Wage for Farm Workers
(16.12.1933)

Sutton Times

Tithe Charges – A Puzzle for Cheam Residents – Schemes for the compulsory redemption of tithes are causing dissatisfaction among residents in one of the newly-developed areas of Cheam ... a number of tithe fields have been built over and the annual tithe-payments divided into units of a few pence each, payable by the purchasers of the houses ... (7.4.1933)

Times (The)

Tithe Resistance (25.11.1932)
Tithe Dispute in Kent – Bailiff's Small Haul (22.12.1932)
Farmers and Tariffs – Tithe Redemption (12.1.1933)
Security in Home Market – Expectation of Farmers – Tithe (19.1.1933)
Offer to Settle Tithe Arrears (25.1.1933)
King's Bench Division – Tithe Sales in Wales (2.3.1933)
Kent By-Election – Labour and Tithe (10.3.1933)
Tithe Distraint in Farmer's Absence (24.3.1933)
Essex Tithes Case (31.3.1933)
The Case for Queen Anne's Bounty (4.4.1933)
Tithe as Property – Two Points of View (15.4.1933)
Tithe Cases at Saffron Walden (29.4.1933)
A Tithe Compromise (31.3.1934)
An End of Tithe (28.2.1936)
Tithe Grumbles (16.3.1936)
The Tithe Bill (6.5.1936)
Tithe Hill – Help for Incumbents – Payment of the Annuities – Cost of Collection (20.5.1936)
Tithe Bill – Labour Peer and the Church – The Primate's Reply – Tribute to Country Clergy (8.7.1936)
Voluntary Tithe – Archbishops' Appeal for the Clergy – Cosmo Cantuar. (1.10.1936)
Sir G Middleton – The Ecclesiastical Commissioner (26.10.1938)
Farmers' March in London (2.2.1939)
Obituary – Alderman Edwin Gooch – Sturdy Champion of Farmworkers (3.8.1964)
Couple 'inherit' £96,000 church bill (29.3.2000)
Gary Slapper – Court of Appeal gives judgement (29.5.2001)

Tiverton Gazette

Farmers and Tithes – Sallies in Verse (7.3.1933)
The Tithe Controversy – Lower Prescott, Tiverton – Recruits claimed from Kentisbeare (21.3.1933)
Farmers and Tithes – Sir, E J Musgrove, Tiverton (28.3.1933)
Distraint for Tithe – Seizure of Furniture (11.4.1933)

Tuesday Express

(The **Kentish Express** mid-weekly)
Judge and Pluckley Demonstration – Comments on Tithepayer's Protest – Judicial Rebuke at Ashford (8.7.1930)
Lively Tithe Meeting at Canterbury – In the Lions' Den – Queen Anne's Chairman meets Tithepayers (10.10.1933)
Mr R M Kedward Wins Tithe Case – Judge Refuses Second Distraint – Receiver Under-Estimates Sale Value (16.7.1935)
Funeral Tributes to The Rev R M Kedward – Ashes scattered at Charing (16.3.1937)

West Wales Guardian

Farmers and the Tithe – Some People Never Satisfied – Pembroke City Edition (5.3.1933)
Where the Tithes Go – Pembroke County Edition (17.3.1933)

Western Gazette (Yeovil)

Tithe – 'Sir, It is repeatedly stated that tithe is a burden on agriculture. Is this true? As a landowner, I hold it is not. Rather it is a burden on landowning.' (23.12.1932)
Tithe – Sir ... George Pitt-Rivers (6 .1.1933)
Tithe – Letters to the Editor (13.1.1933)
Dorset Tithe Protest – Gathering at Hinton St Mary – Captain Pitt Rivers and Land Burdens (24.2.1933)
Tithe Grievances – Conservative MPs Appeal to Government (24.3.1933)
The Tithe Controversy – big gathering at Hinton St Mary (14.4.1933)
Tithe – Can Furniture be Seized in Distraint? – Important Judgement in Salisbury Appeal/Anti-Tithe Leader's Unpaid Tithe – Clergyman's Appeal for the Money – Captain Pitt-Rivers' Reply (20.10.1933)

Western Mail (& South Wales News)

Welsh Farmers Refuse to Pay Tithe Charges – 44 sued in County Court – Burden is More

Than We Can Bear (11.1.1933)
Welsh Farmers and Tithes Payment (14.1.1933)
Settlement of Welsh Tithe Dispute in Sight –
Farmers' Stocks Not to be Sold (20.1.1933)
Tithe Acts Inquiry – Farmers Demand
Immediate Action (17.3.1933)
One Thing Out of Every Ten (28.3.1933)

Western Morning News
Address to Devon Farmers (14.1.1933)
Turning point in Agriculture – Churchman
on Tithes (28.1.1933)
Wool Prices and Tithe Charges – Protest by
Somerset Farmers (24.2.1933)
Tithe Grievances – Conservative MPs Appeal
to Government (22.3.1933)
Tithe Question – Report to Somerset Farmers'
Union (21.3.1933)
Distraint for Tithe in Cornwall – Mevagissey
Farm Case – Protest at Bodmin Meeting
(28.9.1934)

Worcester Daily Times
Another Dispute with the Church – 'Mr J H
Stevens, a Cambridgeshire farmer who figured in
a case three years ago when the ecclesiastical
authorities insisted that he should repair the
chancel of Hauxton Church, near Cambridge, is
involved in a dispute with the same authorities
over the payment of tithes.' (22.11.1932)
Farmers and Tithe – Unconstitutional or
Other Methods? (16.12.1932)

Wrexham Leader
Denbighshire Farmers' Union – The Tithe
(23.12.1932)
The New Tithe War – Why the Vicar of
Gwersyllt was Present at Recent Sale
(3.3.1933)
The Recent Tithe Sale at Gwersyllt – Alleged
Contempt of Court (10.3.1933)
Gwersyllt Farmer and Tithe – Proceedings in
the High Court (25.3.1933)

Yorkshire Herald
A Farmer's Tithe Protest – High Court Sequel
– To Pay – 'Wales: Where They Sing With or
Without Provocation', Counsel (21.3.1933)
Tithe Grievances – Agricultural MPs Urge
Government to Act (22.3.1933)

Yorkshire Post
Lancashire Property Owners' Opposition – 'A
large number of property owners in the Culcheth
district between Leigh and Warrington, which is

in the deanery of Winwick and the diocese of
Liverpool, have received notice to redeem tithe
rent charges. These vary from a few shillings to
many pounds.' (21.12.1932)
The Church and Tithes – Commissioners'
Reply to Charges Protest (10 March 1933)
Tithe Dispute – Argument in High Court
Today (20.3.1933)
Writ of Attachment Against Farmer – Offer of
Payment (21.3.1933)
Tithes (22.3.1933)
Tithe – The Position as to Owners and Payers
(13.4.1933)

In addition, articles appeared in the following
newspapers, among others:
*Bath & Wiltshire Chronicle, Bedford
Standard, Belfast Newsletter, Birmingham
Evening Despatch, Birmingham Mail,
Bournemouth Daily Echo, Brecon Express,
Bristol Evening World, Burton Daily Mail,
Bury Free Press, Caernarvon Herald,
Cheltenham Chronicle, Cheshire Daily
Echo, Cheshire Observer, Chester
Chronicle, Church Assembly News,
Cornish Times, Cornishman, Cornish &
Devon Post, Daily Worker, Darlington
Times, Dartford Chronicle, Deal, Walmer,
Sandwich Mercury, Dorset County
Chronicle, East Kent Gazette, Folkestone
Express, Grantham Journal, Hertfordshire
& Essex Observer, Huddersfield Daily
Examiner, Ipswich Evening Standard,
Kent Courier, Law Journal, Leeds Mercury
Leicester Mercury, Leighton Buzzard
Gazette, Lowestoft Journal, Manchester
Daily Post, Manchester Evening Chronicle,
Montgomery County Times, Morning
Advertiser, Norfolk Chronicle, North
Devon Herald, Oxford News, Pembroke
County Guardian, Peterborough Herald,
Southern Times, Southern Weekly News,
Staffordshire Evening Sentinel, Sunday
Despatch, Sunday Graphic (incorporating
The Sunday Herald and Sunday News),
Sunday Pictorial, Sussex Courier, Sutton
Advertiser, Torbay Express, Torquay Times,
Tunbridge Wells Advertiser, Warwick
Advertiser, Weekly Illustrated, Wellington
Journal, Welsh Gazette, Western Times,
Wiltshire Gazette, Wiltshire News,
Yarmouth Independent*

BIBLIOGRAPHY

Best, G F A, *Temporal Pillars: Queen Anne's Bounty, the Ecclesiastical Commissioners, and the Church of England*, Cambridge, 1964

Brewer, J D, *Mosley's Men: The BUF in the West Midlands*, Aldershot, 1984

Brocklehurst, Rev George, *A Text Book of Tithes and Tithe Rentcharge*, Kent, 1911

Bryant, Mark & Heneage, Simon, *Dictionary of British Cartoonists & Caricaturists: 1730-1980*, Hampshire, 1994

Butler, R A B, *Art of the Possible: The Memoirs of Lord Butler*, 1971

Cooper, Ashley, *The Long Furrow*, 1982

Cross, Colin, *The Fascists in Britain*, 1961

Ecclesiastical Law (reprint from *Halsbury's Laws of England*), 1957

Ernle, Lord, *English Farming Past and Present*, new edition by Sir A D Hall (1941)

Evans, Eric J, *The Contentious Tithe: The Tithe Problem and English Agriculture 1750-1850*, London, 1976

Evans, Eric J, *Tithes: Maps, Apportionments and the 1836 Act*, Chichester, 1993

Forman, Susan, *Loaves and Fishes: An illustrated history of the Ministry of Agriculture, Fisheries and Food 1889-1989*, 1989

Friar, Stephen, *The Companion to the English Parish Church*, London, 2000

Gill, George J, *A Fight against Tithes (with an Epilogue by Henry Williamson)*, Dorking, 1952

Groves, Reg, *Sharpen the Sickle! The History of the Farm Workers' Union*, London, 1948

Groves, Reg, *Seed Time & Harvest*, 1972

Hart, A Tindal, *The Country Priest in English History*, London, 1960

Hawkins, Rev W M, *Key to the Tithe Question: A Handbook on Tithes*, London, 1887

Hitchman, Janet, *Such a Strange Lady*, 1975

Jackman, Francis, *Tithes, Their Origin and Abuse*, London, 1934

Jacobs, Leslie C, *Constables of Suffolk*, 1992

Kain, Roger JP, *Tithe Surveys for Historians*, 2000

Kain, Roger & Prince, Hugh, *The Tithe Surveys of England and Wales*, 1985

Kain, Roger J P & Oliver, Richard R, *The Tithe Maps of England and Wales*, 1995

Kendall, R T, *The Gift of Giving*, 1982

Kilvert, Rev Francis, *Kilvert's Diary 1870-1879*, ed William Plomer, 1944

Lawrance, David M, *Imperial Taxes and Tithe Rentcharge*, 1926

Le Fanu's Queen Anne's Bounty: a Short Account of its History and Work, 2nd edition F G Hughes, 1933

Lockhart, J G, *Cosmo Gordon Lang*, London, 1949

Mayfield, Guy, *The Church of England*, 1963

McCarthy, Justin, *The Reign of Queen Anne, Volumes 1 & 2*, London, 1902

Milford, H S, ed, *The Complete Poetical Works of William Cowper*, London, 1906

Mobbs, A G, *Eighty Years on Suffolk Soil*, 1974 (unpublished)

Moore, A W, *A History of the Isle of Man, Vol II*, London 1900 (Manx Museum & National Trust, 1977)

Morsley, Clifton, *News From the English Countryside: 1851-1950*, London, 1983

Mosley, Nicholas, *Rules of the Game*, 1982

Mosley, Nicholas, *Beyond the Pale*, 1985

Pemberton Leach, George, *The Tithe Acts and The Rules Under the Tithe Act, 1891*, London, 1896

Roundell, Earl of Selborne, *Ancient Facts and Fictions concerning Churches and Tithes*, London, 1888

Rowland, Peter, *Lloyd George*, 1975

Savidge, Alan, *The Foundation and Early Years of Queen Anne's Bounty*, London, 1955

Seaman, L C B, *Life in Britain Between the Wars*, London, 1985

Shepherd, June, *Doreen Wallace (1897-1989), Writer and Social Campaigner*, 2000

Simper, Robert, *The Suffolk Show 1831-1981*, 1981

Strachey, R S, *Freedom from The Tithe Act, 1925*, London, 1932

Trevelyan, G M, *English Society History*, 1944

Twinch, Carol, *Women on the Land*, Cambridge, 1990

Venn, J A, *The Foundations of Agricultural Economics*, Cambridge, 1933

Whetham, Edith H, *The Agrarian History of England and Wales, 1914-1939, Vol VIII*, Cambridge, 1978

William Cowper's Letters, A Selection, ed E V Lucas, 1911

Williamson, Henry, *The Story of a Norfolk Farm*, London, 1942

Woodforde, James, *The Diary of a Country Parson 1758-1802*, ed John Beresford, 1935

Wynn, Bob, *Skilled At All Trades: The History of the Farmworkers' Union 1947-1984*, London, 1993

Also:

Tithe Records: A Detailed Examination (Leaflet 41, Public Record Office)

Chancel Repairs (Legal Records Information Leaflet 33, PRO)

The Land Worker (Journal of the National Union of Agricultural Workers) 1931-1936

The NFU Record (Journal of the National Farmers' Union) 1925-1980

The CLA Journal (also *Country Landowner*)

Who's Who and *Who Was Who*

County Trade Directories

Works by Doreen Wallace, including: *The Portion of the Levites* (1933), *The Tithe War* (1934), *So Long to Learn* (1936), *Old Father Antic* (1937), *Barnham Rectory* (1939), *East Anglia* (1939, 2nd edition 1942-3), *Land from the Waters* (1944)

See **Appendix V** for a selection of newspaper references

Miscellaneous:

Tithe Rentcharge Tables (Shaw & Sons), the following editions:
1837-1859 Henry Pyne (Tithe Commission)
1860-1891 George Taylor Snr (Tithe Commission)
1893-1909 George Herbert Taylor (Board of Agriculture)
Tithe Rent Charge and Redemption Annuity Tables
1910-1937 Percy William Millard (Board of Agriculture & MAFF)

Tithe Collecting in Wales (Daily Graphic, 29 August 1890)

Y Faner (Welsh language newspaper) Distraint on James Davies of Nant-y-Merddyn, Llansannan (1894)

Journal of the Board of Agriculture (The Food Production Programme for 1919) October 1918

Tithe – A Churchman's Reply (*The Field*, 19 November 1932)

QAB and Tithe (*Church of England Newspaper*, 8 September 1933)

The Tithe Questions: The Tithe-payer's Point of View, AG Mobbs, and The Tithe-owner's Point of View, George Middleton (*The Listener*, BBC, 22 November 1933)

Some Monstrosities of Tithe Law, C B Scammell (1933)

Questions & Answers on Tithe, Captain G Pitt-Rivers (*Tithe News Sheet*, January 1934)

The Distraint, Doreen Wallace (*Tithe News Sheet*, January 1934)

Queen Anne's Bounty: Original, History & Work of a Famous Institution, W G Hannah (*The Churchman's Handbook*, 1934)

Tithe: A Monthly News Sheet of Current Events and Opinions (January 1934)

Parliamentary Debates, House of Lords, Tuesday 17 April 1934 (Vol 91 – No 42)

Tithe, "Ye Devour Widows' Houses", Alderman E W Tanner, JP CC (*Liberal Messenger*, Saffron Walden Division, September 1934)

The Church and Housing: Work of the Ecclesiastical Commissioners, George Middleton (Board of the Church Assembly, 1934)

Fascism and the Tithe Question, Alexander Raven Thomson (*The Blackshirt*, November 1934)

The Incredible Tale of Tithe, Doreen Wallace (*Good Housekeeping*, 1935)

The Inferiority Complex in Marriage, Doreen Wallace (*Good Housekeeping*, 1935)

Minutes of Evidence Taken Before the Royal Commission on Tithe Rentcharge (HMSO, 1936)

Resources of the Church: The Ecclesiastical Commissioners and Queen Anne's Bounty, Sir George Middleton (Board of the Church Assembly, circa 1937)

The Land Flares Up! British Democratic Party: The Party of Tomorrow (1939)

The Potato Riots, 1825 (The Isle of Man Natural History & Antiquarian Society Proceedings, Vol IV, 1945)

Facts and Incidents of an Unequal Struggle (Ashford, Kent and Sussex Tithepayers' Association, circa 1950)

"Commit me to Prison" says the tithe war campaigner, Donald Rowland (*Norfolk & Suffolk Farmer*, Nov-Dec 1970)

BUF Intervention in the Wortham Tithe Dispute, Roger Spalding, *and Suffolk and the Tithe War of the 1930s*, John Mead (*East Anglian History Workshop Journal*, Vol 1)

Yesterday's Witness (*Radio Times*, 18 May 1972)

Yesterday's Witness: The Tithe War (Post Production Script, BBC2, 1972)

The Tithe War, S P Andrews (*Suffolk Fair*, Vol 5:4)

Recollections of the Waspe Tithe Distraints, 1932-34 (told by Edward John Waspe to Andrew Mitchell) (unpublished private paper)

Tithe Redemption Annuities (Inland Revenue Press Release, 17 June 1976)

The Demise of Tithe, Francis Holland (*Country Life*, 28 July 1977)

Closure of the Tithe Redemption Office (Inland Revenue Press Release, 24 October 1978)

The Good Old Days, Ruby Pollentine (*Suffolk Fair*, Vol 6, 1978)

The Tithe War (Wales 1886-91), Clwyd Record Office (1978)

Albert Mobbs, Doreen Wallace (*Suffolk Fair*, March 1979)

Recollections of the 'Tithe War', Alf Addison (*Suffolk Review*, Vol 5:1, 1980)

Blundeston & District Local History Society (extracts of AG Mobbs' unpublished autobiography, 1980-1981)

Tithe Memorial, Janet Cooper (Suffolk Local History Council, 1984)

Statutes in Force (Finance Act 1989) Part III Winding up of Redemption Annuities Account & Schedule 17 Tithe Redemption (HM Stationery Office 1989)

The Tithe War of the Twenties, R Edward Spalton (*Faith & Heritage*, No 37, 1994)

He Who Pays the Parson, John Wescott (*The Field*, April 1995)

"The Canterbury Tales" (Transmission Script, Twenty Twenty TV, 1996)

The Tithe War, Robert Halliday (*Suffolk Review*, Suffolk Local History Council, 1997)

Fascism in East Anglia: The British Union of Fascists in Norfolk, Suffolk and Essex 1933-1940, Dr Andrew Mitchell (Ph.D, University of Sheffield, 1999)

Tithe to Support the Church caused Riots, Harvey Briggs (*Isle of Man Examiner*, 24 April 2001)

Judgement in the Supreme Court of Judicature Court of Appeal (Civil Division): Case No A3/2000/0644 (Royal Courts of Justice, 17 May 2001)

Eastern Angles – Tithe War!, David Henshall (*East Anglian Magazine*, 30 June 2001)

Rash Behaviour – Eastern Angles Tithe War!, David Henshall (*East Anglian Magazine*, 7 July 2001)

Tithe War! A musical by Ivan Cutting & Pat Whymark (2001)

Doreen Wallace and the Tithe War, Carol Twinch (*Book Talk*, Autumn 2001)

INDEX

The index is simplified to include only the main players and events.
Further references can be found in the Contents and Appendices.